"I'm sure many parents would agree: raising kids can be challenging. Although we can figure it out as we go along, wouldn't it be nice if there was a manual for each child, one that gave insights into what they needed to thrive? Briana Saussy delivers the perfect parenting road map with *Star Child*, a beautiful guide into using astrology for raising healthy, happy children. Saussy breaks the astrological chart down to the most important parts every parent needs to know. Learn the basics of natal chart interpretation and specific guidelines for each zodiac sign, along with stories, activities, and so much more. If you've ever struggled to figure out what's up with your kid, *Star Child* will show you the way."

THERESA REED
author of *Tarot: No Questions Asked*

"This is THE parenting book to read before all others! *Star Child* is a gorgeous invitation—a practical, nourishing, and magical exploration of the astrological maps of our children. Saussy offers potent and beautiful rituals, stories, and activities to help us parent our children with a deeper knowledge of their unique astrological makeup. This is a book to revisit again and again."

HEIDI ROSE ROBBINS
astrologer, author

"Briana Saussy is a truly magical *starryteller* who weaves astrology, fairy tales, myths, and activities into this absolute gem of a book. Like me, Saussy is passionate about helping people tune in to and embody the cosmic energies, and she does so in a masterful way that will help parents understand their children's needs and help children understand themselves. As a parent of two magical adult daughters, I wish I'd had this to read to them while young. However, the most beautiful thing about this book is that, while it may be aimed at understanding children, adults will also learn about the magic in themselves. Bravo!"

LOUISE EDINGTON
author of *The Complete Guide to Astrology* and *Modern Astrology*

"Briana's work in the field of sorcery is absolutely unique. It is practical, wholesome, and enriching, and her deft and elegant ability to weave folktales, myths, and stories into her craft is exquisite. *Star Child* is an incredible next step in the expansion of her lyrical and lovely praxis, and it is an absolute must for every parent, caregiver, or anyone else who has small humans in their lives. This book is a treasure."

ELIZABETH BARRIAL
proprietor of Black Phoenix Alchemy Lab

"*Star Child* is the rare parenting book that transcends the genre to connect to the inner child within all of us. Briana Saussy provides clear, heartfelt teachings on how astrology works, while leaving the door open for magic and deep soul healing by way of folktales, rituals, and the reminder that you're beautiful just the way you were born."

AMELIA QUINT
astrologer

"In *Star Child*, Briana Saussy roots you in 'the soil of wonder, imagination, and practical application' of modern astrology, not only as a parent but as a person. She masterfully brings the stars down to Earth, unlocking astrology's tools for self-discovery, then widening the lens to the life experiences of our littles. The potent rituals she's designed at the end of each chapter allow celestial wisdom to be embodied as you help your child(ren) discover their place in the universe. Regardless of your current level of star knowledge, *Star Child* will prove to be a stalwart companion as you navigate the precious childhood years."

JENN ZAHRT, PHD
senior editor of *The Mountain Astrologer* magazine

STAR CHILD

ALSO BY BRIANA SAUSSY

*Making Magic: Weaving Together the
Everyday and the Extraordinary*

STAR CHILD

Joyful
Parenting
Through
Astrology

BRIANA SAUSSY

sounds true
BOULDER, COLORADO

Sounds True
Boulder, CO 80306

Published 2021

Cover design by Lisa Kerans
Book design by Meredith March

 The wood used to produce this book is from Forest
Stewardship Council (FSC) certified forests, recycled
materials, or controlled wood.

Printed in the United States of America

BK06059

Library of Congress Cataloging-in-Publication Data

Names: Saussy, Briana, author.
Title: Star child: joyful parenting through astrology / Briana Saussy.
Description: Boulder, CO: Sounds True, 2021.
Identifiers: LCCN 2020044686 (print) | LCCN 2020044687 (ebook) |
    ISBN 9781683646754 (paperback) | ISBN 9781683646761 (ebook)
Subjects: LCSH: Astrology and child rearing. | Astrology.
Classification: LCC BF1729.C45 S28 2021 (print) |
    LCC BF1729.C45 (ebook) | DDC 133.5/86491–dc23
LC record available at https://lccn.loc.gov/2020044686
LC ebook record available at https://lccn.loc.gov/2020044687

10 9 8 7 6 5 4 3 2 1

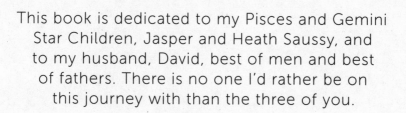

This book is dedicated to my Pisces and Gemini Star Children, Jasper and Heath Saussy, and to my husband, David, best of men and best of fathers. There is no one I'd rather be on this journey with than the three of you.

Contents

Introduction

Every Child Is a Star Child

"I don't think anyone can grow unless he's
loved exactly as he is now, appreciated for
what he is rather than what he will be."

Fred Rogers, *Mister Rogers' Neighborhood*

I t should come as no surprise that Astrology can give us greater
insight into our children and that it can support us in caring for
them, educating them, and fully supporting their interests. We have
consulted the stars for inspiration, knowledge, and self-development
for millennia—ever since we first noticed them in that velvety sky.
From kings and queens to financial brokers and even US presidents,
humans have long sought out the insights that Astrology provides and
have worked with it as a supportive tool in navigating daily challenges
and successes.

Who are these precious children of ours? Who are they, really? How
are we raising and guiding them? Astrology can give us flexible, playful,
more profound information than other schematics and typologies, and
it can support parents, guardians, and family members with immediate new insights into their children. These are the ideas I want access to
for my own kids. These are the observations all of my clients, students,
and friends who are parents ask for. And it's not just something for
adults: the children themselves can get into their Astrology—and participate in it—by connecting with the stories and mythological figures
of the signs and with the wonder that the stars inspire. This book is

both guide and support for raising and connecting to our young ones through the maps of our lives, woven in starlight. It is also an inducement to trust our own experience. It is a call to a quest.

I'll never forget the day in fifth grade when my mother got a call from my guidance counselor. There was a Situation. In mom rushed to the school for a meeting. My guidance counselor—let's call her Mrs. Cartwright—wore the sort of heels that make a brisk, clicking sound on the school's linoleum-floored hall. You could always hear those power heels before you saw her. You could also hear my mother coming long before you saw her. Instead of power heels, however, it was the jingling and jangling of the many charm bracelets she wore on each wrist. I sat there in the counselor's office, dreading each of those sounds. My stomach dropped to the floor. I had no idea why I was there, but I knew the battle of the Power-Clicking Heels versus the Charm Bracelets was about to commence.

I'm the sort of person who likes to read the end of juicy books first, so I'll tell you now that the Bracelets won. But let's return to the story.

What was the Situation? A boy had lavished unwanted affection on me. He told me he liked me, in *that* way. He expected me to kiss him. I told him nicely I did not like him back in *that* way. And that was that.

Well, almost. He wouldn't take no for an answer and continued to pursue me. So I tried again, more bluntly this time. I think I used the word "never." And perhaps something like "over my dead body" for added rhetorical and persuasive effect.

Anyway, it worked. Too well. This second verbal snub of mine upset the guy. But instead of teaching him how to take "no" for an answer, Mrs. Cartwright offered kind counsel to my mom that I had a problem. I was too honest, too blunt, too forthright.

I know what you're thinking, and I agree. Different times, I suppose, and I'm hopeful that young girls today would receive quite different guidance. In any case, my mother responded by explaining in precise and logical terms that Mrs. Cartwright was clearly confused. I did not have a problem with honesty, but Mrs. Cartwright would be the one with the problem if she wanted to pursue the matter further. Turns out, Mrs. Cartwright did not pursue the matter further. The boy stopped lavishing unwanted attention on me. Life moved on. The Situation vanished.

Now, years later, I think Mrs. Cartwright might have been trying to counsel me to be more kind. Choosing kindness is certainly a bedrock principle worth cultivating. But most little girls I grew up with were not encouraged to be outspoken. Kindness was a way to hide our thoughts and feelings, whereas boys were given a free pass to say pretty much what they wanted to, no matter how crass or hurtful, because "boys will be boys." I went on to face this set of attitudes not only as a child, but in college too. Even at the turn of the twenty-first century, ladies at the seminar table still deferred to their male counterparts. The "problem" was that I was just not that sort of girl. I spoke up and told the truth, perhaps to a fault.

As a mother of two boys, I sometimes find myself reflecting on this incident from my school days. What would have changed, I wonder, if the adults in the room had taken certain facts into consideration about me, the boy, and themselves? We of course do not know how Mrs. Cartwright counseled the boy's parents, but what would have happened if she and my mother had been aware that, contrary to my Sun Sign in charming Libra, my Moon is in blunt and truth-telling Sagittarius, indicating that I am very comfortable telling the whole truth, regardless of how people feel? What counsel would have been given if they had seen that my Mercury is in Scorpio in the Eighth House—another sign of blunt, forthright, and, yes, sometimes stinging communication? And then what about the boy? What were his tendencies and challenges?

Some of these terms may be unfamiliar, but you will likely recognize this as astrological language. You may have heard some of these terms in daily or monthly horoscopes, or you may have read books or studied the methods and terms of this ancient art. Mrs. Cartwright might have thought it to be poppycock. Or she might have learned it at her grandmother's knee.

I don't know that having all of this astrological information would have changed the outcome at all. There is so much that goes into the shaping of young hearts and minds that I would certainly never claim that these facts hold the sole key to unlock the mysteries of human personality.

Yet I am convinced these considerations would have helped me (and probably the boy as well) to gain understanding and tolerance of ourselves and those around us. Astrology can provide a counterpoint—even a point of resistance—to some of our most entrenched habits of thinking, in this case about how children should or should not behave. With an understanding of Astrology, we could instead turn to the child himself or herself and make an effort to see them as they are, not as the culture, their parents, or school guidance counselors would have them be.

There are many tools that can help us see and know our children better. Psychology offers one popular set of tools. Whether we make use of the insights of psychology, those of Astrology, or both, the whole point is to be able to see our children for who they are and thus to develop healthy, growing, joyful relationships with them. And that means it's not just parents who can benefit from these insights but teachers, guidance counselors, relatives, neighbors, and family friends. This book is written for the whole village. Experience teaches us that knowing ourselves is hard—there's no way around it. Most of our difficulties with parenting, caring for, and teaching children begin with our inability, or even our refusal, to be interested in the challenge of self-knowledge at all. Even if it proves one of the most difficult of tasks to know our kids and ourselves, it will serve us well to get interested in them, find out about them, and try to see and know them for who they are independent of our own desires for fulfillment, hopes, dreams, and fears.

I am a storyteller, ritualist, practitioner, teacher, and writer in the Sacred Arts by trade. Over the years, Astrology has become one of a core set of disciplines in the course of my work. At the forefront of everything I do—at the heart of the Sacred Arts—is the problem of self-knowledge. My community of soulful seekers follows closely the Delphic Oracle's famous pronouncement to "know thyself"; this is the motivating force behind our work. The consequences of not knowing ourselves are too plain—and perhaps too painful—to spell out. If we want to flourish, the place to begin is with this piece of sage advice. The same can be said about knowing our children and helping to foster their potential. The simple truth is that Astrology, if worked with intelligently and with a good heart, can be an excellent tool for helping us in our pursuit of self-knowledge and happiness.

It is, for instance, a useful thing indeed to go into your Pisces child's parent-teacher conference and already know that you will be told that they are imaginative, highly artistic, and sometimes overly sensitive with their friends. If you were privy to this information, you might feel empowered to encourage the teacher to stop trying to force your child into participating in big and loud group activities and to offer a quiet place in the classroom for them to recharge.

When it comes to life at home, activities shape themselves around the awareness you develop of your child's specific nature. With my own children, Astrology has shown me what to expect when it comes to things like playdates, parent-teacher conferences, academic performance, and selecting extracurricular activities. Moreover, I observe a positive difference when parents take even scant astrological information into account in their parenting, not only in the child or the parent individually, but especially in the relationship between the two.

With this book I hope to remedy two glaring, unexamined issues in conventional astrological practice. The first issue is a twofold problem with Astrology resources. On the one hand, there is an excess of needlessly complicated, jargon-filled books, websites, and teachings that offer very little advice on how to practically implement astrological information in everyday life. You'll get information overload and a big headache trying to sort through all the arcane details. On the other hand, the astrological world is filled with sugar pills—easy-to-swallow, sentimental platitudes. These little pills go no further than giving you the vague comfort of knowing that you are a Libra, that your friend is a Cancer, and that such-and-such might be in store for you today. Astrology is vast enough to do more than provide a passing remedy and is instead able to go to the root of your life and experience, without breaking your brain.

The second issue is the lack of magic in much modern Astrology. Like all forms of divination, Astrology is associated with magic-making, but "magic" can be a dirty word. Magic is about power—so the understanding goes—and power is a problem. The earliest astrologers were also magicians, and the earliest magicians were all aware of the movement and relationships of the stars, Planets, and other major celestial bodies. This is part of what the ancient axiom "As above, so below; as within, so without" speaks to.

I want to offer a middle way between the extremes of information overload and sweet-tasting but ineffectual sugar pills: a way that is super-practical and gets into the nitty-gritty of daily life, and one that's sufficiently radical, meaning it goes down to the roots of life where magic lives.

Let's say you find out that you are going to have a tough transit in the coming year. Maybe your astrologer tells you that there are some funky alignments happening and you are going to be affected financially or with respect to your health. I don't know about you, but when I get information like that my next question is automatically "OK, that doesn't sound great. Now what?" Making magic is the answer to the "now what" question. It is the way that we petition and commune with our celestial holy helpers and take an active role in shaping our fates and fortunes. As we will find out, making magic is a completely natural way to put astrological information into action. In this book, you'll get a better sense of how Astrology shows up in your own life and learn some working methods to try for yourself.

What if you don't believe in magic but are open to Astrology? That's perfectly fine, and I'm not out to change your mind. But you might be interested to know that magic, in the way I teach and practice it, is not really a matter of belief. The practices I offer in this book require no religious affiliation or adherence to a particular doctrine whatsoever. They are fun and creative practices that help you bring the information you will learn here into your daily life. And if you have figured out a way to do this without magic—a way that is both easier or more comfortable and as effective—then go for it!

There are three basic questions this book answers:

1. How will Astrology help me have a more knowledgeable, joyful, and nurturing relationship with my child, the children in my life, and even my own inner child?

2. What are the starting points of Astrology? Where can I begin in the subject of Astrology if I want to make it my own? (Knowing where and how to make a good beginning is more than half of the whole endeavor and is important even for those with experience in the subject.)

3. What do I *do* with the star knowledge I have gained? How do I apply this celestial knowledge directly to my life here and now?

One useful way to think about Astrology is as a map that helps us orient to our place in the vast cosmos. So it is that *Star Child* begins with an overview of the basic features and coordinates of that celestial map with an eye to giving the reader a comprehensive familiarity. Thereafter it is organized according to Zodiac Sign, beginning with the first, Aries, and ending with the last, Pisces. Each chapter opens with a story from the rich folkloric traditions of the world that speak to some of the core qualities of the given sign. Stories and stars have always gone hand in hand, so when we begin to approach the meaning or significance of a particular astrological phenomenon, it can be helpful to approach through story. The original fairy tales were much starker and grimmer than the sanitized versions many of us are familiar with today. Within the folds of these stories there are pockets of pain, death, destruction, deceit, and callousness toward others. There is violence. There is also radiance, wonder, wise guidance, and love.

The stories that I share in the following pages come from all over the world. Some are sweet, some are salty, some are tough, and others are fun. I encourage you to share these stories with the children in your own life, making them your own. At the same time, I would counsel you to not edit out too many of the difficult parts, for this is often where the sauce gets most savory, and in my experience children love these best of all. When applied correctly, stories heal many of the heart wounds we sustain and dole out to each other.

After the story, we survey basic information about the sign, including its date range, Ruling Planets, alchemical element, quality, symbol, House position, and season. These considerations are followed by general points about the core personality, outlook, and attitude of each sign: a list that is necessarily limited in scope but handy as a quick reference. We then move into the depth of each chapter, broken up into several subsections. These include personality, friends and play, academics, physical activity, art and creativity, extracurricular activities, technology, sleep and waking, and discipline. I am consistently asked about these areas of focus by parents, students, and clients when discussing a child's astrological makeup. We also have a "How Best to Connect" section for each sign. Deeper and more sustaining connection is one of the most useful gifts of understanding our astrological makeup and that of our children.

Finally, each chapter concludes with three practices to help put to work the ideas of each chapter in your life. The practices I offer here are simple and, in many cases, everyday activities that are given a bit more breadth and scope. At the end of each chapter there is an activity and a little ritual that a child can do alone or with an adult, and then there is a final practice that is meant for the adult who wishes to get in touch with their own inner child. Our child-selves are still part of us—our memories, our stories, and our current experiences. It is remarkable how much insight we can gain into our adult lives when we reflect on our inner child through the prism of Astrology.

While this book is a handy reference, my best advice is to read it all the way through. Take it in whole. All the signs are interrelated and are all present in everyone's story, so the best use of this information is to develop a feel for the whole of the Zodiac and the Houses and to reflect on, as you read through the signs, all the people in your life, both children and adults. Don't try to fit people into the boxes of the signs, but let your living experience of them lead the way. You will find as you read that more than one story or chapter is relevant to your child, to yourself, and to others in your life.

Those of us who have children know that it does indeed take a village to raise a child. While parents will find this book helpful, I have made an effort to include all of the adults whom a child has a deep relationship with including their teachers, extended family members, family friends, and other caregivers. Finally, it should be noted that this is written primarily to address the life and times of school-age children and that a further assumption is that children are in a conventional, public-school-type setting. If your child does not fall into that category, there is still much of worth and value here for you, and all sections can be adapted to specific life circumstances. After all, Astrology is all about giving a complete and comprehensive picture as well as a good story to share.

Every child is a Star Child. And long after youth has faded, every grown-up still carries their own childhood within. In this way, every adult is a Star Child too. These facts are easily forgotten or ignored. What would happen if we started remembering?

CHAPTER 1

Star Light, Star Bright:
Finding Our Place
in the Heavens

"More heavenly than those glittering stars we hold the
eternal eyes which the Night hath opened within us.
Farther they see than the palest of those countless hosts.
Needing no aid from the light, they penetrate the depths of
a loving soul that fills a loftier region with bliss ineffable."

from *Novalis: Hymns to the Night I*,
translated by George MacDonald

No matter what advanced tools you use, Astrology begins not by interpreting charts and numbers, but stargazing. This is what we call "naked eye, naked sky" Astrology. Now part of this might involve learning names of stellar objects, but really it is a craning of the neck, a throwing back of the head, and an opening of heart and mind to the awe of universe. You literally look up at the sky, regularly, and pay as much attention as you can. Notice what is happening. What stars, star patterns, and Planets are you able to see with your naked eye?

Astrology is really astronomy asking for a human scale, for relationships. We take the same data of astronomy and ask: What and who are we in the middle of this grandeur? What was here before us; what will be here long after we are gone? What are we in the middle of the incomprehensible vastness of the universe?

In the ordinary business of life, it can be easy to forget how interconnected we are. That is, it can be easy to forget *who* we are. The starting point of our journey to the stars, with the aim of learning about our children, begins with remembering who we are. To help facilitate this process, we need learn to achieve some small changes of perspective that bring big results.

I'll give you two examples to practice on. Think about Earth, but in the earthiest way possible—from the point of view of your locale, where you are right now. Is it a separate realm from the stars? It seems so. We are here, and the stars are up and out there somewhere. Now let's shift our perspective. Imagine Earth as whole. You've seen pictures from space. You can see now that Earth itself—revolving around a star, the Sun—is *in* the stars and is, in fact, stellar. Earth as a whole is a member of a whole solar system. It's not an isolated mass. So we have the same body, Earth, understood in two different ways. Both are true, and both are useful under different circumstances. This shift in perspective is vital for the work we will be doing in this book, vital for Astrology and our relationships to our children.

Here is another shift of perspective—one that can be useful—and it concerns the meaning of home. I unpack this shift at length in my book *Making Magic*. We usually regard home as a realm separate from the world, from nature and the wilds, and from magic. That is one perspective—and it is a legitimate one. But then, with a small shift, we may discover the wilds in our own homes, unfolding, as it were, like worlds. Water, Earth, Air, and Fire, for starters, are at work at the very center of the home, the kitchen. We don't have to go very far to find the powers of the cosmos at work in our everyday lives. Everything we need to track down that wild "something" we call magic is right here the whole time, hidden in plain sight. This perspective, by the way, can be incredibly helpful during shelter-at-home experiences, or other situations in which you find yourself and your mobility restricted.

Now that we have practiced on two examples, let's turn to the matter at hand: our children and ourselves, remembering where and who we are. To do this, we practice our shift in perspective.

First of all, I want to take a common example that many parents might appreciate: the "This is not forever" approach to mundane chores such as washing and folding children's clothes. You could apply "This is not forever" to grading papers if you're a teacher or to doing the dishes at home. There are piles of dirty clothes, piles of papers, piles of dishes. On the one hand, you could find any chore burdensome because it's a burden you are taking on. But then, with a small shift in perspective, you remember: This is not forever. Children grow up so fast, in the blink of an eye. Your parents and grandparents said this, and they were right. As a result of the small shift in perspective, your relationship to that chore changes. The burden can actually seem lighter, easier to carry.

This shift in perspective is one that can be practiced and developed into a keen-eyed perception of things you never lose. In the following pages you'll find an activity and two rituals that will help you foster the sense of interconnectedness that is so foundational to a genuine understanding of the stars. Take them as guidelines, not gospel truth. I expect you to experiment and adapt according to your own needs and own sense of things so that it's just right for you.

Astrology will begin for you when you start to become aware of just how interconnected the firmament is to your own life. What relationships could you discern if you showed up to watch the night sky repeatedly for many nights in a row? And perhaps most importantly, what stories were told about the stars we see, and what stories did the stars want to have told about them? As you continue to ask these questions, you will pick up more and more knowledge, putting theory into practice immediately in your own life.

Many people think that the only way to understand Astrology is to be "good at math" or to be able to make sense of complicated lists and charts, rulers, graphs, and computer programs. But Astrology and all star lore begins with what the naked eye can see in the nighttime sky, and star magic begins in the relationships that unfold for us as we pay attention.

I started learning Astrology early on, inheriting it from family members who were plainspoken country people. Had I given them an astrologer's natal chart (which provides a snapshot of the sky at the time of someone's birth including the positions of Planets, Zodiac Signs, and the relationships between different celestial bodies), they would have looked at me sideways and given it right back. But they lived by their Farmers' Almanac, knew exactly what phase the Moon was in at any given time, and were more than fair hands at predicting the weather. That's Astrology, though they didn't call it that.

There is a common-sense attitude in all of this that we want to always retain, much like keeping extra sugar and flour in the cabinet. Astrology can be cloaked in so much mystery and intimidation for many that it appears to be the most complicated and arcane of the Sacred Arts, something only really smart people could understand. This technical and exclusionary approach to Astrology does not work because Astrology—literally "the speech of the stars" if we parse the word down to its ancient Greek roots *astra* and *logos*—is a Sacred Art firmly rooted in the soil of wonder, imagination, and practical application. Farmers pay attention to the stars so they can plant at the right times, harvest at the right times, and care for their livestock in the best possible way. Medieval magicians consulted astrologers (or learned the art themselves) so that they could advise people on the best time to marry, to have a baby, or to start a business. And in my experience, everyone who pays attention to Astrology cannot help but reflect on the stories the stars might have to share about us, our lives, and the most choice-worthy ways to lead them right now.

PRACTICE

Our first step for engaging with Astrology is to go to the stars themselves, observing and connecting with the night sky. As we begin to delve into the content of *Star Child*, I cannot overstate how useful it is to never once lose sight of where all of this work begins: under the starry firmament with just you looking at the stars and wondering. It is both an inspiring and a humbling experience. In this space, we feel more capable of reflecting on our lives in ways that can open our hearts and minds and bring great benefit to daily life.

Activity
Naked Eye, Naked Sky

Many of us live in cities with so much light pollution that it is difficult to see the Milky Way Galaxy strewn across the sky. But the stars are not so lost that we cannot see heavenly bodies like the Moon, Venus, Mars, or even Jupiter and Saturn.

If you want to look through a telescope or binoculars, that's wonderful, but don't feel pressure to do so. So many of us don't bother spending much time simply looking with our own two eyes because we feel that we need special equipment or apps—and we assume our eyes are somehow not enough. But they are, and *you* are.

Find a location that will be safe and suitable for stargazing. Pick a night that's not too hazy, with relatively few clouds, and go. It may take some trial and error to find the right location and the right time, so be sure to give yourself space and time to get settled with "your spot."

If it works with your situation, bring a friend or take the kids along. Make it a star party. Your spot could be in the backyard, on the front porch at the grandparents' house, or even in a park. Most summers we journey to the mountains of New Mexico and do a lot of stargazing with the kids from the back of our pickup truck.

Establish your exploration of the sky as a periodic practice if you can. It doesn't have to be every day, but try your best to pick the same time and day every week, every two or three weeks, or even just every season—a periodic occurrence of whatever frequency works with your life. Aiming for some kind of regularity will help support you at whatever level you happen to be working. If children are involved, and hopefully they are, it will help them build a good habit of observation and experience, and it will help them remember. The regular meetings will also begin to create a pathway between yourself and the sources of assistance that are most appropriate for you to work with at this time. Just by showing up and nothing more you are sending out a message to the cosmos that you are ready to get to work.

At first, for this practice, make it a goal to simply visit the stars themselves like you are visiting an old, forgotten friend who is always there for you. Enjoy the fresh air and open sky, letting your mind and imagination wander freely. What are some things you notice? Is there something you've never noticed before? Don't try to be sophisticated.

Remember always: the astrological charts and symbols and all the technical terms and the jargon of Astrology have their roots in this direct encounter with the night sky.

Ritual
Setting Your Celestial Compass

You have found a location or locations that will be safe and suitable for stargazing. You've started paying more attention to what is happening in the aerial realms, you visit this spot as a regular practice, and now you're ready for more. What's next?

From where you stand or sit under the night sky and stars, first call out and identify the seven directions: North, East, South, West, Above, Below, and Center. I like to hold out my arms and hands when I do this, as a way to feel the scale of the space surrounding me. Feel yourself come into alignment with the heavens and the earth: it's amazing!

Notice the horizon. Can you see it? If you can look in all directions, notice that the night sky from horizon to horizon is like a great dome. Directly above you is what is called the "zenith."

Pick a star—any star—and reach up to touch it or pluck it from the sky. The angle your arm is making when you do this is the "altitude" of the celestial object. Notice, as well, how the stars move in circular paths around a celestial pole. In the Northern Hemisphere, the celestial pole is Polaris, also known as Ursa Minor. In the Southern Hemisphere, the Southern Cross constellation is used to find the Southern pole.

See if you can locate the Planets. Have you noticed how they always seem to travel in a line? That line is called the "ecliptic."

There are many ways to orient ourselves in the world. We often use our address or the name of the city we live in to let people know where we're from. Remember that we are also literally made of stardust, so setting your celestial compass is another, much vaster way of finding your unique place in the wide cosmos.

Ritual for Your Inner Child
Storytelling and Star Lore

Around the world and in many different cultures, Astrology is always rooted in stories and in everything the telling of stories implies. In fact, it seems plausible that it was precisely under the stars, next to a roaring fire, that storytelling and the "endless eyes" of the imagination were first awakened. From this place, the whole universe positively glows with inner vision.

Storytelling conveys important basic meanings and lessons, but just as important is that it gives the listener an idea of the appropriate frame of mind we might cultivate as we delve into the sacred art of Astrology. After you begin looking at the actual night sky and orienting yourself to the stars, you will find that you start seeking out stories about them. Some stories will make themselves known to you naturally and organically; some may appear in your dreams.

You might seek out other stories during your course of study. *Star Child* contains stories that support us as we explore the given material. These stories illustrate for us the various ways we can begin putting this information to use in our lives right here and right now.

All children love stories and love to be told stories, but I have learned that the inner child in many of us carries a wound of story deficiency. At some point, many parents stopped telling stories to their children. They may have read books or watched films, but the oral tradition of telling stories has become something of a rarity. The wound this causes is twofold. On one hand, we suffer from a lack of stories; on the other, we often feel that we do not have any stories to tell our own children. So this ritual addresses those feelings—with a little help from our friends, the stars.

Keep track of any "stories written in the stars" you might come to know as you spend more time under the night sky. How does the night sky help you understand the story or stories you yourself are living?

At some point when it feels comfortable to you, you might try picking a story from this book, one that speaks to you and yours. Or you might research the body of stories specific to the constellations we see in the sky. One of the interesting things about Astrology is that there isn't just one Astrology, but many. Most cultures have their own names for the constellations they see, meanings for how those astral patterns influence daily life, and best of all, stories about the shapes in the sky and what they are up to. There are many resources for getting acquainted with the ways that people throughout the world and through time have conceived of the stars. When you find a story about the stars that particularly resonates with you, learn it by heart and then tell it under the stars to the children in your life, young or old, whom you love.

CHAPTER 2

Navigating the Celestial Map: A Guide to the Natal Chart

"The most important places on a map are the places we haven't been yet."

from *The Map of Salt and Stars*
by Jennifer Zeynab Joukhadar

I f you could make a picture of all the celestial objects exactly as they appeared on the day you or your child were born, what would it look like? It's wonderful to try to imagine the sky as it might have really looked in all directions, above and below the horizon line.

Where we can get this information? How can we know where the Sun, Moon, Planets, and signs of the Zodiac were at the time of birth? Do you know what was coming up just over the eastern horizon? If it weren't for astrologers, these facts would be unremarked upon. Fortunately for us, centuries of practice recording and calculating such information has given us what we call a "natal chart."

Most people are familiar with horoscope astrology, the sort that gives information about "your sign." This is what traditionally is called the Sun Sign: the Zodiac Sign that the Sun is in at the time of one's birth. Thus we can easily get the idea that Astrology is about typecasting people into different Sun Signs: I'm a Libra, you're a Pisces, he's a Cancer, they're a Virgo, etc. The truth is that this typecasting is a vast oversimplification of the information your natal chart actually reveals. It's as if we were told that music made by a symphony orchestra was really the music of a single instrument—one violin or one oboe—rather a hundred instruments playing together.

Just remember that at the moment of your birth, there is not just one celestial object in the sky (the Sun) but an entire cosmic symphony surrounding you. If you want a more nuanced and truer understanding of the children in your life (not to mention yourself), you would do well to avoid overidentifying them with only their Sun Sign.

A natal chart is a geometric representation of the precise configuration of those symphonic planetary and celestial energies at your exact time and place of birth. It is the unique piece of music attuned to you that the cosmic symphony plays. The chart looks a little like a wheel with spokes, a pie cut into twelve pieces or wedges, or a dial. A horizontal line bisecting the circle into upper and lower hemispheres represents the horizon. The upper hemisphere of the circle represents what was above the horizon and could be seen at the time of birth, and the lower half is below the horizon or what could not be seen.

Every individual's chart is made up of a unique arrangement of celestial objects. The arrangement differs from person to person, just as two pieces of music have different notation patterns. All natal charts, however, are built on the foundation as illustrated, which is unchanging in its order and sequence. Thus the natal chart is always subdivided one through twelve in this manner: one through six is below the horizon, and seven through twelve is above the horizon.

The wedges you see in the chart are what we call Houses. From a psychological point of view, the Houses give information about your personality or character in relationship to various life themes. Most astrological information you will find works with natal charts exclusively in this way, as a tool to reveal major and minor personality traits and challenges.

Another way to view the natal chart is like a game board. If you've ever played board games such as Monopoly or Clue, all the pieces move through the areas on the board. In Monopoly, it's properties like Boardwalk or Park Avenue or a railroad; in Clue you move to different chambers of the mansion where the murder might have taken place. In a natal chart, the Planets,

Natal Chart with Labels

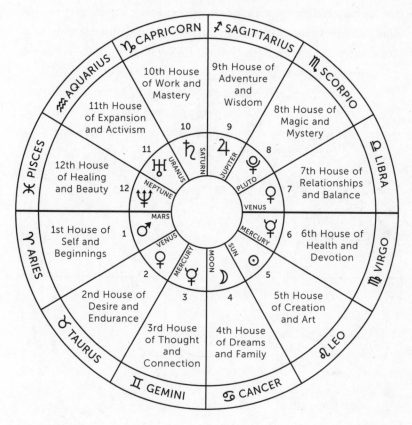

A "blank" natal chart with the planets and houses in their natural positions.

celestial objects and Zodiac Signs all vary in position from chart to chart, moving through the fixed order of Houses. Every chart is different, and it is where all these objects land on the board that is the point of interest for us.

Let's go on a scavenger hunt with a real natal chart. For the purposes of this book, there are only three things in particular I would like you to look for.

1. The Sun: Where is the Sun?

2. The Moon: Where is the Moon?

3. The Ascendant: What sign of the Zodiac is rising above the eastern horizon?

Discovering these three elements will help us start down a path of developing a richer, more nuanced understanding of ourselves and our children rather than focusing exclusively on the Sun Sign, as horoscope astrology does.

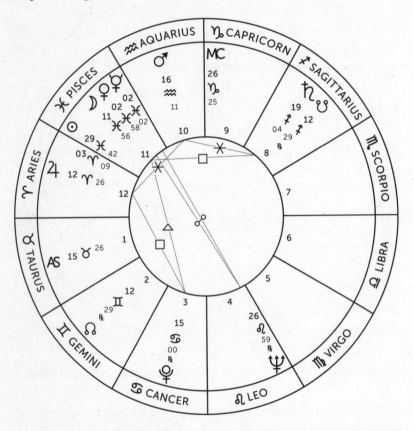

This is what the sky looked like on March 20, 1928, at 8:20 a.m. in Latrobe, Pennsylvania. The chart is packed full of information and might seem overwhelming at first. To get started, however, overlook all the details and just notice the interior ring of the circle that's divided into twelve numbered wedges. There's your "game board" with its twelve Houses. Remember that numbers one through six represent activity *below* the horizon. Seven through twelve are *above* the horizon, and these are always the same, no matter what chart you are examining.

After you've observed the Houses, look at the outer part of the circle, where you will see all twelve Zodiac symbols.

The word "Zodiac" comes from the Greek, *zōidiakòs kýklos* (ζῳδιακός κύκλος), which means "little circle of animals." While most of the Zodiac Signs are representation of living creatures, one of them is not: Libra is a scale or balance. The circle of Zodiac symbols represents a specific area of the sky associated with twelve specific constellations, the Zodiacal Belt. As you observed in the Naked Eye, Naked Sky activity, the Moon, the Planets, and the Sun appear to move along this same belt across the sky.

The sequence of signs, from Aries to Pisces, is always the same, but they appear to move through the sky as if on a dial, while the Houses are stationary.

Each segment of the Zodiac is a 30-degree segment of the full 360-degree circle of the sky. This 30-degree slice is known as a House. Just as there are twelve Houses, there are also twelve signs of the Zodiac. When astrologers analyze or interpret a natal chart, they are primarily looking at the Houses, the Signs each House is affiliated with, and the Planets within the Houses and how they interact with one another. It is a sort of snapshot of our place in the universe at the time of birth.

Now back to our scavenger hunt. We want to find where the Sun, the Moon, and the Ascendant appear in our sample chart. First, let's find the Sun. The Sun is represented by a circle with a dot in the center. In this chart, the Sun appears inside the Eleventh House. Moreover, it is positioned in the sign of Pisces.

Now let's find the Moon, represented by a crescent-moon shape. In this natal chart, you see the Moon is in the Eleventh House—and also in the sign of Pisces.

As for the Ascendant, find the horizontal line on the chart. On the inside ring, there are letters AS, standing for "Ascendant." Once you find that, then look to the outer ring: Taurus. When this person was born, if the conditions allowed it, the constellation of Taurus appeared to be rising over the eastern horizon.

Let's now look at the significance of each of the three elements we've found in our little scavenger hunt.

Sun: The Sun Sign represents a person's general nature and approach to life. Here the Sun is in Pisces. Some of the qualities most present in those born under the sign of Pisces include a spiritual and artistic bent, gentle and kind personalities, and a desire (and often corresponding ability) to help others heal. Pisces Sun Signs are also known to be dreamers who often have potent nighttime dreams and are tasked with carrying those dreams and visions into reality.

This individual's Sun is also in the Eleventh House. The Eleventh House is all about stirring things up; bucking the status quo; and looking for new, better, and more ingenious ways to get from point A to point B. Eleventh House energy is like lightning hitting the ocean—mega electrical currents are generated here. Typically this House encourages us to review our relationship to ideas like conformity and fitting in. It encourages us to make full use of available technology and to broadcast our work far and wide.

Moon: The Moon represents a person's emotional and interior life. Here the Moon is also in Pisces. A Moon in Pisces describes someone who is deeply spiritual or religious, intuitive, and most comfortable when creating art, music, or playing make-believe. Writing fiction or creating an entire town of fictional characters would be quite enjoyable for those with this Moon.

We notice that the Moon is also in the Eleventh House. The Eleventh House gives the Moon a visionary quality: Pisces brings a dream, and the Eleventh House turns it into a working vision of what could be. The Eleventh House is also the area where neighbors, community, and congregations are emphasized.

Ascendant: The Ascendant has two qualities. The first is that it often describes the ways we are perceived by others, and the second indicates an aspect of our work and journey that we are meant to fully step into as we develop. Taurus at the Ascendant would give this gentle Piscean soul a spine of steel when needed. When Taurus is at the Ascendant we display to others a sense of being calm, grounded, and certain when it comes to our work. Taurus at the Ascendant is easygoing about things it doesn't care about and absolutely unshakable in its convictions and things it *is* dedicated to. Taurus at the Ascendant also gives off an air of wealth and richness that can be both financial and artistic in nature. When someone has Taurus at the Ascendent, their work is to manifest their dreams and artistic visions into the world and to make them tangible and concrete in some manner so that many people can benefit from them.

Bringing it all together, we get a picture of an individual who is highly imaginative, creative, and gentle in spirit. This person might be deeply devout in their chosen religious or spiritual tradition; they might even be a minister, priest, rabbi, or imam—or they might fill some other ecclesiastical role. This is an individual who is able to intuit where there is a wound that needs healing and can create a response that brings a sense of healing to the situation. They might do this through imaginative means, such as putting to use things like fantasy or "playing pretend." They have an awareness and concern for the greater community, neighbors, and the public, and they are not satisfied with the status quo; in fact they are most comfortable when challenging accepted societal norms but in a gentle, subtle way. While this individual is most likely deeply kind and gentle, they are also determined to bring their vision into concrete reality as indicated by the Taurus Ascendant. They can handle the practical details, are not afraid to talk about money, and will not budge on the matters they find most important.

So who does this sound like? Why, it's Fred Rogers, of course, who lives in Mister Rogers's Neighborhood! Fred was a Presbyterian minister who took his message of kindness and inclusion to children through the Public Broadcasting Service (PBS) with his TV show, *Mister Rogers' Neighborhood.* The show had an incredibly long run of thirty-one seasons (that Taurus endurance!), and it focused on family, neighborhoods, and healing the wounds that children experience.

Fred Rogers explored topics that were considered too hot to handle by many politicians and was a powerful voice for desegregation and women's rights, even when those topics were still considered taboo in many areas of society. He engaged with children through his Neighborhood of Make-Believe and his wonderful stories. Mister Rogers also provided one of the strongest and most heartfelt defenses of continuing funding for PBS in front of Congress. Do you see some of his Astrology at work in all of this?

Activity
Star-Studded Scavenger Hunt

Procure a natal chart for yourself, your children, or a loved one, and print it out. (Astro.com is a long-standing website that still offers free natal charts, but there are many others.)

Find the Sun ☉, the Moon ☽, and the Ascendant AS on the chart. In which Sign and House does the Sun appear? The Moon? What is the Ascendant, the Zodiacal sign that is rising above the horizon at the moment of birth? What Houses are the Sun and Moon in?

Note these placements in a journal so you can refer to them as you read the chapters that follow. You'll first discover the significance of each House, the Planets, and other features of the chart. Each sign of the Zodiac then has its own chapter, primarily devoted to its significance as the Sun Sign, but also its general significance and particular influence as the sign for the Moon and Ascendant.

If little Fred Rogers were our child, we would first read his Sun Sign in Pisces, to help us better understand not only his general nature, but his inner life. Next, we would read about his Pisces Moon to gain insight into both his emotional life and matters that pertain to his Moon's position in the Eleventh House. (Remember, that's the area of the natal chart where communities, congregations, and neighborhoods are emphasized.) Finally, it would behoove us to read about his Taurus Rising Sign, which would give us clues as to how others tend to see him as well as the ways he would step into his work over time.

Keep notes on your findings, and reflect on them. Get familiar with the Houses and what areas of life each one speaks to. Then, if you started with your own chart, move on to your child's and the charts for the other members of your family. As you look at your chart and the charts of your loved ones, focus especially on the Houses that represent the life areas you are currently most concerned with. At the same time, start paying attention to the Planets and the meanings behind each of them. Houses, Planets, and other essential elements of the natal chart are covered in chapter 3. If there is a Planet that seems especially resonant to you, then notice where it is in your chart. As you apply your new understanding to your nearest and dearest, notice where the information really resonates and feels right, but also notice what feels off or not accurately descriptive. This will give you clues about what part of the chart to peruse next.

Ritual
Wish-Upon-a-Star Sacred Vessel

Many children first encounter stars through the idea of making a wish upon them. This essential act of childhood is actually a door that opens up to, and reminds us of, our deep relationship with the stars and all of the magic they possess. This ritual is designed to get the creative juices flowing, give you insight into your child, and strengthen that connection to the stars.

What is a sacred vessel? Some of the oldest magical objects in the world are sacred and ceremonial vessels—horns full of healing herbs, eggshells full of precious stones, and mason jars full of sugar. A sacred vessel is easy to put together as long as you understand the basics.

First you need a vessel or container. This can be a box, jar, glass, bag, vial, bottle, eggshell, skull, or hollowed nut. Next, gather the sacred materials you will be working with. These might include botanicals, personal concerns, petitions, supplications, images, and curios.

Sacred vessels are useful because they can sit on a bookshelf like an innocuous trinket, they can be buried at a threshold where they transfer your magical intention to all who cross into the space, or they can be temporary holding places that host magical intent. Sugar jars, witch bottles, box spells, prayer bundles, mojo hands, gris-gris bags, magical lockets, ritual rings, and Archangel Michael packets are all examples of sacred vessels. Of course the most primary sacred vessel is the very body you inhabit.

In order to do this ritual you will want to set aside at least an hour of time and make sure that you have the following items: a container of your choice (glass mason jars work particularly well for this), pictures, stickers, glue/tape, paper, a pencil, glitter, and any talismans your child might wish to add to their project.

Start out by asking your child if they enjoy wishing upon a star. The answer will be yes! Then explain that you are going to make a special wishing bottle (or box, or jar, etc.) that is only for them. Tell them that they can use whatever materials they want to decorate the jar. If they are young, make sure you assist them with cutting and pasting or taping. Work on the outside of the jar first; it will look like a glorious collage when you have finished. Once the outside of the jar is complete, invite your child to put special objects into the jar that they want to keep safe and that feel magical to them. Note what items they put in the jar, as this will already give you unique insight into your little one and what they are attuned to.

Once the jar is complete, explain to your child that this is a wishing jar and that any time they wish on a star they can go to this jar, write down or draw the wish on a piece of paper, and put it in the jar. Tell them to make a wish, and walk them through the process the first time if they are younger. Once they put their wish in the jar, they can top it off with a bit of loose glitter, put the cap on the jar, and then shake it quickly before scampering off. Later, you can peek into the jar to see what your child is wishing for and make those wishes come true!

Throughout this book are activities and rituals designed to help you and your child connect to some of the specific astrological qualities you feel most attuned to. These rituals are simple by design—because our relationship to the stars is simple too—so we start with what we see. I would much rather have readers come away from this book with one or two good stories about stars they see in the sky and a great Wish-Upon-a-Star Sacred Vessel they can play with instead of a deep or sophisticated understanding of astrological signs, elements, and aspects. Star knowledge, like all knowledge, works best when we root it in our lives and put it into practice. Keep it simple, and let your sense of wonder lead.

Ritual for Your Inner Child
Rooting to Rise (Grounding, Centering, Anchoring)

Rooting ourselves to the ground in the here and now and looking far and wide is not something that many of us are accustomed to doing. Recognizing that we are a point on a line that stretches back into earliest history and far into a future we have not yet begun to dream up can be a disorienting experience. Stars are quite good at helping us find our way. They are the original navigation maps and signposts that point us to True North. This is especially true for raising our children. To fully understand and appreciate the unique miracles that our beloved children are, we need to immerse ourselves in a specific language: the stellar, stardusted poetry of Astrology.

Grounding and Centering are both activities that we do prior to active imagination meditations, making ceremony, and any time we need to be extra-centered. Anchoring is a physical gesture that is given to us or perceived by us during the active imagining and may be used in everyday life. If possible, go outside to perform this ritual.

Grounding

1. Sit or stand in a position that is comfortable for you. Begin to notice your breathing, and allow yourself to take a slightly deeper inhalation and a slightly fuller exhalation. You may close your eyes or have them slightly open, whichever works better.

2. As you are ready, see, sense, touch, know, hear, and feel your feet on the land. No matter where you are standing, indoors or outside, your feet rest upon the face of the Earth. Allow your awareness to pool in the bottom of your feet and then sink deep into the layers of Earth's crust—past tree root, past bedrock, past water table and great layers of historic time. Note how this particular land feels underneath you. What brings it joy? What causes sorrow? How might you be of service here?

3. See, sense, touch, know, hear, and feel your feet touching Earth's molten core and drawing up a golden-green light into their soles. See, sense, touch, know, hear, and feel that light rising up through your legs, into your knees, your

thighs, warming your sex, and illuminating your abdomen and solar plexus until it comes to rest at the center of your heart. Breathe in this light from deep Earth and breathe out thanksgiving.

4. Now become aware of your shoulders, face, neck, and head. See, sense, touch, know, hear, and feel that they are rising up and reaching high above the ground and into the starry heavens. Affirm and acknowledge that in this moment there is a particular star or Planet that resonates with and for you. Connect with it, reaching all the way up so that the crown of your head is dusted in starlight. Feel that stellar light wash down over you—over your face, shoulders, neck, and head—until it meets the Deep Earth light in your heart.

Centering

1. Breathe in the light from Deep Earth and High Heaven.

2. Breathe out gratitude.

3. Breathe in the light from Deep Earth and High Heaven.

4. Breathe out awareness of connection to this specific place and time.

5. Breathe in light from Deep Earth and High Heaven.

6. Breathe out affirmation of alliance and right relationship with all beings.

7. See, sense, touch, know, hear, and feel Earth Light and Stellar Light swirling through your heart and moving through the core of your body. Here is Center amid all that moves.

Anchoring

1. Return your attention to the light at your center. Fill your mind with a thought of joy and bliss as you connect to that core.

2. Now create a key that will allow you to access that center immediately. This can be a thought, a date, a word, or a physical gesture. Keep it simple so you may have immediate access to it.

3. Next time you see the Moon or look up at the Planets and stars, take a few moments to think about your Ancestors from long ago and those who come after you. Whether by blood or spirit, the ones who came before once gazed upon the same Moon, the same rising Planets and stars, the same Sun. A long time from now—far in the future—your Descendants, whether blood or spirit, will see the same stellar objects. In a very real way, the celestial realm is something we all share in. It is something that unites us, no matter where we live and no matter what time period we live in. I encourage you: never lose sight of this as you make your way through this book.

How do we care for our young ones? How do we care for ourselves? So often we try to answer these questions only by looking at what is immediately in front of us, easily grasped and put to use. It is important to know where you are, but it is also important to know where you come from and where you might be headed in order to fully and meaningfully answer those questions. Look at where you are, look down at the good earth under your feet, and then raise your head up and look at the stars. They have such stories to tell.

CHAPTER 3

The Language of the Cosmos: Signs, Planets, Houses, and More

"One of the ways you can work for freedom is to change your mind and to move away from the space of binaries, of simplistic either/ors, and to be able to look at the picture that offers us complexity."

bell hooks

For readers who are brand new to the Sacred Art of Astrology and are still trying to figure out the difference between an Ascendant and an Aspect—or what it means if your Sun Sign has a cardinal, fixed, or mutable quality—the following chapter will serve as the orientation and reference you need in order to begin really understanding your natal chart and the charts of your children. Readers who are more experienced in Astrology may desire to skip over this chapter, as it will contain many familiar terms. Speaking as someone who is paid to cast and analyze natal charts, however, I always appreciate revisiting the basics of my craft—and I find that every time I do, I learn something new. So with that in mind, let's get familiar with some of the most common astrological terms and features.

THE TWELVE SIGNS OF THE ZODIAC

Each of the subsequent chapters in this book goes through the twelve signs of the Zodiac in detail. For now, however, this list of mottos for each sign will assist you in becoming more familiar with them.

Aries
I am here to protect.

Taurus
I am here to make.

Gemini
I am here to speak.

Cancer
I am here to dream.

Leo
I am here to create.

Virgo
I am here to serve.

Libra
I am here to relate.

Scorpio
I am here to empower.

Sagittarius
I am here to teach.

Capricorn
I am here to master.

Aquarius
I am here to envision.

Pisces
I am here to heal.

A word on date ranges for Sun Signs: it is useful to know the general date range during which people are born under a specific Sun Sign. However, if you read different Astrology books, you will also notice that these date ranges change by a day or so from year to year. Sometimes the dates overlap. For instance, those who are born on the cusp days (days that are split between two signs like Pisces and Aries or Aries and Taurus) will need to know the time of their birth to find out what their Sun Sign actually is. This is one reason why it is a good idea to have a natal chart cast for yourself.

POLARITY

Every Zodiac Sign has an opposing sign, also known as their polarity. Knowing about the Polarity can be extremely helpful as this sign often has the exact lessons and teachings we need to feel balanced. In the chapters that follow, I list the Polarity for each Zodiac Sign and how it influences the child's personality.

THE SEASONS

In each chapter I mention the season that a given sign is associated with. Traditionally it is understood that this season is one of the times in the year when those influenced by that sign naturally flourish, so I find this to be practically useful information. Likewise, the season that is opposite from a given sign can be a time of year when those influenced by the sign may have a more difficult and challenging time. Do note that we are working with the seasons as they appear in the Northern hemisphere. Readers in the Southern hemisphere will experience the opposite seasonal time from the ones mentioned.

THE FOUR ELEMENTS

There are many ways to read a natal chart, and one of the easiest is to look at what elements are the most predominant in an individual's chart. For the purposes of this book, the elements we are referring to are the four classical elements from ancient alchemy and magic: Earth, Air, Fire, and Water.

Each element has its own set of characteristics and focal points, so a good way to start getting a sense of your Star Child's makeup is to discover what elements are very present (or conspicuously absent) in their charts.

Earth

The Earth element is seen as feminine, heavy, strong, and deep, and is associated with the Planets Earth, Jupiter, and in some cases Pluto. The star signs associated with this element include Taurus, Virgo, and Capricorn. Earth is the slowest moving of all of the elements, it is heavy and sedentary like a giant piece of granite. Individuals with a great deal of Earth in their charts tend to be slow moving and slow to speak, but they are very thorough. They often communicate most effectively through touch and are kinesthetic learners. They are often physically strong and have great endurance but may prefer to be sedentary when given the option. These individuals prefer the hours of deep night and often have a hard time waking up. They appreciate organization, tidiness, industriousness, responsibility, and a practical approach.

Air

This element is seen as masculine, cool, light, and dry and is specifically associated with the Planets Mercury and Uranus, and sometimes Saturn. The star signs associated with this element include Gemini, Libra, and Aquarius. Individuals with a great deal of Air in their charts are quick thinkers and smooth talkers. They often communicate most effectively through audio-verbal means and can be gifted writers. They are often physically light, lithe, and flexible. These individuals prefer the hours of early morning and tend to like to go to bed earlier. They appreciate connection, relationships, harmony, social justice, fairness, sharing, and intelligence.

Fire

The element of Fire is seen as masculine, hot, light, dry, and associated with the Planets of Mars and the Sun. The star signs associated with this element include Aries, Leo, and Sagittarius. Individuals with a great deal of Fire in their charts tend to be passionate and creative. They often communicate most effectively through visual aids and are strong visual learners. They are often physically powerful and energetic with lots of zest and enthusiasm for contests. These individuals prefer the hours of midday and need to be allowed to wind down before going straight to bed. They appreciate color, sound, excitement, parties, enthusiasm, romance, adventure, discovery, physicality, and power.

Water

Elemental Water is seen as feminine, cool, dark, and moist and is associated with the Moon (of course), as well as the Planets Neptune, Venus, and in some cases Pluto. The star signs associated with this element include Cancer, Scorpio, and Pisces. Individuals with a great deal of Water in their charts tend to flow easily and occasionally feel overcome by waves of emotion—they are the most sensitive and empathic members of the Zodiac. They often communicate most effectively through sound; musical qualities such as timbre, rhythm, and pitch aid them in learning. They are often physically agile and have finesse but tend to shy away from competitive endeavors and prefer collaboration. These individuals prefer the hours of twilight and dusk and often have a hard time waking up. They appreciate beauty, spirituality, unconditional love, healing, devotion, art, music, and mystery.

THE THREE QUALITIES

Another interesting way to look at the natal chart is by tallying up the Qualities. Each of the signs has a corresponding quality attached to it. There are three of them, and they are cardinal, fixed, and mutable.

Cardinal

The cardinal signs are Aries, Cancer, Libra, and Capricorn. These are the natural leaders of the Zodiac. They are the individuals who are most frequently picked for leadership positions, and they are the ones who find it easy to organize and inspire teams of people and initiate projects. Cardinal signs must watch their tendency to become bossy, and they should remember to invite everyone to participate in creating an overall effort. They also need to make sure they finish what they start.

Fixed

Fixed signs include Taurus, Leo, Scorpio, and Aquarius. Fixed signs are slower to move, thorough, and exacting. They do not initiate, but they follow through and make sure the endeavor is completed to their specifications. Fixed signs are the endurance runners and workers of the Zodiac; they see the job through to its end, and they know who they are and what they are about. Those with a number of fixed signs in their chart can find that they sometimes suffer from tunnel vision and a "my way or the highway" approach that excludes other people and fresh ideas.

Mutable

Mutable signs are the unsung heroes of the Zodiac in my (cardinal sign's) opinion. The mutable signs include Gemini, Virgo, Sagittarius, and Pisces. These signs are the connective tissue that allows the other qualities to communicate without killing each other. The mutable signs are the ones in the background, sometimes mistaken as wallflowers, who actually make sure there's enough food, the decorations are on trend, and the music is lively for the dance. Then everyone shows up and they seemingly disappear. Mutable signs need to take credit for their work and learn to allow themselves to be complimented and appreciated. They also need firm boundaries.

THE TEN PLANETS

In Astrology, the Planets include celestial bodies such as the Sun, Moon, and—yes!—Pluto. Each Planet is associated with at least one, and sometimes more than one, Zodiac Sign. The Planets are also associated with various divinities, have days of the week named in their honor, and each has a unique tone and flavor. In any given person's chart, the presence of some Planets will be more "felt" than others, and it is useful to begin noticing what Planets we are especially attuned to.

If the natal chart is a descriptive story about an individual's life, then the Planets are the major characters in the story. We have relationships with all of the Planets, but just as we have some relationships that are more intimate and some that are less so, we have a similar dynamic with the Planets. You will find it helpful to familiarize yourself with their particular qualities and associations.

Sun

The Sun rises every day and sets every evening. Its presence allows life to exist on Earth. Our Ancestors felt dread during solar eclipses, when the Sun was seen to be devoured by darkness. They reveled during the long night of Winter Solstice when the Sun "returns" and the days begin to grow longer. Because the arc of the Sun can be followed through a single day and also through an entire solar year, it is a celestial body that has always been strongly associated with the cycles of growth, fullness, and then decay. As the Sun is the source of light and warmth, it has also been tied to the magic of abundance, prosperity, and good fortune as well as intellectual endeavors. The Sun is the Ruling Planet of Leo, the Fifth House, and is traditionally honored on Sunday. When someone asks you what "sign" you are, they are asking you what Zodiacal constellation the Sun was in at the time of your birth.

Moon

Lunar energy traditionally represents the mother, home, family, nurturing, poetry, and our emotional lives and reactions. The Moon is also strongly associated with women's mysteries and magic in the West. In the East—especially in China and India—the Moon is associated with the reflective mind and intellect referred to in Sanskrit as *Buddhi*.

In Astrology, the Moon represents the way we emotionally cope: Do we get stressed out? Angry? Sad? When looking at yourself and your child, the Moon's position should be noted because it can give you clues about how the two of you will emotionally relate to one another. The Moon speaks to the theme of mom, home, and comfort zone. Many of us must learn to dance with our Moons (and our moms!), taking the best parts of our lunar energy for nourishment and depth and leaving behind the tendency to stay where it's safe and comfortable. The Moon rules Cancer, the Fourth House, and is traditionally honored on Monday.

Mercury

This little Planet has a big impact on people! The fastest-moving Planet in our solar system, Mercury is symbolic of thought, speech, and communication, just like the Roman deity who is its namesake: Mercury, the Winged Messenger. This Planet deals with how we think and learn, how we communicate ideas, and the role our minds play in our lives as well as what we like to focus on. Mercury is the natural ruler of Virgo and Gemini. In Virgo, Mercury is concerned with the containers for our ideas. Having beautiful ideas is great, but not if they are scattered all over the floor! In Gemini, Mercury is interested in how we relate to others through communication, but sometimes, if not balanced by other Planets and signs, this Planet can be all talk and no content. Mercury is the natural ruler of the Third House of Thought and Connection and the Sixth House of Health and Devotion. He is honored on Wednesdays.

Venus

Venus is the Goddess of Love and Beauty. This Planet is at home in both the Second House of Desire and Endurance and the Seventh House of Relationships and Balance and is honored on Fridays.

Venus is concerned with how we relate to people; the roles that love, romance, and sex play in our lives; our choices of romantic partners; how we demonstrate love; and how we honor and value beauty. Venus also rules over two signs: Taurus and Libra. Like Taurus and the Second House, Venus is all about sensuality—what feels good—with special attention paid to the fertile earth and pleasures of the body! This is all wonderful, although if tipped toward excess, Venus can get lost in love and self-indulgence. When Venus appears in Libra, she is more social and she concerns herself with partnerships, marriages, and connecting to people through love of different types, with a focus on relating to others in beautiful and balanced ways.

Mars

Mars is well known as the God of Warfare and the natural ruler of the first Zodiac Sign: Aries (the name of the God of War in Greek mythology). Mars is most at home in the First House of the Zodiac, the House of Self and Beginnings, and he rules Tuesday. Sometimes Mars energy gets a bad rap—kind of like a little boy in school. He is too unruly, aggressive, competitive, and unwilling to cooperate or collaborate. This is the shadow side of Mars. The Moon can be overly needy and attached, and the Sun can be too much ego. But Mars also has many wonderful qualities. Through Mars, for example, we learn how we relate in the world through *action*. What do we do? How do we do it? What type of physical exercise works for us? Where do we feel especially passionate and who/what are we willing to stand up for and go to battle over?

Jupiter

This potent Planet rules the sign Sagittarius and the Ninth House of Adventure and Wisdom. Jupiter is honored on Thursday. In mythology

Jupiter is the King of the Gods, considered benevolent, wise, and generous. On the shadow side, this energy can also be spoiled, indulgent, and selfish. When Jupiter is working correctly we feel expansive and positive. The largest Planet in the solar system, Jupiter energy makes us feel *big*. Jupiter rules over our actual wealth as well as the areas where we locate security. Jupiter, however, goes far beyond our bank accounts. This Planet encourages us to open and broaden our horizons—to go to new places, meet new people, have adventures, and be a blessing wherever and whenever we can. Jupiter loves parties and festivals. There is also a sharp emphasis on the natural world with Jupiter's influence.

Saturn

Saturn's energy is the perfect complement to Jupiter's. This Planet rules the sign of Capricorn, is at home in the Tenth House of Work and Mastery, and Saturday is its sacred day. In mythology Saturn is the Roman version of the Greek God Kronos, or Father Time. Saturn reminds us to make today count, as we move closer to our death with every single breath. Saturn deals with restriction, binding, and shedding. This tough work doesn't sound as fun as Jupiter's expansion and generosity, but the truth is that without restriction there cannot be meaningful expansion. Without shedding the stuff that no longer matters, we won't have the freedom to focus on what does. Saturn is also discipline—the workhorse—so both Capricorn and the Tenth House are related to career development for this reason. Saturnian energy can devour life force, leaving us feeling harried, bitter, and deeply unfulfilled if we are not careful. This darker side is represented in the story of Kronos trying to eat all his children—overworked and underpaid is a typical Saturnian rant. This needs to be balanced by the shining personality of the Sun, the quick wit of Mercury, the receptivity of the Moon, the sweetness of Venus, the action of Mars, and the benevolence of Jupiter.

Uranus

Uranus rules the sign of Aquarius and the Eleventh House of Expansion and Activism. In Astrology, Uranus is considered the first "outer" Planet (in astronomy the outer Planets begin with Jupiter). Uranus means "heaven," and it is specifically associated with lightning. Each of the outer Planets has a resonance with one of the inner Planets, so while there is no day of the week that specifically represents Uranus, the Planet resonates with Mercury, making Wednesday a good day to work with this planetary energy. Like Mercury, Uranus deals with intellect, but takes it to a deeper level. Uranus wants to go beyond the superficial or everyday and look at, think about, and talk over the *big* questions. Uranus also likes excitement, ingenuity, inventiveness, and enjoys stirring things up. Uranus is forward thinking and future oriented. It likes to take the big questions and meld them with new ideas. When not in alignment, Uranus can feel scattered—as if it is suffering from bad writer's block. This Planet is a wonderful energy to work with when exploring new opportunities, opening roads of opportunity that seem to be blocked, or undertaking a fresh endeavor. Uranus gifts us with the desire to connect, especially through innovative technology and in larger groups.

Neptune

Ruler of Pisces and the Twelfth House of Healing and Beauty, Neptune does not have a designated day of the week, but as a deeper presence of Venus, Friday is a good day to honor this Planet. If Uranus is the idealist and future-forward thinker, Neptune is the visionary, dreamer, and sometimes sentimentalist. Neptunian energy allows us to dream big, bigger, and biggest. It thrives on beauty, love, and spiritual quests. Neptune also rules psychic powers; along with Pluto and

Scorpio, Neptune deals with the occult, magic, and things that are hidden from plain sight. Neptune, like Venus, is concerned with feeling. Whereas Venus deals with our personal feelings and sometimes our feelings in relation to others, Neptune deals with feeling for the world. Remember that Pisces's phrase is "I heal," and part of what goes with that mission to heal is the quality of unconditional love and the desire to save whatever is in need of saving. These aspects are truly oceanic in their scope—appropriate for Neptune, God of the Sea. However, if not tempered by all the other energies, these deep qualities can lead to escapism, addiction, and martyrdom.

Pluto

Always considered a Planet by astrologers, Pluto is the Planet farthest from the Sun with the longest orbit. It rules Scorpio and the Eighth House of Magic and Mystery, and it resonates with Saturn, so Saturday is an appropriate day to honor Plutonian energy. In Roman mythology Pluto is the God of the Underworld. Pluto asks us all to descend into the depths so that we might come to truly know ourselves. Going into our darkest places and dealing with our roughest experiences requires the whole lineup of planetary characters to be on our side, and Pluto includes them all. Even more than Uranus, Pluto is not satisfied with surface anything. It wants to go deeper, deeper, and ever deeper. Plutonian endeavors include our anger; our deepest desires around sex, intimacy, and money; and the unfolding of our true purpose. In the extreme, Pluto can become unhinged, controlling, and obsessive. We must remember that spending *some* time in the underworld is necessary, but staying there forever is perilous and can lead to complete loss of self. On one hand Pluto can go "nuclear" and, like its element plutonium, can be radioactive and incredibly harmful. On the other hand, some radiation is what allows life to happen in the first place!

THE TWELVE HOUSES

As discussed in chapter 2, the Houses are the unchanging part of an astrological chart, like a game board through which the signs and Planets move.

First House: Self and Beginnings

The natural ruler of the First House is Aries, and the Planet Mars rules this sign and House. The First House deals with "firsts": the ways we begin, the first impressions we make on other people, the ways in which we process first impressions others make on us, and how we enter a room. It speaks to our physical appearance as well as our core sense of self. The First House also speaks to our attitudes toward risk-taking and adventure.

If our children are considered loud, problematically behaved, or very distinctive in appearance or impression, we should look at this area of the chart for more insight into what gifts and challenges may be part of their story.

Second House: Desire and Endurance

The Second House is naturally ruled by Taurus and is the happy home of Venus. Here we deal with personal wealth—both the money and material belongings we possess through inheritance as well as the wealth we create in our own lifetime. Underneath the theme of wealth lies the idea of security—what makes us feel secure. Desire plays an important role for the Taurus child, and we can see their desires and strong preferences indicated in the areas of food, finances, and sensual experiences.

If our children are finicky eaters, lethargic, curious about money, and/or exceedingly stubborn and focused, then it's a good idea to look at this area of the chart because the Second House concerns these qualities.

Third House: Thought and Connection

Naturally ruled by Gemini, the Planet Mercury thrives in the Third House, which deals with personal communications, ideas, and intellectual liveliness. There is a "networker" aspect to the Third House and a real need to bring a personal message to the wider world. This House is also about friendships and learning—especially in childhood, sibling relationships, voice, and connection. Every parent and caregiver should therefore pay close attention to the Third House. Here we see information about how children relate to friends and other children, how they get along with their siblings, and what their learning styles are. If there are difficulties in the classroom or with learning, then the Third House should absolutely be consulted.

Fourth House: Dreams and Family

The Fourth House is naturally associated with Cancer. The Moon rules this House. Here we gain insight into our family (both genetic and spiritual), tribal groups, tribalism, the home, and the mother. This includes our physical mothers, the way people of any gender mother one another, and what mothering issues we need to take a good long look at. In the Fourth House, we think about how our experiences with family, social groups, mothering, childhood, and home define and inform us and how we emphasize them. Dreams are especially important in this area of the chart; often those with strong Fourth House placements find that their dreams provide vital information. When we want to find out the best ways to mother, nourish, and create stable homes for our children, we can take a peek at their Fourth Houses.

Fifth House: Creation and Art

The Fifth House is naturally home to Leo and is ruled by the Sun. Here we experience freedom, creative expression, and a desire to be seen or to stand in the spotlight (or not). We also pay special attention to love affairs and father figures—both literal and metaphorical. When we engage in Fifth House work, we ask ourselves where we come alive creatively, what aspects of our personality we wish to highlight or draw attention to, what our relationship is to the children in our lives, the influence of father figures on us, and how we father. The Fifth House is concerned with the art of living well, and that includes information on how children best play and enjoy themselves. This House also speaks to a child's creative flair and style.

Sixth House: Health and Devotion

The Sixth House is ruled by Virgo, and the Planet Mercury rules this part of the natal chart. The Sixth House is affiliated with health and healing as well as organizations, system building, innocence (the Virgin), and devotion to others. When we work on Sixth House concerns, we're asked to consider what in our life needs a better "container." What area(s) sorely lack structure and clarity? What can we embellish or make more beautiful, pleasing *and* functional? What needs to be healed, and how do we help heal each other? What do we need to pay attention to when it comes to our physical health?

If a child is experiencing health problems, the Sixth House is an important area of the chart to consult. Here we can discover information about physical, mental, and emotional health issues and can receive clues about what remedies would be most beneficial. We also discover what kinds of structures and levels of organization work best for our children.

Seventh House: Relationships and Balance

The Seventh House marks the transition from the part of the chart that is all about the individual to the part of the chart that is all about an individual relating to others. It is fitting, then, that Libra calls this area of the chart home and Venus is its Ruling Planet. In the Seventh House the work is all about relationships: entering into them, maintaining them, not getting lost in them, and knowing how and when to end them. The only quality the Seventh House focuses on as much as relationship is balance. It is here that we become deeply concerned with what is fair, right, just, and equitable—not only for ourselves but for everyone else. Beauty continues to be a strong theme here—as does sensual pleasure—but in this House the emphasis is on creating pleasing experiences for groups of people and taking on social responsibility to make sure that beauty is available to all, perhaps by patronizing the arts. The Seventh House also deals with diplomacy and acute negotiating skills. The relationships covered here include romance and marriage but also business and even friendships.

As children get older and potential flirtations and relationships loom over the horizon, the Seventh House is a useful place to look in terms of what kinds of relationships will be most supportive for our children and what kinds of relationship patterns they should steer clear of.

Eighth House: Magic and Mystery

The Eighth House is where Scorpio lives, and its Ruling Planets are Mars and Pluto. Mars is the Planet that ancient astrologers associated with this House and sign. Pluto became associated with the Eighth House and Scorpio after its discovery in 1930. I jokingly say that the Eighth House is all about sex, drugs, and rock 'n' roll. It's actually about mystery, power, intimacy, death, and money. The Eighth House challenges us to relate to and understand our relationship with Mystery—to the Unseen Worlds, the things we do not know, and the shadows within ourselves. The Eighth House has a reputation in Astro-land of being intense, dark, and mysterious, but its ruler Scorpio also possesses incredible charisma and deep potential for lasting, evolutionary-level change, which is why this House is also associated with power. This House teaches us about power: how we wield it, how it influences us, and what its gifts and limitations are.

If our children experience any kind of wound or trauma (psychological or physical), then the Eighth House is an area to look at because it will provide clues on how they can recover and heal from those experiences. Sometimes we have children who feel strongly called to the magical or the spiritual, and the Eighth House is an area to examine in those cases too.

Ninth House: Adventure and Wisdom

This House is naturally ruled by Sagittarius and Jupiter. Adventure and wisdom are the focus here, especially in the areas of philosophy, religion, and worldwide culture. The Ninth House is a powerhouse of religion and philosophy with a potential rigidity that is counterbalanced nicely by a genuine interest (that should be cultivated) in how other people, places, and cultures do, see, and experience things. Freedom is of paramount importance to those with strong Ninth House placements, which is why they are so partial to going on adventures. The Ninth House also speaks to the realm of wisdom in the world including teaching, higher education, and nonprofit organizations.

Whereas the Third House tells us what kind of learners children are, the Ninth House tells us what kind of teachers they will best respond to. It can also help teachers and educators keep in mind a particular child's strengths and challenges in various learning environments. This area of the chart can also give us great information on how well—or not—children will travel and deal with relocations.

Tenth House: Work and Mastery

The Tenth House is naturally ruled by Saturn, and Capricorn is happy as a clam—or Sea Goat—in this House. It is about career building and relating to both the world and other people/creatures through work and mastery. Because it deals with career, the Tenth House also concerns wealth and money. It relates to how you want the world to see you. The Tenth House speaks to how well one is able to perform in public.

For children, the Tenth House speaks to competitiveness. Here we discover how children react to competition and collaboration. We also can find valuable information about how they will fare in high-pressure situations and/or when facing their peers in a public setting—for example, presenting a project to the class.

Eleventh House: Expansion and Activism

The Eleventh House is ruled by Uranus, and Aquarius rocks out in this House. The Eleventh House is expansive in its energy and deeply concerned with communities, congregations, and large gatherings of people. This area of the chart deals with technology and our affinity (or lack thereof) to it. It also speaks to social media and how technology and communities interface with each other. This House deals with the rebel who has a cause, the inventor with a strong vision of what is possible, and the activist who is willing to agitate for what is right.

If you're concerned about your child's relationship to technology, the Eleventh House is a good area to look at. This sector of the chart can tell you much about screen time and the ways that children relate to computers and e-books. This is also a good area to look at when considering how children thrive in various community settings or organizations.

Twelfth House: Healing and Beauty

The Twelfth House is naturally ruled by Neptune and is home to Pisces. The Twelfth House is often said to be the "wisest" House because it has learned the lessons from the other Houses. It is the House of Healing and Beauty because the lessons and insights brought to us by the Twelfth House support us in healing on all levels and allow us to retrieve, through the healing power of beauty, what may seem forever lost. Here we look at our relationship to our inner worlds and worlds beyond the visible. We are interested in dreams, shamanic journeying, myth, and story—really any vehicle that will help us access and explore the unseen. Art and music are essential for the Twelfth House to do its vital work, and that work is not always easy. The Twelfth and Eighth Houses are the most likely spots in the chart where we can get weighed down by depression, substance abuse, and generally addictive and negative behavior.

For children, the Twelfth House often speaks to their dream lives, sleep habits, the role spirituality plays in their daily experiences, and a desire to help heal and restore. This area of the chart can also indicate what our children have inherited from us and from other family members in terms of looks, attitude, talent, ability, and interests. Sometimes this area of the chart can indicate children who are gifted healers and/or in need of rich spiritual and religious traditions.

ASTROLOGICAL COMPASS POINTS

There are six points in your natal chart that can give you extremely useful information about yourself and the children in your life. These points answer fundamental questions we all have, such as: What is the best way to recharge after a stressful time? What aspirations are we uniquely suited for? What do we have ease in drawing and attracting into our lives? I call these Astrological compass points because they make it possible to orient yourself even if you have minimal knowledge about Astrology or your natal chart.

Sun Sign

We probably already roughly know the position of our natal Sun. When someone asks, "What's your sign?" we answer: "I'm a Gemini" or "I'm a Scorpio," which refers to the position the Sun was in at the time of our birth. The position of the Sun in our natal chart provides the center point of the compass. This is where (and who) we are now: How do we show up? How do we like to meet and socialize with people? What are our general priorities?

When we look at our Sun Signs, or those of our children, we also want to pay attention to what House the sign occurs in, what Planets or points of interest may be near it, and what relationships it has to other areas in the chart. A child's Sun Sign gives us clues about the basic personality that they're in the process of waking up to and fully occupying. This book is organized so that most readers will reach for the chapter the deals with their child's Sun Sign to get a clear picture of what to expect. As we will learn, this can be a useful approach, but it is also somewhat limited because the Sun Sign tells just part of your child's entire star story.

Moon Sign

Our Moon Sign is more of a map "key" than part of the compass rose because the Moon Sign speaks to our emotional lives. What are we like when left to our own devices? What is our relationship to our emotional lives and feelings? How well do we rest, and how deeply do we dream? Where could things be made more comfortable and where have we perhaps become stuck in a rut?

Getting familiar with our natal Moon allows us to begin thinking about those questions in a meaningful way—both for ourselves and our children. The Moon Sign of a child gives us information on how they might express difficult emotions, where they are likely to feel stuck or inert, and how they handle stress. This sign can also give us good insight into how our children might want to be nourished—in terms of food, love, and guidance. Finally, knowing a child's Moon Sign can help us create a bedroom for them that feels like a harmonious sanctuary. We spend over half of our lives sleeping, so understanding what can best support us in getting a full night of rest is quite important. The following chapters, which are dedicated to individual Sun Signs, include some basic information about the Moon's significance in that sign.

Ascendant or Rising Sign

The Ascendant is also known as the Rising Sign. It is not a celestial body like the Sun or Moon but rather a specific point where one of the Zodiac Signs rose over the horizon at the time of our births. This point serves a twofold purpose: initially it speaks to how we show up in the world as well as to the ultimate purpose that may most resonate with us. The Ascendant is reflected in our personal style and appearance; it also speaks to how we enter a room, the kinds of first impressions we are likely to make on people, and the way we best begin projects and endeavors. On the other hand, the Ascendant also points to the work, life, and path that we are best able to grow into—it is one way to begin understanding the promise and purpose that every soul carries. Much of adult life and work is about growing into our Ascendant. Children are busy growing into their Sun Signs but, interestingly, many of the children I know firmly occupy their Rising Sign. It is as if they come in knowing what they're here for, and then as they grow, they forget. Grown-up caregivers who know this point in a child's chart can plan well and help the child find their own unique style and voice.

Descendent

The Descendent is not the most widely known or discussed point in Astrology. It is opposite the point of the Ascendant, and it marks the point where one of the Zodiac Signs is setting beneath the horizon line in the Western Hemisphere. The Descendant is always in opposition to the Ascendant. In Fred Rogers's chart the Ascendant is 15 degrees Taurus and his Descendent is 15 degrees Scorpio. While the Ascendant speaks to purpose and promise, the Descendent tells us what qualities, abilities, tools, and talents we can easily draw to ourselves. What can we attract with ease and efficiency? Where is the road naturally open? Where does life give us a big *yes*?

For children the principles are the same: the Descendent indicates what things our children can naturally call to themselves and where they can easily excel. This point also speaks to how our little ones finish projects and conclude endeavors. Though I do not think parents and caregivers should overemphasize the Descendent, it is a good idea to at least familiarize ourselves with the basic qualities of that point and then look at how they might show up for your child in this area of life.

Midheaven

The Midheaven is a point at the top of the natal chart and is determined in a couple of different ways depending on what House system the astrologer (or astrology program) is using. However, for our purposes it is simply enough to know where the Midheaven is in a given chart. This point is the place we want to home in on when it comes to our work in the world, the skills and talents we are known for (and paid for), and the story of our careers. The Midheaven is especially useful for those who are trying to discern their path or purpose within the greater world. It is useful to look at the Midheaven in a child's chart to get a sense of what broad and general areas they are likely to excel in as they get older. The Midheaven is often translated as the "career" sector of the chart, and while it does speak to career, it also speaks to the more general principle of being at our life's height and fully flourishing. We can look at the Midheaven in our children's charts to get an idea of where they will flourish at the height of their life and also what qualities and characteristics will best support them throughout life.

IC (Imum Coeli)

The *imum coeli* (Latin for "bottom of the sky") is a point opposite our Midheaven that's found at the bottom of our chart. This little point is essential to get familiar with because it tells us all about how we recharge, recover, and energize ourselves. The IC of our charts shows the best kinds of self-care for us as individuals. In addition, it tells us how we deal with trauma, pain, and journeys into the psychological underworld. Parents and caregivers should familiarize themselves with this point in the chart to discover how to create the most restful and nourishing environment for their children and also to learn how their children will best handle and cope with difficulty, pain, and loss.

ASPECTS

When we look at Mr. Rogers's chart in chapter 2 (page 22) we see that there is a smaller circle in the middle that's filled with lines connecting the Planets or other special points in the natal chart to other objects. Just as is our experience in life, some of these connections are easy and favorable while others are more tense or difficult. In Astrology, these relationships are called Aspects. There are many different Aspects but there are five that I believe are the most important ones to look for.

Conjunction

Sometimes we have Planets in a chart that are sitting right next together. This is considered a conjunction. When two Planets are conjunct they complement each other's energy and they bring the life concerns and experiences of the House(s) where they sit into clearer focus. Conjunctions are powerful alchemical blends that show where the individual has qualities ready to partner together.

Square

A square occurs when two Planets are 90 degrees (roughly three Houses) apart. When Planets are squared they are in a conversation—each one needing to learn a lesson from the other. Often this can feel very tense and manifest as challenging or stressful situations in your life. But if work and awareness are brought into the picture, our squared Planets can be a deep source of wisdom for us.

Trine

A trine occurs when Planets are 120 degrees apart—one-third of the wheel of the sky. This Aspect indicates that the road is open and the way is clear because this relationship is so supportive. In this case the two Planets, or points in the natal chart, are speaking to each other in a powerful manner and encouraging the building of something that incorporates all of their energy.

Sextile

A sextile occurs when Planets are 60 degrees apart and also indicates ease of work. It is not quite as potent as a trine but is still quite useful. The energies are supportive, mutually beneficial, and work best when combined.

Opposition

An opposition occurs when two Planets are 180 degrees apart and opposite one another in the natal chart. This Aspect indicates that the two Planets are in deep polarity with one another, and this will speak to stress and tension in an individual's life until the teachings of both Planets are integrated together.

Activity
Ruling Planet Recognized!

Now that you have a bit more astrological knowledge, you should be able to determine what the Ruling Planet is for your Sun Sign. Once you have figured this out, select an item that you can wear on your body that represents the way that Ruling Planet feels to you. This could be a piece of jewelry or a talisman of some kind. It could also be a special item of clothing or even a particular color that you strongly associate with that Planet. Example: I have a pair of earrings that I strongly associate with the energy of my Ruling Planet, Venus. Whenever I need to be extra sociable, charming, and convincing, I put on those earrings so that I have just a bit more Venusian mojo! Developing a relationship with your Ruling Planet is one of the most powerful things you can do as you begin your astrological journey.

Ritual
Weekly Honoring of the Planets

Each day of the week is named after and associated with a Holy Helper, a divine deity who in turn is associated with a planetary energy. A great way to get to know the different Planets we work with in Astrology is to recognize or honor them on their given day of the week. You may wear a color or item you associate with each Planet on that given day, or you can make an offering of incense smoke. One of my favorite things to do—and to have my children do—is inscribe the glyph of the day's Planet(s) in incense smoke at our front door, welcoming that Planet's energy into our home. This also really helps get rid of the archaic notion that there are "good" and "bad" Planets. Every Planet has lessons to teach and gifts to bestow.

Here are the days associated with each Planet:

Monday: Moon

Tuesday: Mars

Wednesday: Mercury/Uranus

Thursday: Jupiter

Friday: Venus/Neptune

Saturday: Saturn/Pluto

Sunday: Sun

Ritual for Your Inner Child
Make a Master Candle

A Master Candle is a candle that represents yourself. It is placed on an altar, shrine, or sacred space and kept either perpetually lit, or is lit first and then used to light any other candles in the space. There are many ways to create Master Candles that come out of the Hoodoo tradition of folk magic, but one excellent way is to make a candle that is the color of your Ruling Planet. You can add layers of color to speak to the different planetary influences as you become more familiar with them. For instance, someone who is a Leo with a Moon in Gemini and an Ascendant in Sagittarius would be ruled by the Sun, but this person would also have a strong affinity for Mercury (the ruler

of Gemini) and Jupiter (the ruler of Sagittarius). Different people associate the Planets with different colors, so
rather than giving you a list of color–Planet associations, I
encourage you to ask what color a specific Planet feels like
to you. For instance, some people feel the heart-centered
energy of Venus to be green, while others associate it with
pink or even gold. From this example, once the individual
has decided what color each Planet feels like to them, they
could fashion their candle and incorporate all three of
those shades.

CHAPTER 4

The Aries Child

"Freedom lies in being bold."

Robert Frost

(Aries, born March 26, 1874)

BIRTHDAY: March 20–April 19

RULING PLANET: Mars

ELEMENT: Fire

QUALITY: Cardinal

SYMBOL: Ram

HOUSE: First House of Self and Beginnings

STATEMENT: I am here to protect.

SEASON: Early Spring

GUIDING STORY: "Jack and the Beanstalk"

Children, gather round me now. Cast your eyes up to the heavens and see if you can find the constellation of the Ram, Aries. There are two stars within it, Hamal and Sheratan, that are still used for navigation today. This medium-sized constellation is most visible during the month of December. But perhaps it is too bright still to see it.

The winds are picking up and the sun is beginning to set. Look at how the sky is full of crimson ribbons. They remind me of the kinds of ribbons you would find at a fair: bright-red silk and soft to the touch. But such things happen only when the fair and the merchants and the land itself is wealthy—and not all places and not all times are. So now sit still, or move about as you will, and listen to my tale. This is a story of a young man, quite likely influenced by the sign of the Ram, for he was willing to try anything. This telling will be familiar to you and comes from the United Kingdom, but its root story is quite ancient and springs from the lands of Iran and India.

There is time for everything under the heavens: a time for laughter and a time for tears, a time for rest and telling stories, and a time for hard work and daring deeds. Once upon a time there were no stories, no smiles and laughter, because the land was dry and everyone was so very hungry.

A woman who was more bone and breath than flesh and blood took a worn leather lead and placed it in the hand of her only child with whispered instructions to take the pathetic-looking white cow to market so that it could be sold. Perhaps—just perhaps—some bread could be purchased.

The young man did as he was told, but along the way he met a stooped old one, so wrinkled and gnarled that he could not tell if this figure was a man or a woman. They whispered a few words with a gleam in their eye, and Jack thought, "Why not?" Soon he was on his way back home with a spring in his step. He had no money, and no cow, but he had magic. Three magic beans, traded for that skinny cow, and now they belonged to him!

But when Jack returned home his mother was so angry that she wept bitterly and refused to look at him. Jack felt angry too, and he tossed the seeds out onto the hard, dry ground and then shut himself up in his room, trying his best to ignore his belly. He fell into a fitful sleep.

Upon waking Jack saw that the beans had taken root and that a big, strong, supple green shoot had shot up from the ground into the heavens. It was big enough for Jack to climb, and so he did. Using his anger and frustration for energy, he climbed. Using his creativity and courage he climbed, and soon he reached the top of the stalk high in the clouds.

Now here was a castle, a beautiful palace that seemed empty. Jack went into the fortress and saw the biggest woman he had ever seen, eating a fruit pie. She startled him, but he also startled her, and after she warned him of her husband, they came to an agreement, and Jack was hidden away in a kitchen pot.

Soon the thundering footsteps came and then "Fi, Fie, Fo, Fum. I smell the blood of a human one. Be he alive or be he dead, I'll grind up his bones to make my bread."

Jack was deathly afraid but stayed put, and he saw the giant count out stacks of gold coins as he yelled at his mistress to fetch him food and drink. Jack watched. He fidgeted and grew impatient, but he kept his wits about him and he saw treasures in turn: the coins (one of which would buy food for a year), a plump hen who laid solid-gold eggs, and an enchanted harp that magically played the most beautiful music. Jack watched, and then Jack acted, his light fingers cleverly lifting this priceless item and then the next.

He went down the beanstalk, sharing the wealth with the whole village and beaming at his mother's pleasure, and then up again he went. And again. On the third time down the giant took note and followed the pesky human. But his weight was too much for the stalk, and the giant fell to the earth, vanquished once and for all. Jack took his position as defender of the village and sought out council on how to plant and tend the land so that none would go hungry again.

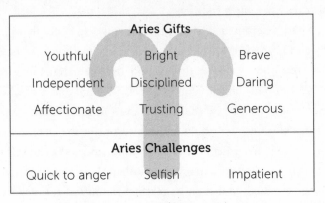

Aries Gifts		
Youthful	Bright	Brave
Independent	Disciplined	Daring
Affectionate	Trusting	Generous
Aries Challenges		
Quick to anger	Selfish	Impatient

THE ARIES PERSONALITY

The "Jack and the Beanstalk" story places many traditional Aries qualities front and center. The emphasis on Jack's youthfulness reminds us that because Aries is the first sign of the Zodiac, it is also the sign most connected to the newness of youth.

The Aries child is bright, enthusiastic, and fun! If you need a big *yes*, then go talk to an Aries kid. They end sentences with lots of exclamation points, and they love to be moving and engaged in some group venture or activity pretty much all of the time. Aries is the first sign of the Zodiac and is ruled by Mars, the martial Planet. This means the Aries child loves to be first, to take risks, and to take on dares. It also means that if the Aries children are having a bad day, not feeling well, stressed out, or tired, they can become demanding, rude, impatient, and aggressive.

These qualities are what we see in our guiding story, "Jack and the Beanstalk." Jack's anger and frustration, which come and go quickly, mimick Aries's own experiences with hot emotions. The youth's impetuous decision to trade his cow (the family's last valuable asset) for some beans points to both the impetuous behavior and gullibility we often see in Aries children. The fact that the beans turn out to be magic directs our attention to the fact that for all their bluster, fun, and motion, Aries children can also be highly sensitive and intuitive.

These little rams are incredibly loving and quite often very generous. Aries children are creative, often athletically or kinesthetically gifted, and their minds tend to move quickly. They do not verbalize everything they feel (or even half of what they feel) and instead often express themselves through physical motion. When directed in the right way, the Aries child will defend those who cannot defend themselves and fight for justice; if not given direction, the Aries child can easily become a bully.

Underneath the loud volume, enthusiasm, and unceasing motion, the Aries child is engaged in constant optimization—this is the drive for perfection that shows up anytime Mars is around. From their physical appearance (which often matters very much to Aries) to their physical and intellectual prowess, the Aries child is always trying to improve on the one hand and spot out flaws on the other hand.

They are often drawn to soldiers, stories of war and conflict, and military themes because they themselves understand the mentality of soldiers and military operations—it is native ground for them. Parents and caregivers can emphasize the positive aspects of this culture—including order, responsibility, cleanliness, caring for others, courage, and bravery—to great positive effect in their Aries children. Responsibilities such as caring for a younger sibling or a pet makes the Aries child happy, as does plenty of physical affection. These Ram children know who they are and what they want. Their development should move in the direction of being aware of and considerate of the needs of others.

Aries children may be little fashion plates who are drawn to the latest styles and trends and who are enthusiastic about makeup and cosmetics. This speaks to Aries's position as the first sign of the Zodiac, the area where appearance, first impressions, and being on trend matter so very much. You can support an Aries child's interest in these areas by revealing the work and dedication that go into creating good fashion and by explaining the quality control of cosmetics and accessories in order to teach them to value quality over quantity.

Friends and Play

In our story, Jack loves being greeted as a hero upon his return home. The young man's ability to wheedle his way into the giant's lair points out that Aries children are often able to fit into many different crowds due to their bright and optimistic natures. They tend to be popular, at least until they get mad or make someone else get mad at them. These children are full of enthusiasm and fire. As we see above, they have a strong sense of adventure, daring, and self. The Aries child *knows* who she is and is not waiting for anyone to tell her. As all cardinal signs will, an Aries will naturally take on a leadership position within their social groups. They will come up with games, set rules (and change them as they need to in order to win), and organize their friends. They especially love any kind of competition or contest. One issue that will come up in Aries children's play is that of bossiness. For this reason, an Aries child should be encouraged to share responsibilities, duties, and control.

Aries children have quite the temper, so getting mad and falling out with friends is almost a daily affair. As they get older this tendency will lessen, and it is not unusual for Aries adults to be good friends with people they knew in grade school: they are one of the most loyal signs. Emotional blowups will come, but they go just as fast—sometimes leaving parents and caregivers feeling whiplashed. Aries children are naturally demanding and perfection-seeking, and their friends are included in this. Parents will do well to teach their Ram children to be more accepting, tolerant, and flexible.

Academics

Jack's theft of the giant's treasures teaches us that although Aries children have a definite sense of moral right and wrong, they are willing to transgress it if it serves the bigger picture. Jack's ability to ignore his own desires in order to accomplish a greater goal (and the giant's inability to do the same) is part and parcel of his overall success. This sense of a greater goal when it comes to academics is something that speaks to Aries children, guided as they are by disciplinarian Mars.

Aries children are naturally bright and optimistic. They are often the first ones with their hands up in the air or blurting out an answer—right or wrong—before anyone else has a chance. The typical young Ram wants to be called on first and is happy to volunteer for pretty much anything as long as it doesn't involve being quiet or sitting still. Though they can be chatterboxes in their early years, Mars-ruled Aries children can develop impressive diligence and discipline when given the right tools, and they find that they can easily focus on tasks they're engaged with. This interest and a sense of purpose are essential.

If an Aries child is suffering in school, it's usually because they're bored with the subject matter or are having a difficult time mastering a concept—yet they avoid telling anyone about their challenge due to the influence of Mars-inspired stoicism. I know an adult Aries who failed first grade because he needed glasses and couldn't see the chalkboard. He never said anything about the difficulty until it was too late! Aries kids may also have a difficult time academically if their physical needs for movement are not being adequately met or if they are overly exhausted from participating in every activity.

Typically, Aries, like all cardinal signs, has one or two areas where they burn brightly and like to focus their attention. This is especially true as they get older. The biggest challenge the Aries child faces academically is not being thorough and rushing through their work. It is common for an Aries child to miss problems in class or in homework because they do not read all the instructions carefully. Skipping problems or leaving work half done is typical, as is waiting until the last minute to complete bigger projects. Because Aries children like to be first, they tend to rush through their work so they can turn it in before everyone else. This can lead to mistakes that would otherwise be avoided. Aries children enjoy solving problems, and they are naturally solution oriented. They often respond better to visual learning and cues rather than an audio-verbal approach. They are show-me, not tell-me, people. The Aries child tends to thrive in noisy, group-centered work and can feel lonely or isolated when working by themselves. Keep this in mind when it comes to homework. Teachers and caregivers should watch out for Aries's self-critical aspects—these are not easily noticed because the kids tend to be so bright, boisterous, and cheerful—but Mars has a melancholy aspect that leaves its children feeling dissatisfied with their performance or rewards.

As Aries children grow and consider education and training beyond high school, they often choose paths that allow them to begin working faster in the "real world" instead of going through more years of schooling. *Action* continues to be one of the key words for those born under the blessing of the Ram, so vocational training, trade schools, or college programs that have a strong practicum element—such as many business schools—are attractive to the young-adult Aries. Rams who are forced into formal colleges or long-track academic programs often find that they do not have the stamina or inclination to finish this type of schooling—they are ready to get started! The result is they may drop out. Family members and caregivers can support the young-adult Aries best of all by encouraging them to try things out, experiment, and learn by doing, as this is how they naturally thrive anyway.

Physical Activity

Jack's relatively effortless climbing of the beanstalk calls to mind the Aries child's natural athletic and kinesthetic gifts. Movement is of paramount importance for the Aries child, who needs to move and is often drawn to sports and athletics early on. In mythology, Mars is the warrior, so Aries children respond especially well to competition and "battles" on the sports field. Caregivers should be on the lookout for that and nourish development early. Ideally there is some time set aside for movement every day for the Aries child. Many of the behavioral issues we see with these children stem from the fact that they have an incredible amount of energy and not enough physical movement to burn it off or channel it.

As Aries children get older they will need to be reminded about good sportsmanship as sometimes this sign is prone to bragging and boasting. They will also need to be encouraged to balance their love of movement with times of stillness and quiet. Resist the temptation to put the Aries child in all the physical activities they ask for, otherwise you'll have one pooped Ram on your hands. Caregivers and teachers should notice if Aries children need to move around more than other children in the classroom, and exceptions should be made so they can.

Art and Creativity

In our story, Jack's gullibility is an asset. Accepting the magic beans leads him to make amazing discoveries. Jack has immense creative potential, although it wasn't initially recognized as such.

It is easy for parents, caregivers, and teachers to label Aries children as the athletic or sporty types and leave it at that. However, this would be a mistake as Aries children also possess deeply creative souls. They respond especially well to bright colors and lots of different mediums when it comes to visual art. However, there are potential drawbacks of making art, including its messiness and the fact that it's often a solo activity. Aries children tend to like things neat and organized, and they love group endeavors. Aries kids can be little drama kings and queens, and they love praise, so they might find that theater acting is something they enjoy and excel at.

Arts that involve physical activity—dance, singing, or even martial arts—can be especially beneficial for the Aries child. Young Rams love to make noise, so another fruitful area to explore is music and learning to play an instrument. They are especially drawn to drums and electric guitars, as they are little rockers in training.

Extracurricular Activities

When considering after-school activities for an Aries child, parents and caregivers must be on their guard. As our guiding story shows, Jack willingly and whole-heartedly accepts his adventure, and it is all-consuming. The Aries child's inclination is to say *yes* to new adventures, to dares, to more activities. This can lead to a child who is fussy, bossy, and apparently ungrateful—in other words, an exhausted little Aries! One of the paradoxes of Aries (and one of the lessons that Aries children and adults alike must discover) is that although their first impulse is to try anything, their actual desire is usually to develop excellence and mastery in a couple of different places. Therefore choose extracurricular activities with an eye to this. One sport per season, two at most overall, is good for an Aries. It is also good to encourage balance: if your Aries child is very athletic, embrace that but also encourage learning a skill in the arts, such as dance, acting, or playing an instrument.

Remember that Aries thrives best in group activities, so team sports or playing in a band or orchestra are preferable for them rather than solo sports like tennis or studies like piano. The most important thing is to keep an eye on your little Ram and make sure they're not getting overly exhausted by their extracurricular commitments—and keep in mind they will also be requesting frequent playdates and overnight visits with friends along the way.

Technology

For Mars-ruled Aries children, screens can easily become addictive, the focus of all of their desire and interest. This is because these children—who yearn for connection and purpose, motion and excitement—feel they are connecting and accomplishing a specific purpose or mission through on-screen experiences. Though it's actually a passive endeavor, screen time can give the Aries child the illusion of being active and engaged in a feat of skill and daring. Some Aries voluntarily eliminate screens altogether; others embrace them fully and completely. The question is: When are they making much-needed connection and engaging in fulfilling activities, and when are they not? Lurking beneath the issue of screens is the allure of the magic harp in the story: Jack's choice of a magic harp in the giant's lair—a harp that plays music by itself—speaks to the timeless allure of technology. Is it good? Is it bad? Neither? There are no hard and fast rules when it comes to screen time. If you are engaged with your children, you will see what helps them flourish and what does not.

The Aries child is likely to seek out more screen and TV time than many other children. You might find it helpful to place limits on that time early and often. These children will also seek out games and TV shows that emphasize subjects like war, crime, action, and adventure; it is part of the martial aspect present in all Aries. An alternative way for your Aries child to engage with technology is to discover how it works, preferably within a group setting. As they get older, Aries children can enjoy technological challenges like coding and robotic competitions, which combine the energy of contest with the social factor of a group. Caregivers and parents might also encourage their Aries child to step away from the screens and go outside to play.

Sleeping and Waking

When Jack returns home with the magic seeds, he returns to a furious mother. Angry with himself and his life, he tosses the seeds away, shuts himself in his room, and tries his best to ignore the fact that he is going to sleep hungry. No wonder he falls into a fitful sleep. The Aries child often goes to bed hungry for more adventure, raw from the conflicts that this brings, so sleep can come with great difficulty.

Aries children require at least eight hours of sleep, and often nine or ten. This is because during sleep they are best able to replenish the energy burned throughout the day. Although these children are sometimes the last to want to go to bed, they need an enforced and consistent bedtime. One effective way to nurture Aries sleep is to make sure their rooms are dark and with no electrical items turned on near the bed. They often do not need an activity like a bedtime story to help them wind down, as they tend to be either on or off, with not much in between. However, they are some of the most physically affectionate children, so they appreciate and respond well to before-bed snuggles.

If an Aries child has slept long enough, they will generally be in good spirits even though they may be slow moving when they get up. If they haven't gotten enough sleep (and this is often the case), they will be grouchy, difficult, and may wake up looking for a fight. Parents may be tempted to gradually wake up their Aries children and ease them into the morning, but these children actually often respond better to a lights-on, everybody-up kind of approach.

Discipline

No one in Jack's community expected that he would be the Boy Who Did Good. The Aries child often finds themself in trouble with parents, teachers, and caregivers, especially during their early years. The little Ram's exuberant nature, sense of daring, inability to sit still, and innate leadership—which may come across to their peers as either a bossy or demanding attitude—can all come together to create the perfect storm.

Aries children have an especially hard time learning to control the volume of their voices, to not interrupt others, and to sit still. For these reasons, parents may find that they receive a lot more phone calls and discipline notices about their little Aries children than other parents do. Regular punishment is not nearly as effective as random positive rewards, and this is especially true in the case of Aries. One really fun idea is to keep a drawer full of small, age-appropriate toys (I often get mine from the party-favor section at our local party store) and give them to your little one when they do something exceptionally great. For older children, privileges may be taken away when there is problematic behavior, but privileges can be gained when there is especially kind behavior or a big accomplishment. Mars-ruled Aries is already in a habit of looking to see how they can be better, stronger, faster, and generally more perfect. They hide that behind good cheer and strength of personality, but Aries children find it easy to fall into deep wells of self-criticism. Because of this, a demanding parent or caregiver who continually lists an Aries child's failings won't have a good impact if the goal is correcting behavior. An Aries will become angry and then petulant when they hear someone pointing out issues that they're already quite aware of.

Instead, random positive reinforcement can work wonders with those born under this sign as they love to be praised and flattered. Their naturally generous natures respond in kind to someone else's generosity, and they appreciate kindness. Teaching the Aries child mindfulness techniques that include regular and rhythmic motion (such as meditative walking or a physical gesture such as a yoga *mudra*) can help the child to anchor themself to the present moment and can help with avoiding time-outs and detentions. Left unchecked and unparented, the Aries child could easily turn into a bully. It's not unusual for both female and male Aries children to get physical with those around them. Remember, the sign is ruled by war-loving, battle-hungry Mars. Aries children, especially when angry or sad, can and will go looking for a fight.

One of the best ways to counterbalance this is to make sure that you give Aries children tasks and responsibilities. This is tricky because what parents and teachers often see when they look at an Aries child is a bright mind that cannot focus or sit still—in other words, not the most responsible person. But like a good soldier, an Aries needs duties and responsibilities to round them out. Give them tasks that really do help others: the more physical the better. They love being chosen and called on, and they will respond well to being given more responsibility and authority in service to others.

How Best to Connect

In our version of the tale, Jack's final move is to seek out knowledge that will help his people do a better job of caring for the land. Every Aries child needs to learn when to admit they don't know something and then ask for help, yet this is something that can be hard to do. Through his courageous efforts, Jack restores peace and prosperity not just to his own family but to his entire community. When standing on solid ground and held by love and guidance, Aries children are absolutely capable of the same feat.

Aries children are doers, movers, and shakers. Their favorite way to connect is by sharing in an activity with others—whether by playing a sport, learning a new skill, going shopping, or even cooking together. Those born under this sign learn about themselves and their inner lives through activity. Aries children who are less activity prone do well to remember that movement and activities are not always distractions from the more serious and meaningful aspects of life.

Connection with the Aries child happens primarily by participating in whatever they are up to at the moment. They love it when people join in, and though they may not always voice it, they dislike doing things by themselves. These little Rams are also very physical. Words and verbal expression are typically not their strength but physicality is. They love hugs, to be picked up and swung, to have their hair tousled, and to have piggyback rides. Aries is the sign that rules the head, so head and face massages are very soothing to the Aries child and provide physical connection. Incorporate them into your bedtime routine to help the little Ram in your life turn down their energy and get ready for sleep.

Polarity: Libra

Libra teaches Aries to refrain from always putting themselves first and to consider how their actions and words affect people around them. Libra also encourages Aries to stop always looking for a fight or conflict and to work to achieve more harmonious ends whenever possible.

Aries Ascendant

When Aries is at the Ascendant, the child often comes across as physically striking and beautiful, bold, and bossy. They often show great enthusiasm at the beginning of a project but may have a hard time following through. Aries Ascendant children do best when they are able to take their experiences and put them into action. Part of the work of these children is to develop a strong sense of individual identity so that they can be leaders and pioneers.

Aries Moon

The child with Aries Moon usually has tranquil emotions and is comfortable surrounded by half-finished projects, loud noises or people, and difficult tasks. Their idea of a good time is optimizing and perfecting everything they can get their hands on. No matter what their Sun Sign is, with an Aries Moon these children can show flashes of an extremely hot temper that might take others by surprise.

Walking with Intention

Take the Aries child in your life out for a walk. Encourage them to really feel the minute motions involved in taking first one step and then another. Support them in feeling the pressure of first the heel, then the center, then the ball of the foot, followed by the toes landing upon the earth. Call their attention to their breath, to the way that air and light feel on their skin, and to what they see with their eyes, smell with their nose, and hear with their ears. This ritual will encourage each child to take motion to a deeper level and to begin to see the relationship between movement and stillness.

Ritual
Candle Light, Candle Bright

Light a candle before bedtime. Let your Aries child watch you do it, and when they are old enough, let them help you do it. Allow them some time to just watch the flame without any agenda. Once they grow still, blow the flame out and snuggle them down into bed. This ritual encourages the relationship between the child and their natural element of fire.

Ritual for the Inner Aries Child
Embracing Action

In my work with adults who are nurturing their inner Aries child, I often find that one of the most damaging things they heard, over and over again while growing up, was the command "Sit still!" This is painful for any child to hear, but for an Aries it is akin to "Don't breathe!" Our inner Aries child is the seat of our bravery, our boldness, and our core sense of self. These are important elements to be familiar with if we are going to help the inner child heal.

The ritual for supporting this healing work is one of movement. First ground and center yourself in whatever way works best. (The Grounding, Centering, and Anchoring activity in chapter 2 is a great exercise to use.) Then, as you are ready, ask your inner Aries child how it wants to move. Listen with your body, and then allow those movements to be expressed. Move for as long as you want, in whatever ways you want. Once you have finished, write about your experiences in your journal.

CHAPTER 5

The Taurus Child

"The most important thing is to enjoy your
life. To be happy. It's all that matters."

Audrey Hepburn
(Taurus, born May 4, 1929)

BIRTHDAY: April 19–May 20

RULING PLANET: Venus

ELEMENT: Earth

QUALITY: Fixed

SYMBOL: Bull

HOUSE: Second House of Desire and Endurance

STATEMENT: I am here to make.

SEASON: High Spring

GUIDING STORY: "The Race for the Mango"

Now children, come together as night begins to truly fall. Draw your eyes up to the sky once more so that you can find the Bull. This is a large constellation taking up much space in the sky. You may see it most clearly in November when the Taurid meteor shower seems to fall from its stars. Aldebaran is its brightest star—do you see it now? Good. The Bull represents many things, but among them is the understanding of where we truly come from and what sustains us. Settle in now, as we travel in story to the rich land of India, where there were once two divine brothers . . .

Once upon a time, Lord Shiva was given a splendid gift: a mango that would bestow upon whomever ate it knowledge and deep wisdom. Shiva was grateful for the gift but was also concerned, for he had two sons and was not sure which one should have the precious fruit. So, he sought the council of his beloved wife, the Goddess Parvati, and she suggested he create some kind of contest between the boys to help him decide.

He gathered his two sons to him. One was the elephant-headed Lord Ganesha and the other was Lord Kartikeya, the God of War. Shiva challenged each boy to race around the entire universe and all of its worlds and promised a fantastic prize to whomever won. He explained that this feat would call upon all of their strength, endurance, and magic. As Shiva was speaking, Lord Ganesha found a bit of milk-sweetened rice and was eating it happily while also listening to his father. Kartikeya clapped his hands together in delight; everyone knew that he was stronger and faster than his tubby brother who liked to do nothing more than eat sweet things, read, and write. As soon as Shiva had finished speaking, Kartikeya called to his side his racing peacock, saddled up on it, and went off into the skies.

Ganesha slowly got up, for his belly was quite full, and he went through the house until he found his mother, Parvati, the Goddess of the Universe and all living things. Ganesha took her hand within his own, and he walked around her three times. Then he sat down, happily waving his trunk in the air, and declared victory. As soon as he had done so, Kartikeya returned, out of breath and with a tired-looking peacock.

The great lord was surprised that his oldest son had completed the task first. As for Kartikeya, he could not believe his big, slow brother had bested him. Ganesha explained that the challenge was to race around the universe, but he knew that his mother—and all mothers—contained the entire universe in their bodies and within their families. Shiva could find no fault with this unique way of understanding things, so he gave the golden, juicy mango to his oldest son. Ganesha took it gently in his trunk, sniffed it once, and then gobbled it up whole!

Taurus Gifts		
Strong	Consistent	Artistic
Sensual	Physical	Gentle
Skilled	Practical	Grounded
Taurus Challenges		
Lazy	Self-Indulgent	Stubborn

THE TAURUS PERSONALITY

In the tale of "The Race for the Mango" we see many hallmarks of the second sign of the Zodiac, the lovable Bull known as Taurus. The Taurus child is gifted with patience, strength, focus, and endurance. Like Ganesha, these children are looking to play a long game and are often able to outlast others when it comes to contests of strength or focus. There is a natural intelligence in the Taurus child that seeks out solutions that are elegant, simple, and above all practical. When it comes to this latter virtue, practicality, the Taurus child shines. It is not uncommon for even very young Bulls to talk in pragmatic terms about subjects like career, money, and even romance and sex. You may suspect that when they are not engaged in feats of strength on the playground, they are considering what stocks to invest in or what their 401K might look like—and you might not be wrong!

Sometimes this practical side of the Taurus child can get them into trouble. They tend to do what makes sense from a pragmatic, as opposed to a moral, standpoint. One of the places the Taurus child is most practical is with money and finances. Taurus is the first sign in the Zodiac that has a definite relationship with money, finances, and cash flow. They tend to do well in calculating sums for this reason, and they enjoy games like Monopoly. Taurus children are often interested in how much money their family has and how much money others have as well. This kind of talk can leave adults feeling uncomfortable. As fixed signs, Taurus children are especially hard to shake. They will circle back to the subject of finances whenever they see an opportunity to do so and keep asking questions until they receive answers that feel adequate. For this reason, we might find it helpful to be completely open with the Taurus child about money. They will respond well to behavior expectations when those expectations are monetized, and they will enjoy learning the ins and outs of money: making it, saving it, spending it, and managing it.

Economics is an area of study a Taurus will probably feel drawn to in some form or fashion. If the interest in money and finances is not honored, then the young Bull can develop an overly strong fixation on wealth, become selfish, and/or want to acquire lots of status through possessions (e.g., designer clothes, fancy shoes, and pricy jewelry). You could talk to your bank about opening an account for the Taurus child and check to see if there are any investment clubs they could play in and learn from. And don't be afraid to talk money with them.

Pleasure is another area that the Taurus child has a natural affinity for. These children tend to be picky eaters, not because they want to be difficult but because they are all very particular about what they eat—and they want something that is yummy. They often have strong ideas about what is delicious or the appropriate way to prepare a dish—and you will not be able to change their minds once they have been made up, so don't even try. The Taurus child has a knack for finding delicious food and also the most comfortable spots to hang out, whether at school or at home. They are often very selective about clothes. The little Bull child may desire outfits that make them feel good and that are pleasant to the touch as well as stylish.

Sensual pleasures are one of the domains of both the Taurus adult and child. This is another area that can make adults feel uncomfortable as these children are often ready to have honest conversations about sex, pleasure, and the body long before their peers are. Sensuality, of course, goes beyond sex. The Taurus child is not the most verbal, but what they don't communicate in speech they often communicate through touch and physical contact. For these reasons it is important for caretakers and parents to honor their little Bull and allow for age-appropriate sensory experiences. Educational philosophies like those of Waldorf and Montessori schools have many fantastic resources for sensory education that the Taurus child will respond to beautifully.

Because the Taurus child tends to be on the quieter side, it's sometimes difficult for adults to know what's going on with them. These children do not display their emotions as easily as the Aries or Pisces child. Typically, Taurus children have relatively pleasant and grounded dispositions. They are, after all, ruled by Venus.

Two words powerfully describe the mental facility of the Taurus child: thorough and deliberate. Taurus children often take longer to complete their work, and tasks in general, but this is only because they are methodical and exacting. They do not like to be rushed but typically do respond well to timed activities because they are cool under pressure. If the activity is presented as a game and there is a monetized reward for completion, all the better!

Friends and Play

In our story, Ganesha is slower and more thorough than his sibling. He takes his time and enjoys himself. He is selective, as we can see from his choice not to take the obvious route to victory. Instead he does something unexpected and creative. In the same way, the Taurus child is selective when it comes to friends and play. Though they may have a wide circle of friends, they typically have only a handful who are really close friends. Taurus children, blessed by their Ruling Planet Venus, tend to be popular, but guarded about who they really let in. If your young Bull plays sports, often their team members will become close friends. This is in part because Taurus children communicate especially well through physical contact, so situations in which they're allowed, encouraged, and rewarded for expressing themselves physically tend to be good settings for long-lasting friendships. The Taurus child would rather be alone than engage in vapid socializing. It is common to see the Taurus child hanging out by herself if she has not yet discovered the friends with whom she truly connects. Taurus is a fixed sign, and this can prove sticky in social situations because Taurus adopts a "my way or the highway" attitude, often refusing to shift ground, adjust expectations, or make exceptions. The moment Taurus starts feeling bossed or bullied they dig in—and good luck moving them. Taurus children possess a very focused personality: they tend to be able to concentrate on one project for a long period of time. For like-minded friends this can work out beautifully, but for other friends (especially when Taurus is younger) this can be very frustrating and perceived as boring. They will thrive best in social relationships when they are encouraged to collaborate and adapt. Since a Taurus can initially be a bit shy, they can be greatly helped if their caregiver reaches out and arranges one-on-one playdates on their behalf.

Because Taurus is such a pragmatic thinker, they can have issues at school when morality comes into play. If the Taurus child in question is good at reading social cues, they will deliver the answer they know they're supposed to give—even if they secretly don't believe it. If they have a hard time with social cues—or they just don't care about other people's opinions—they may give responses that are much less concerned with moral qualms and more interested in practical results. Learning that involves being outside or working with plants or animals is especially pleasant for a Taurus child, and they do well in any academic setting that encourages such interactions.

Academics

In "The Race for the Mango," we see how no one expected Ganesha to win. His brother was a shoo-in for obvious reasons, and so everyone overlooked the tubby Elephant God. Shiva was astonished to see Ganesha and hear how he came to finish the race. The Taurus child is usually very smart, tends to have a natural facility with numbers and often with languages as well, and can excel at reading if they are not rushed in their early years to learn to read. But like Ganesha, the Taurus child can be easily overlooked or unrecognized in the pursuit of academic excellence.

There are several factors contributing to this child's invisibility. The first reason has to do with communication: a straight-up Taurus is not the best verbal communicator. They do better when making, doing, or showing, and they will also do better on written work. Taurus's innate perfectionism may also contribute to their lack of recognition by teachers or peers: they are so consistently good that their excellence can be taken for granted.

Anything that requires detail-oriented thinking or technical proficiency will appeal to Taurus children, who are thorough and often slow-going. They may even seem to be falling behind. They're not going to be the first ones to raise their hands in most cases, and they may not even offer an answer to the current question at all, even though they probably know it. The fact that a Taurus moves at his own pace and is seldom willing to budge means that he may become stressed by assignments in which time plays a big factor or there is a rush to finish. On the other hand, if time is managed well, the little Bull has a tremendous capacity to get it right like no one else. As an Earth sign, Taurus can be fairly slow to get started but often will endure longer than most other children. For this reason, special care needs to be taken when transitioning the Taurus child from one activity to another. These little ones often need extra time to get settled and acclimated before they can begin working on the task at hand.

These young Bulls are not afraid of work or struggle. They actually embrace it and look forward to difficult problems that take an extra-long time to solve—they may even become bored if given tasks that are too easy or simple to navigate.

In addition to perfectionism and a preference for nonverbal communication, Taurus often does not respond best to audiovisual instruction. They prefer a hands-on, visually demonstrative approach and are often more kinesthetic learners. The Taurus child who is well supported in her learning styles and habits shows herself to be a creative thinker capable of great focus and patience, and a student especially adept at tackling bigger, multilayered problems with patience and endurance.

Because a Taurus child is always a pleasure seeker, watch out for fussiness when it comes to *things*—from the food at lunch to the temperature of the classroom. These children can be distracted if things are not just right. This sense of having things be just right, on the other hand, is one of Taurus's greatest assets if it is well-directed. Rather than commanding them to quit being so fussy, nurture them by helping them sense when to let things go as they are, while at the same time honoring their need to have things just right.

The young-adult Taurus who is considering college may find themselves drawn to art or design schools and typically will do well with those programs. Though Bulls are practical-minded, they also appreciate and seek out opportunities for mastery. A maturing Taurus child may value teachers for who they are and what they know more than the name of the university or the prestige that a certain college degree carries. Likewise, if there is something practical and worthwhile to learn, the Taurus will commit fully, but if the academic subject is deemed unimportant, the Taurus adult won't be interested even if it's taught at an impressive institution. For the Taurus who is not interested in a school for art or design, trade schools that teach practical skills are often appealing. Ruled as they are by the Second House of Desire and Endurance, young people born under Taurus will always want to know how what they're learning will translate into a paycheck.

Physical Activity

Taurus children benefit greatly from physical activity, but they may not seek it out on their own. Like our beloved Ganesha, these little ones tend to be very happy being sedentary and left to their own devices. But they have great reserves of strength and endurance that make them excellent assets to many sports teams. Team sports are best for the Taurus child, though if pushed in the direction of sports they may opt to do a solo sport like swimming or tennis if given the option. Team sports are great for Taurus because one of their primary challenges is learning to move from their own viewpoint and to understand a more collaborative framework. They may also benefit from solo sports, like cycling, that can transition into team sports. The Taurus child, once physically active, will usually do really well and impress others with their abilities and sustained energy levels. They may be slow to start, but once they get going, watch out! The combination of strength, endurance, and the Taurus child's ability to solve problems means that they are valued members of a team and can be excellent strategic and tactical players.

As the Taurus child ages, they may drop out or reduce their participation in organized sports because other interests like art or science occupy their schedule. This is fine, but the Taurus child should always be reminded that they need to move, get their heart rate up, and physically exert themselves regularly. If not, they run the risk of health issues due to an overly sedentary lifestyle.

Art and Creativity

In "The Race for the Mango," Ganesha is a creative thinker who solves the challenge in a way nobody else could imagine. In the same way, the Taurus child tends to enjoy and be adept at artistic and creative endeavors. Taurus is one of the signs strongly affiliated with the arts, especially the visual and tactile arts. In fact, art-making is one of the things that so many Taurus children excel at because it combines their ability to problem-solve and work on complex ideas with their Venus-inspired love of beauty and pleasure. As Earth signs, Taurus children are perfectly happy taking their time and making sure that their art project is exactly how they want it to be, and they may eschew the conventional methods for producing a piece of work in favor of something more simple and direct. They also may find that their creative juices flow more in the direction of a tactile experience like gardening.

Taurus children do not like to be micromanaged in their creative lives. They may find themselves on the wrong side of the teacher if they choose to focus on something other than the class lesson. On the other hand, they can respond well to basic direction concerning an overarching vision, but then they prefer to be left alone or in the company of a small group of friends while carrying out the vision in the way they see fit. Trying to redirect a little Bull once he has gotten started making art is a fairly futile effort because by that point in time he has a fixed notion of where he's going and how to get there. The Taurus child may seem to lack imagination due to her orderly approach and insistence on not deviating from a specific path once she has decided on it. In fact, she is deeply creative and sensitive, and art is one of the few places those qualities can have free rein. If your Taurus becomes anxious, get their hands dirty with clay or carving—they will immediately relax and have an excellent time!

Extracurricular Activities

One of the most striking qualities of Ganesha is the way he balances repose and enjoyment of life with the pursuit of excellence. Ganesha can serve as a model for the young Taurus. Like her fellow Earth signs of Virgo and Capricorn, Taurus has to balance the desire to chill and enjoy life with a desire for excellence and the development of skill.

Juggling these different qualities is often trickiest around extracurricular activities. The Taurus child may need coaching, encouragement, and—in some cases—gentle coercion by parents or caregivers to initially get involved in any activity. Ideally, the Taurus child would be involved in one creative/artistic extracurricular activity and one physical activity. In the best scenario, the Taurus child is committed to a small number of activities that they can focus on, develop their skills around, and fully engage in while the rest of their after-school hours is time off.

If the Taurus child has activities booked every day of the week, the caregivers will discover that they have a very unhappy (and stressed out) Bull on their hands. Taurus children are often too willing to become couch potatoes, munching on after-school snacks and watching TV or playing video games for hours on end. As children of Venus these children naturally like pleasurable activities, and as Earth signs they will go with a sedentary activity when they can. But the answer is not to have them moving 24/7. Instead, find a happy medium between letting your Taurus child unwind and enjoy free time after school and participating in some meaningful activities. Once the Taurus child is engaged in an activity he really likes, he will usually do quite well with it as he is able to bring his focus and concentration to bear on it. Creative activities in the arts, especially the tactile arts like pottery, weaving, or even cooking can really appeal to Taurus on many levels. Also, caregivers should keep in mind that Taurus is the sign that rules the throat. That means many of those born under the sign of the Bull have naturally beautiful singing and speaking voices!

Technology

The Taurus child tends to have an all-or-nothing attitude when it comes to digital media. As an Earth sign, some Taurus children exhibit very little interest in technology. They would rather be outside climbing trees, curled up in a sunny spot with a good book, or building something challenging. A great deal of our tech gadgets make things go faster, and Taurus is a sign that doesn't believe faster is always better. Screens, artificial lights, and lots of sounds and noises can stress them out, so they avoid them as much as they can. In fact, some young Bulls may find that when learning via digital media is introduced, their grades go down and it takes them a while to acclimate to the new program.

In other cases, however, the Taurus child will find that they love screens. They are especially prone to passively consuming movies, video games, and all matter of electronic entertainment to unwind at the end of their day. Parents and caregivers should keep in mind the Taurus child's tendency to be sedentary above all else and closely monitor screen time so that plopping down with their computer or tablet is not the only thing the Taurus child does all afternoon. The Taurus child does tend to like games, so educational games that come with tangible rewards and involve higher-level problem-solving skills will appeal to them. The Taurus child will also be interested in the tech aspect of finance, so as they get older expect them to explore concepts like blockchain, e-commerce, and crypto-currencies. If caregivers see that their Taurus child is already in love with all things math and money, it is a good idea to introduce them to spreadsheet- and budget-making tools and apps.

Sleep and Waking

In our story, Ganesha is not a fast mover like his brother. In the same way, the Taurus child is not a fast mover, and this Venus-ruled child enjoys sleeping in when given the chance. Taurus children tend to think they need more sleep than they really do and are particularly resistant when roused awake. At bedtime, there are a couple of things to watch for. First of all, make sure that they have had a good dinner. A hungry Taurus is a Taurus no one wants to be around, and if these children go to bed hungry they won't sleep well and may not sleep at all. An hour to ninety minutes before bedtime, caregivers should turn off anything that might stimulate the child and keep them awake. Being Venus ruled, Taurus children often like a nice bath (with good bath products) and comfortable pajamas that feel good on their skin. These children can be fussy about their external environment and may have a hard time sleeping in a messy room or a room that is too hot or cold. Having a natural affinity with animals, Taurus children may want the family dog or cat to sleep with them, or, if that isn't possible, a stuffed animal may help them feel secure.

Often upon waking the Taurus child is hungry and will need to have a good and balanced breakfast. Grabbing a quick breakfast bar on the way out the door does not work for these children. The Taurus child can be a bit of a clotheshorse and take a really long time deciding what to wear, so it is a good idea to encourage them to pick out their outfits the evening beforehand. Some Taurus children like to create uniforms for themselves so that they don't have to think about clothes. This may be very unofficial (jeans and a white or black t-shirt) or there might be certain elements that always need to be in place (like a specific pair of shoes or a particular handbag). Taurus does not like to be rushed, and if pushed tends to dig in and simply refuse to move. Given that, it is a good idea to give a Taurus child extra time in the morning to wake up, which will make sure that they have plenty of time in the morning to get ready for school.

The Taurus child appreciates order and organization, a decluttered room, and a predictable morning routine. Some forethought about the morning can go a long way toward reducing stress.

Discipline

Ganesha doesn't get in trouble very often—not just because he is lovable but because he is not one to rush into every and any new deed. Similarly, Taurus children tend to be well-behaved for the most part. The biggest challenge with these children comes when they feel that they are being pushed to do something in a specific way and they dig in their heels. It is very hard to move a Taurus child once their mind is made up. This digging in can look different depending on the situation. On one hand, the Taurus child may not say anything to indicate that they are not listening, and they will simply proceed as they were before being corrected. In this case, their behavior often takes on the flavor of deliberate disobedience and can make teachers, parents, and caregivers deeply frustrated.

Another form of classic Taurus stubbornness is a refusal to do what they are being asked to do verbally and with no further explanation for why they are choosing not to follow directions. (Honestly, the Taurus child feels that if you cannot figure this out yourself, you probably shouldn't be telling them what to do.) Things can quickly devolve at this point, as the Taurus child and their adult caregivers are at loggerheads with each other. A better option is to give them several options or alternative behaviors to choose from, and invite them to pick the one that suits them best. This allows the child to have some say in what happens next and know that their backs are not against the wall, thus forcing them to dig in their heels. Conventional corrective techniques like time-outs do not tend to work on these little Bulls. They often enjoy time out! It gives them a chance to be quiet and alone with their feelings and thoughts. Systems of reward and punishment, especially if they involve actual goods or tokens that can be traded in for goods, often work very well for these children.

How Best to Connect

In "The Race for the Mango," we can sense how Ganesha is a great lover of touch and tactile sensation. The Taurus child is similar. Connecting through touch and tactile sensation will therefore help to build trusting relationships with them. The Taurus child tends not to be a big talker, but this does not mean that she doesn't have thoughts and feelings or that she doesn't want to share. Verbalizing those emotions is especially hard, which means that caregivers need to make sure there are other avenues of expression for the Taurus child. Visual art, making things together (even cooking a meal together), and physically snuggling are all ways the Taurus child can feel safe and connected with her caregivers. Once that connection is in place, and in her own time (please do not rush these children), the Taurus child can open up and share with their people. Another excellent way to connect with these children is by doing things outside: gardening, hiking, picking fruit, or doing something that involves animals. Outside, in nature, and with four-footed friends, the Taurus child often feels more relaxed and at liberty to really share their rich, inner world with those whom they trust.

Polarity: Scorpio

Scorpio reminds Taurus to go beyond the surface of things and that not everything that is worthwhile is necessarily going to be pleasant or feel good. Scorpio encourages Taurus to apply their strength and skillfulness to moving beyond the surface and examining their shadow sides instead of settling only for the things that come easily or the paths of least resistance.

Taurus Ascendant

The child with the Taurus Ascendant comes off as strong, determined, quiet, and stubborn. They often have a beautiful voice and give off a grounded, earthy vibe. These children can also seem a bit uncommunicative or lazy. Taurus ascending asks that whatever paths the child follows, she manifests the work she brings into the world in a physical and tactile way. The ultimate mission of these children is to allow themselves to feel pleasure and enjoy themselves.

Taurus Moon

Children with their Moon in Taurus love to be outside with their hands in the dirt. These children often have a strong affinity with nature and may be more comfortable around plants and animals than they are around people. Also, Taurus Moon children are often naturally gifted healers and very much enjoy making natural remedies/cosmetics/potions. These little ones need plenty of sleep and are quite comfortable doing nothing, so they may have to be encouraged to get exercise and be social with peers.

Activity
Tending the Garden

Introduce your Taurus child to the delights, responsibilities, and pleasures of tending a garden. Provide them with a small bit of earth (or even a pot) and allow them to participate in the entire process: choosing what they wish to grow, digging the hole, planting the seeds, and caring for the plant. This will teach the Taurus that hard work bears tangible fruit. It also allows them to connect with Earth which is, after all, their element!

Ritual
Saving Up Your Coins

Honor the Taurus child's love of finance with a magical piggy bank. For this ritual I recommend that you purchase a bank-box type of bank so that the Taurus child can open it and see how many dollars and coins they have. Give them a coin every day and make a ritual of placing it in the bank for safekeeping. When they let you know there is something that they would really like to have, remind them of their piggy bank and help them figure out how much they need to save or spend out of their funds. This ritual will also allow your Taurus child to ask the natural questions they have about money in a safe space.

Ritual for the Inner Taurus Child
Allowing for Luxury

Many adults focusing on their inner Taurus child realize that their interest in money and the finer things was a source of stress and shame when they were growing up, and may even be one today. They were often told, "Don't be greedy!" I've heard from many of my adult Taurus clients that they were taught from a young age that money is something you just don't talk about, and they were shamed for wanting to think and talk about money. This ritual addresses those wounds.

Cultivate calmness in whatever way works best for you. Ask yourself the following question: What little luxury have I been denying myself? Instead of writing down your answer, create the answer visually, through painting or clay or collage. Once you know what the little luxury is, give yourself intentional permission to procure and enjoy it.

CHAPTER 6

The Gemini Child

"I change during the course of a day. I wake
and I'm one person, and when I go to sleep
I know for certain I'm somebody else."

Bob Dylan
(Gemini, born May 24, 1941)

BIRTHDAY: May 20–June 20

RULING PLANET: Mercury

ELEMENT: Air

QUALITY: Mutable

SYMBOL: Twins

HOUSE: Third House of Thought and Connection

STATEMENT: I am here to speak.

SEASON: Late Spring

GUIDING STORY: "Diamonds and Toads"

Children, your chattering now should begin to quiet, and I can see the hope for the sweet candy that Ganesha likes best of all shining in your eyes. Turn your attention to the skies once more as we speak of the sign of the Twins: Gemini. It is best viewed during the month of February and may be spotted by its two brightest stars, Castor and Pollux. These brothers were divine twins from ancient Greek myth, and were so loved that they never died but instead were turned into stars. Our next tale, from France, features one character who might also be turned into a star—she is that virtuous. But she has a stepsister who is decidedly not, as you will soon see. Now, listen.

There was once a man who had been blessed with a daughter as beautiful as she was kind. Sadly, not long after the child was born, her mother died. A few years passed and the man decided he might take a new wife so that his daughter would have another woman in the house.

He went off to the big city, found a suitable bride, and brought her and her daughter back to his home. But the man had not chosen well and his new bride was both cold and vain, her daughter as lovely as she was cruel and hateful. Above all, both women were exceedingly jealous of the first daughter and filled their days with plots determined to make life a misery for her. This went on for some time. The first daughter was moved from her grand rooms into a cellar. She was blamed any time something went wrong, and she was made to do all of the hardest household tasks. Among these tasks was going to the center of the village where the well was in order to draw enough water for the house's daily needs. She did this first thing every morning, and she did it without complaint.

One morning the girl approached the well and found another figure there—a withered and wispy old woman who smelled like sour cheese and whose mouth was full of blackened teeth. The old woman was cursing and cackling and struggling fiercely with her heavy bucket. The girl intervened, bowing with respect, and asking if she could help the old woman carry the water back to her home. As soon as the words had left her mouth, the old woman changed into a magical fairy queen and made a sign of blessing on the girl's head, proclaiming that everything she said from this point on would bring wealth, fame, and wisdom.

The girl, amazed by what she had seen and heard, thanked the fairy queen, finished drawing up the water and went home where she began to explain her encounter to her family. But as soon as she started speaking, diamonds and pearls and all manner of priceless gems fell from her mouth to her feet. Large crowds began to gather to hear her words, for they were both beautiful and true. The stepmother was enraged at the first daughter's good fortune. She roughly shoved the wooden bucket into her own daughter's arms and bade her hurry to the well, for if the worthless first daughter had been so blessed, what might happen to her own perfect child?

Angrily the girl went to the well, but she saw nothing there except a stinking old woman. She drew up water and then moaned and groaned about having to carry the heavy bucket all the way back home. While she had been drawing the water, she had ignored the struggles of the stinky old hag. Finally the crone turned to her and—with a mouth full of those blackened teeth—asked for aid. The daughter rolled her eyes and moved away from the biddy, laughing at her and refusing to help. The old woman squinted one eye and then the other and made a sign over the girl's head, and then she disappeared. Enraged, the girl made her way back to her mother and found herself stepping over piles of priceless gems and treasures. Her stepmother greeted her and wanted to know exactly what had happened and the girl began to tell her that *nothing* had happened, but as soon as she spoke, a slug, then a snail, then a toad and a worm all fell from her mouth. She began to emit a terrible odor, and no one wanted to be near her, not even her own mother. It was then she realized that she was cursed. Not long after, the stepmother and her spoiled daughter left the home never to return again. The first daughter fell in love with and married a wise and noble prince, and they had many beautiful children whom her father spoiled and whom she taught, above all, to be kind—especially to strange old women.

Gemini Gifts		
Intelligent	Friendly	Kind
Optimistic	Inclusive	Articulate
Adaptable	Agile	Imaginative
Gemini Challenges		
Flighty	Unreliable	Distracted

THE GEMINI PERSONALITY

Gemini children and adults are known for having dual natures. It is for this reason that the image of the Twins is particularly fitting for the third sign of the Zodiac. And, as the tale "Diamonds and Toads" illustrates, one of those natures is often sweet, beloved, and kind whereas the other is difficult, lacks noblility, and is shadowed. The crux of this tale has to do with speech and the actual substance of our words. The tale of "Diamonds and Toads" encourages all of us to ask if our words had physical form, what would they look like?

The Gemini child is bright and charming, cynical and fussy, friendly and engaging, shy and retiring. Can one child really be *all* of these things? When you are dealing with a Gemini child the answer is *yes*, and then some! In fact, when it comes to understanding the core personality of the Gemini child the only constant is change.

These little Twins are ruled by the original Trickster: the sandal-footed, quicksilver-tongued, Messenger God Mercury. Like their ruling Planet, a Twin is usually incredibly bright and intelligent, full of wit, smooth tongued, articulate, and able to move quickly from one place/feeling/experience/thought to the next. Because Gemini is ruled by heady Mercury and is an Air sign (also known as the intellectual powerhouse of the elements) caregivers might make the mistake that Geminis are all in their head. But Mercury rules *all* change, including vascillating emotions, so be prepared for the Gemini child you know and love to be moody and emotionally mercurial as well as smart.

One interesting aspect of Gemini is that this is the sign for *all* children. The time of childhood is the time of Gemini, so for that reason it is a good sign for everyone to pay attention to. The Gemini child, in the way of a true Air sign, is a great talker who loves to communicate and is typically most comfortable communicating verbally. Gemini children are thinkers as well as feelers, but above all they are connectors. When it comes to connecting and feeling connected, Gemini is a triple threat: these children are ruled by Mercury, the God of Messages, they are mutable signs (who are like the connective tissue and nervous systems of the Zodiac), and they are ruled by the element of Air which values relationships above everything else. For these reasons, it is very important for the little Twin to feel both heard and seen. If they feel that they are being ignored or overlooked, then a clever and emotionally manipulative side may quickly emerge to wreak havoc.

If the Gemini child has an older sibling, caregivers should prepare themselves for a serious case of hero worship because the little one wants to do everything their older sibling does. If a Gemini has a younger sibling, caregivers can expect them to take the role of older sibling very seriously. Typically, these children are comfortable with other children of all ages and all that goes along with them. Gemini children can come off as flighty, unreliable, and distracted if they are fatigued or overstimulated—and the sign in general can seem a bit shallow and superficial. Nothing is further from the truth. When Gemini is in his full power, he is discovering what the message is he wants to share with the world, and generous Gemini loves to support others as they discover theirs.

Friends and Play

The guiding story "Diamonds and Toads" reveals another aspect of Gemini: genuine versus counterfeit connection. We can see this with the two sisters in the tale. The heroine fosters a real connection with the older woman and is not reticent in assisting her, despite the woman's decrepit appearance. In the same way, the Gemini child who truly connects with someone sees past the obvious features and homes in on something deeper and more essential. The cruel sister, however, also displays a tendency of the Gemini child, which is the fostering of a surface connection motivated by shallow reasons or exclusively for personal gain.

The tension between genuine versus counterfeit connection, which is native to the Gemini, directly bears upon friendships, but also shows up in the area of art and creativity (see below).

The young Twin excels in the area of friends and play. A big concern for caregivers of the Gemini child is that they can easily become overstimulated by too many companions and too much activity. A balance must be struck because friendships are so important to Gemini children. They make friends quickly and are often the ones who can and do move between different groups or cliques as they get older. The Gemini child has friends from every possible social circle: nerds, artists, jocks, popular kids, and techy kids. These little Twins are one of the most inclusive signs in the Zodiac. They genuinely love all kinds of different people and figure that the more friends they have the more they can connect and learn (two favorite activities for the Gemini child). Caregivers should support the Gemini child's love of friends and make sure to arrange playdates, have friends over, and allow their child to connect with many different types of friend. Do not try to make Gemini stay in a single social box; they will rebel and show the dark and manipulative side of Trickster energy.

One area to watch when Gemini are with friends is that they tend to go along to get along. As mutable signs, these children tend to be the ones who are least comfortable making waves. As Air signs, Gemini children are people-pleasers and want to be well liked. When paired with other children, Gemini children may find that they are constantly doing what others want to do instead of doing what they would like to do. At the most extreme, sweet and affable Gemini children may be easily bullied. Teaching our Gemini children how to articulate and stand up for what they want will go a long way in preventing unwanted experiences and unpleasantness. Another area to be aware of is Gemini's ability to be influenced by others. The Gemini child will change, but when we see a Gemini child intentionally changing to be like someone else that they know, a red flag should go up. This is a case of our little Twin being influenced in a problematic manner and losing their sense of who they are and what they care about.

When the Gemini child is with their friends, they want to play! Play is important to all children, but it is especially important for the Gemini child who loves to share (both toys and experiences) and to connect with their friends. Gemini children are often the popular kids; they have an innate sense of what is trendy and what people will respond to. When we watch a Gemini child work a crowd, even at the earliest age, we can see that being charming just comes naturally to them.

Gemini children love games of all kinds: sports, video games, and games based on imaginative storytelling. They're up for all of it, but if there is a physical component involved, they're especially happy. Play can become a trouble area when the Gemini child wants only to play and discovers that she does not want to focus on anything perceived as work. This is when some gentle guidance can come in handy as you help them build good work habits—either making work tasks feel like a game or explaining (when the child is ready) that sometimes we have to put down our toys and do something that is needed but not necessarily fun. The sign of Gemini rules the hands, and Gemini children often find that they're very gifted and facile with their hands, so play that incorporates the hands (such as cards or jacks) can be really satisfying.

Academics

In our story, "Diamonds and Toads," words may look like toads and snails or they may be diamonds and pearls. Either way, there are definitely words—lots of them! The Gemini child loves to communicate and connect through speech, and this potency helps with academic work.

In addition to being at home with playing, Gemini children excel at learning. They want caregivers to engage and converse with them. The mutual exchange of ideas and information makes little Geminis feel safe, secure, and loved. This is the first area of the Zodiac where learning and learning styles come up for discussion. The Gemini child loves to learn and is usually quite smart—in fact, this sign has the reputation as one of the smartest in the Zodiac. Because they love to talk, Gemini children may get in trouble for talking out of turn or blurting out answers. Focusing on impulse control can help, but most likely this will always be a challenge for Gemini, especially in their early school days.

Though they are incredibly bright, Gemini children often struggle in school, at least at first, because they love to talk and have a hard time focusing on one activity at a time. The little Twin's fast-moving mind gets bored easily, and even sitting still for periods of time can pose a challenge for this active and aerial child. School environments that allow for more freedom of movement tend to work well for these children. Teachers and caregivers can work with a Gemini to return their attention to the task at hand in a loving and gentle manner. Curricula that are best for the Gemini child span a broad number of topics. As Gemini children get older, with a little support they are usually near the top of their class academically. Although Gemini children may get in trouble at school, they often like school and feel especially comfortable there. As they get older, the Gemini child will most likely be called out for distracting their friends; for instance, they have something they need to tell their friend *now*, and no, it cannot wait until after second period! Cheating can also be a problem. Specifically, Gemini children often allow others to copy or cheat off of them.

The blend of raw intelligence, kindness, desire for connection, and difficulty saying no mean that Gemini children are often too willing to accommodate more forceful classmates.

As the Twin matures, school and education are likely to take on an ever more important role in her life. Gemini young adults often find that they are drawn to staying in school; these youths run the risk of being perpetual students, happy always to learn but more resistant to actually doing something with their knowledge. Four-year degrees, masters programs, and even doctoral studies often appeal to Gemini. A Gemini who isn't given the opportunity to continue their education after high school may feel they are lacking something fundamental and may enter a higher learning program later in life. As these children mature into adults, they are most likely to become lifelong learners and will take an interest in nurturing others in those pursuits.

Physical Activity

As a Mercury-ruled Air sign, the Gemini child loves to move and is typically quite gifted when it comes to physical prowess. Gemini children often have good hand-eye coordination, and if caregivers notice that their Gemini child doesn't have this ability, it's a good idea to take them to the eye doctor as there may be an issue with vision.

The Gemini child also has a natural sense of rhythm, so different forms of movement and dance can appeal to them. As aerial signs these children often have a gift for tumbling and gymnastics. Sports that involve intricate hand motions—basketball, tennis, football—will appeal to the Gemini child. Because they work so well with others, the Gemini child is often the glue that holds a team together—encouraging those who need a boost and criticizing those who are bringing the team as a whole down. These children can be competitive, especially if adults around them are displaying that behavior, but they much prefer to be collaborative and work together.

Unlike their next-door neighbor Taurus, the Gemini child does not have a great deal of endurance; they have short bursts of energy and activity followed by a need to replenish and relax. An excellent way to help your little Twin do this is to give them a book because they love to read! Caregivers will see Gemini start to lose steam when physical activities that had been for fun suddenly become serious, usually in middle school and high school. At this point the Gemini child often takes a step back, preferring to keep things light and not enjoying the high-pressure stakes of serious competition. As in the areas of friends and play, caregivers do best for Gemini children when they encourage a moderate amount of physical activity but not too much—otherwise the Gemini child will be tired and unpleasant.

Art and Creativity

"Diamonds and Toads" teaches us that the Gemini child's primary work is to discover what really speaks to him and also what messages he wants to share with everyone else. The question is, will Gemini's message make the world more beautiful, or less?

If Gemini children don't know an answer, they have no problem making up one that sounds good. This may bring to mind the duplicity that Geminis are known for. You even may have heard the unkind phrase, "Don't rely on a Gemini." However, the truth is that Gemini children are natural storytellers, and often Gemini adults make successful careers in writing and publishing. Encourage the Gemini child in your life to tell stories from their imagination or to discourse on their interest while also teaching them about the difference between fact and opinion.

That reputation for duplicity can be channeled into another arena as well: acting and theatre. In fact, one of the best illustrations of the inner life of a Gemini is the theatrical Comedy and Tragedy masks. A Twin can move through many different emotions with ease, and this gives them versatility on stage and an affinity for the dramatic.

The Gemini child is naturally creative and makes all kinds of mental and emotional connections that lend themselves to art and creative activities. This sign rules the hands, and Gemini children are often very gifted at making things with their hands. That is the good news. The tougher news is that art requires a level of focus and concentration that is hard to come by for the Gemini child. They may be naturally talented musicians, but getting them to practice consistently is a battle. Or they might be gifted visual artists who float from one topic to the next, never exploring one in great detail. These habits can be corrected and supported, but a Gemini is never going to have the natural focus of a Taurus or the intensity of purpose that a Scorpio has. Instead, their gifts lie elsewhere. One exception to this is writing. Gemini children love to read, and as they get older, they often discover a love for writing as well. Fiction, creative nonfiction, and even scientific how-to writing appeals to the young Twin. Because writing concerns the world of words and ideas, there is always something new to consider and some new story to tell that keeps the Gemini child engaged and active. In close kinship to writing is the art of storytelling. Mercury-ruled Gemini definitely has the gift of gab, and caregivers should support both their writing and storytelling habits.

Extracurricular Activities

The two sisters in "Diamonds and Toads" are polar opposites, yet both have very malleable characters. It's as if the furthest thing on their mind is to offer any resistance to the experiences they have. They will try anything or do anything. Like all Air signs, Gemini children are likely to spread themselves too thin. They want to be involved in *all* activities and to say yes to *all* opportunities. This leads to a tired, worn-out kiddo, and when Gemini is tired she gets *cranky*. Tears, tantrums, and pouts are all part of the territory of the unhappy Gemini. For this reason, caregivers should keep an eye on their Gemini child's pace, social life, and activity list.

When it comes to extracurricular activities, there really is too much of a good thing. As we have seen, this child's tendency is to say yes to everything they possibly can. First of all, they don't want to miss out on anything. Second, they don't like saying no, and third, they want to be with friends. The Gemini child thrives best when there is a balance between physical, mental, and creative activities as well as a mix between competitive, collaborative, and solo activities.

Yes, solo activities are especially important for this child, who sometimes will discover that he has a hard time being by himself. The little Twin also needs unscheduled free time in which she can play, dream, imagine, and revive herself. If she has no extracurricular activities, she will resent the fact that she is missing out on the fun stuff her friends talk about. But if she is overloaded, she will become overwhelmed, trying to please too many people, and end up not really enjoying any of her commitments. Caregivers should be selective in what they encourage their Gemini children to do and should make decisions with an eye to social bonds as well as the merits of the activity itself.

Technology

In the Gemini's guiding story, each sister has a different relationship to the old woman who turns into the magical fairy, and thus each possesses a different relationship to magic. The first sister connects immediately and effortlessly with the crone and her magic; the second one takes on all of the crone's worst qualities (like her scent). Because so much of modern technology is shrouded in secrecy and arcane symbolism, there is often an analogy drawn between technology and magic. Technology mystifies and has a magical effect on us and especially on our children, even though the truth is that the systems of technology are thoroughly mapped out and rationalized from top to bottom.

In classical Astrology, Mercury is the ruler of both magic and technology. So the Gemini child is often at home with technology. In one way, Gemini is naturally connected to what is new "now" and on trend. But most of all, Gemini children will find only certain uses of technology alluring—like social media of all kinds—because of the promise of connection they might bring. Other aspects of technology will be interesting too, but nothing will appear more attractive to the Gemini than the promise of connection by means of technology. Certain Geminis, with their native love of connection, might just as easily turn the other way, and look down on technology as being counterfeit rather than a genuine way to connect with other people.

Naturally curious, these little Twins may want to understand how their technology actually works. Born communicators, these children have a knack for coding languages and an almost an intuitive knowledge of how different kinds of machines work and learn. Robotics and engineering are areas that the Gemini child might be naturally drawn to, and these children also tend to excel in the sciences.

From a consumption point of view, the Gemini—like all children—won't say no if you give them a fun game and flashing screen. But unlike other kids, the Gemini child may play one game for a little while, switch to another, and then get up and do something completely different before returning to their original game. In other words, long-lasting and focused video game marathons are not what these children are interested in, unless they are multiplayer games.

Sleeping and Waking

Gemini children are light sleepers and often, like other Air signs, don't need that much sleep. Because they are light sleepers, it is extra important for these children to be given time to wind down before they head to bed. Make sure that there are no distractions, especially noises that could interrupt their sleep.

Gemini children often forget to eat, or to eat enough, so make sure these little ones don't go to bed hungry or thirsty; if they do, they'll be up in a flash. Getting the young Twin to turn off his mind at bedtime can be a significant challenge, especially in the younger years. Reading or telling bedtime stories is an excellent way to get the Gemini child to focus, relax, and settle down so they can sleep well. Just be prepared for them to ask a million questions when the story is over!

After a good night of rest, the Gemini child is usually up early and is ready for fun. The Gemini child often hits the ground running and does not need time to wake up. In fact, they may already be well into creating their first game of the day while everyone else in the household is reaching for the coffee maker. This bright-eyed, bushy-tailed attitude makes getting ready for the day easy! That said, caregivers will need to keep a close eye on her as she's getting ready; even though she is up and awake, she is liable to lose focus and go off track unless she is gently guided to do each task in turn. The Gemini child can also be a bit forgetful, so when she is young, caregivers will do well to double-check that everything she needs for school is present.

Discipline

Just like the two sisters in the story "Diamond and Toads," Gemini children display multiple sides of their personality—and this complexity speaks to the issue of discipline. By and large, the Gemini child is good natured, and their sweetness and desire for connection can lead them into situations in which they are bullied. Yet the Gemini child has another side: one that can be aggressive. When Gemini children get physical, pulling, pushing, pinching, or hitting can ensue, especially if the Gemini child feels they're being left out of a group activity and/or if they feel that other children they are socializing with are not really seeing or connecting with them. What's more, Gemini children's natural intelligence and acting abilities can encourage them to be emotionally manipulative and apply peer pressure to other kids if they're left unchecked. Finally, the Gemini child can have a shallow side that values style over substance and so can be a bit thoughtless and uncaring at times.

The best solution to these potential issues is reminding the Gemini child about how their actions and words affect others and encouraging them to make solid and real connections. When they are younger, the Gemini child may also get into consistent trouble for blurting out answers. As far as discipline goes, Gemini children know how to play the game. They will say their apologies and do what needs to be done to make amends, but caregivers would do well to watch the Gemini child in the aftermath of being disciplined, to make sure that their understanding of what they did wrong is more than skin deep. One type of correction that will get the little Twin's attention is restricting their play, removing a specific toy, and/or withholding a favorite book for a time. Because Gemini loves connection, it is important to spend time with them and engage their interests. A reason for the bad behavior is their craving for connection. Instead of correction, perhaps all it takes is getting down on their level and sitting with them while drawing or talking or playing.

How Best to Connect

The issue of disciplining Gemini children leads us to the question of how best to connect to Gemini. As we know now, connecting is one of their strongest suits—so all the caregiver has to do is show up and pay attention. We have to make time for them. The primary ways that these children like to connect is through words, thought, and language. Talk to and with them. Read them books, tell them stories, imagine with them, and trade ideas. Though Gemini is the sign of the young child, they are very aware when they are being talked down to, so don't do that. Instead, treat them with genuine respect and take their ideas and their words seriously. Above all, with so many things that are liable to change for your little Twin, help them discover the ideas and values they have that are least likely to change, no matter what. This brings a stabilizing influence into their lives. Just letting them do their own thing will not be enough for them as it can be for a Pisces child, who is perfectly content playing for hours in her own world.

Polarity: Sagittarius

Sagittarius encourages Gemini to cease their fluttering from subject to subject and develop real wisdom in the areas that matter most to them. This sign also supports Gemini in taking all the different strands of ideas and experiences and forming one coherent life philosophy with them, and embracing their abilities as teachers, not just learners.

Gemini Ascendant

The child with Gemini at the Ascendant often appears to be younger than all of the other children either in looks or behavior. They come across as bright, curious, chatty, and popular. They may also display that two-sided quality that Gemini is known for. A child with Gemini at the Ascendent is being asked to formulate a message and network of connections that allows them to take that message out into the world.

Gemini Moon

Children with their Moon in Gemini love learning and are often quite comfortable in a classroom making discoveries. These children are busy and always asking questions, playing with words, and, as they get older, writing out or telling stories. Something to watch out for with children who have their Moon in Gemini are those Mercurial mood swings: one moment everyone is happy and cheerful, the next there are tears and tantrums. The good news is that these fits of emotional weather come as quickly as they go! Gemini Moon is comfortable talking but much less comfortable with silences. Learning to commit and focus stretches them in positive ways.

Activity
Write It Out

As your Gemini child gets older, you may find that writing is a deeply creative and powerful way for them to relate and connect. Get a blank book and leave letters in it to your Gemini child, and suggest that they write letters back to you. You will discover more about their thoughts, feelings, and concerns through this shared journal than you ever thought possible.

Ritual
Raincloud/Rainbow

Gemini children are natural storytellers, but as mutable Air signs they often take their feelings and thoughts out of the picture and instead focus on the relationships that matter most to them. Help your Gemini come into contact with their thoughts and feelings by encouraging them to tell you a story about their day. One of my favorite ways to do this is the raincloud/rainbow approach. Ask your little Twin what the "raincloud" of their day was: What was hard, not fun, or challenging? Then, ask them what the rainbow was: What was fun, exciting, or encouraging? In our home we try to pick one experience for each, which always leads to a bigger, more complicated story.

Ritual for the Inner Gemini Child
Speak Up!

The adult who works on embracing their inner Gemini child often suffers from the wound of being told, "Be quiet!" Gemini children are often shamed for talking too much or at inappropriate times, which in turn leads them to feel that no one really wants to hear what they have to say. In many Eastern traditions the space between our collarbones is where the throat chakra (Vishuddha) is located. This is the energetic point in the body that resonates to our voice and our ability to wield our voice effectively—whether through speaking or writing. Honor your voice by anointing this area of your body with a favorite ritual oil and/or selecting a talisman that you can wear around your neck to remind your inner Gemini child that your voice is blessed and one of a kind.

CHAPTER 7

The Cancer Child

"Family is the most important
thing in the world."

Princess Diana
(Cancer, born July 1, 1961)

BIRTHDAY: June 20–July 22

RULING PLANET: Moon

ELEMENT: Water

QUALITY: Cardinal

SYMBOL: Crab

HOUSE: Fourth House of Dreams and Family

STATEMENT: I am here to dream.

SEASON: Early Summer

GUIDING STORY: "Sleeping Beauty"

*Now that you have grown a bit quieter, let us look up
at the sky once more. This time see if you can spot the
constellation Cancer. It can be hard to find as it is relatively
dim and is best seen at the end of March. Look for its
brightest star, Beta Cancri. Now I see you are all getting
sleepy. But sleep is its own adventure, and you must have
a care even when resting. Here, let me tell you about
the magic of sleep in this tale, which comes to us from
many different regions, but most immediately from Italy.*

A time long ago, and yet not so long ago, there was a queen who ruled over a kingdom both beautiful and populated with good people. She was married to a wonderful and kind king, and from an onlooker's view they had everything they could possibly want. But the truth was that the king and queen both longed very much for a child and yet, try as they might, no child was born.

One day the queen sat in her garden grieving by the river. Suddenly the water stirred and out jumped a brightly colored fish with a silver hook in its mouth. "Oh please!" wailed the fish. "Please have mercy on me and help me!"

The queen immediately grasped the fish and removed the spiteful hook and gently placed the creature back into the water.

The fish emerged from the ripples once more and made a courtly bow to the queen. "Good mistress, in return for this kind deed, I shall grant you the deepest wish of your heart—simply name it."

The queen did not hesitate, and she asked for a child as beautiful and good as her kingdom. The fish announced it would be done and bade the queen to always keep her troth with all creatures of her kingdom. She agreed, and nine months later a beautiful baby girl was born. The king and queen were so elated that they decided to hold a great feast that all members of the kingdom would be invited to attend.

The queen set herself about making the proper arrangements. She and her husband had invited not just all of the people but also all of the creatures of the kingdom, including the most elusive: the fairies who dwelled in the great forest. The queen knew that there were thirteen fairies who ruled the realm and kept all in balance. They were all sisters, and the twelve youngest ruled over various realms like the realm of birds, of weather, and of flowers. The thirteenth fairy, though, was the oldest, and her realm was death. The queen felt uneasy inviting such a one to her daughter's royal name day, but she had made a promise long ago to a fish, and she intended to keep it.

So it was with some horror that she saw the palace had only twelve golden plates. She had intended to give these finest plates to each of the thirteen fairies, but now she had only twelve and would have to offend one of them. It was an impossible choice, for what was a kingdom without birds or flowers, or one with terrible weather? Finally the queen decided that the twelve golden plates were a sign from the heavens, and she struck the name of the thirteenth fairy off the invitation list.

The celebration occurred exactly as planned with all invited attending and having a marvelous time. As the name-day festivities drew to a close and the sun began to set, the twelve fairies all blessed the child—with beauty, wisdom, kindness, the ability to speak to all creatures, and more. The twelfth fairy was just about to bestow her own blessing upon the child when the great hall darkened and a peal of thunder rang out. The thirteenth fairy had come after all, and in her haughty beauty, the queen saw she had made a grave mistake by not inviting her. Both she and the king begged for mercy, but there was none to be had. The thirteenth fairy leaned over the child's carved cradle and pronounced that she would grow and live for thirteen magical years, but on the day of her thirteenth birthday she would prick her finger on the spindle of a spinning wheel and die. As soon as the curse had been laid, the thirteenth fairy disappeared. The twelfth fairy, who had not yet given her blessing, stepped forward. She could not undo the curse, she explained, but she could mend it a bit. And so she did, promising that the child would not die, but that she and all of her kingdom would fall into a deep sleep only to be woken by the embrace of her true love.

And so it happened as foretold. Though the king burned every spinning wheel he could find, on the child's thirteenth birthday she did prick her finger and fell into a deep sleep. The fairy folk carried her to her chamber and laid her in her beautiful bed and watched as each member of the royal household—and then the kingdom itself—fell into a peaceful, ageless slumber. A great hedge of roses grew all around the kingdom, protecting it from the outside world, and it was not until many years later that an intrepid young prince would make his way through the brambles and find his Sleeping Beauty. Wake her with a kiss he did, and she was delighted to see her family awaken as well. Eventually she and her prince married, and she remembered what her mother had forgotten, to always honor all creatures.

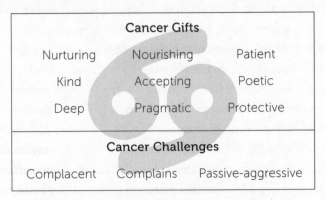

Cancer Gifts

Nurturing	Nourishing	Patient
Kind	Accepting	Poetic
Deep	Pragmatic	Protective

Cancer Challenges

| Complacent | Complains | Passive-aggressive |

THE CANCER PERSONALITY

When you think of a young child lost in a daydream one moment, and then off to do something artistic and creative the next, chances are, you are thinking of a Cancer child. Cancerians are the dreamers of the Zodiac. Like the story of Sleeping Beauty, there is something otherworldly about them. At the same time there is a deeply pragmatic quality. These children are similar to the title character of "Sleeping Beauty" in the sense that they are sheltered in some way from adversity—even Cancer children who grow up in extremely adverse conditions find ways of coping and sheltering themselves that make them quite sophisticated and tough.

Named for the Crab, Cancerians have much in common with their namesake animals. They too seem to exist in a vast ocean of imagination, and their emotions come in and flow out much like the tides. This is emphasized by the fact that the Cancer child is ruled by the Moon. Often these children have a deep love of water and waterscapes, as well as animals that live in the water.

Little Crabs are often not noticed at first by caregivers. They tend to be on the quieter side and are often lost in their own dreamtime or thoughts. What often makes people pay attention to them is an over-spill of emotions because Cancer children are very emotional and, especially when they are young, they have a difficult time regulating those feelings. If attention is drawn to the Cancer child, they often retreat under it. These children can have a hard time making eye contact, speaking clearly, and in general connecting with others due to their very private natures. They will happily chatter away about their day to their mothers or their primary caretakers, but they tend to clam up around teachers, coaches, and administrators. The Cancer child needs to feel safe and protected in order to share themselves with others. If they don't, then they will simply not be forthcoming about much of anything.

Typically the place that the little Crab feels most at ease and able to be themselves is at home. These children are very centered around home and family. Their families often play a very significant role in their lives, and they may be especially close to one parent—often the mom—long after their other peers have started to individuate from their families. For this reason, what happens within their families deeply affects the Cancer child more than it will other children. It also means that involving the parents or primary caregivers of the Cancer child in their learning and general set of activities can be a very useful thing to do, especially if teachers want the child to be more engaged. After the family, the next category is tribal group, and though they tend to be quiet and shy, Cancer children do have their tribes of friends, and once they do, they are fiercely protective of them.

For all of their imagination, Cancer children also have a profound pragmatic streak. Like Taurus children, they are often interested in money and finance and, as they get older, in having assets. Real estate, especially, will matter to security-loving Cancer.

Nourishment is a huge theme for Cancer children, who often love learning how to cook and enjoy sharing food and socializing over food. Finally, these Moon-ruled babies have an intrinsic love of the wild and wild things, including plants and animals. When Cancer is overwhelmed, letting them be around water, plants, or animals is a sure-fire way to restore their energy and happy natures.

Friends and Play

In our guiding story, one of the themes is a retreat from the world. Sleeping Beauty's parents try to shield her from outside influences and spinning wheels, then she is shielded by a hedge of thorns around the palace, and then there is her deep slumber, which lasts over a hundred years in many tellings. Often we find that Cancer children are sheltered by close connections with their family—especially by mothers or primary caregivers. Unlike Gemini or Aries children, Cancer may not have a huge group of social connections, but those they choose to foster are important and meaningful to them. Cancer children are selective about whom they associate with socially. These little ones tend to have a small group of friends but they take their friendships very seriously and love their friends very much. It is not unusual for a Cancer adult to still be close to their childhood friends.

These little Crabs love to engage in imaginative and creative play. They often include fairly sophisticated narrative stories in which they and their friends all play a role. And, because Cancer is a cardinal sign, it is not uncommon to see Cancer directing and art-directing the scene in a gentle yet firm manner.

The Cancer child is deeply intuitive—some might say psychic—and so they have a good sense of social expectations in the realm of play and friendship. For this reason, they may play a game or sport they do not personally enjoy because they know everyone else wants to play.

In such cases, these children usually put their own imaginative spin on things and stand out in a unique way.

When it comes to playdates, the Cancer child does much better with one-on-one scenarios than with groups, large or small. If things go awry with a friend, do not expect your Cancer child to talk about it immediately, if at all. She may take quite a while before she explains what went wrong, and during that time you can expect some sulking and passive-aggressive behavior. Once the Cancer child is ready to share, she is typically interested in a step-by-step process to mend and repair the relationship. Cancer children are so sweet and lovely that they can usually fix any damage.

In some cases, social connections may take a back seat to family relationships. Children born under the sign of the Crab who have strong bonds with family members typically want to stay at home and be with their people. Encourage the Cancer child to be social with others but do not push her—she may become defensive and withdraw completely. As Cancer children get older, they may feel blocked about leaving the home and family in order to discover themselves. Consistent encouragement can go a long way in helping them individuate themselves outside of the family. A final area to watch: Cancer children often have an air of delicacy or fragility that inspires others—especially those in their immediate family—to shelter and protect them. Caring for your little Crab is well and good, but do encourage them to develop relationships outside of the home.

Cancer children are lovely, pleasant, and inspiring to be around, and for this reason they are generally well-liked by everyone. However, when the Cancer child becomes too tired or gets overwhelmed by too many external stimuli, watch out because the claws start to pinch! Specifically, the Cancer child can become defensive—these children have no issue making up a (really good) story to explain why they could not have possibly done whatever it is they are being accused of doing. They do not like to take personal responsibility, and they want to people-please as much as possible, which can lead to defensive posturing. If a defensive retreat doesn't work, the Cancer child may become passive-aggressive, especially if they think they are being targeted or judged by others. They can speak nicely to your face while shooting daggers out of their eyes, and their typically gentle nature does not preclude them from cruel emotional manipulation at which they can excel because they are so emotionally intelligent. Fortunately, it takes quite a bit to push the Cancer child in that direction!

Academics

The "Sleeping Beauty" story embodies the quality of imagination that is central to a Cancerian child's life. As a consequence of their tendency to retreat from the world, they are at home in the realm of imagination. Cancer's brilliant imagination allows them to be exceptional, big-picture thinkers. That quality, paired with their natural leadership abilities (as a cardinal sign), makes them great at heading up and directing all kinds of endeavors, including academic pursuits.

Cancer children see not only what is there but what is possible. And they typically see *many* different possibilities. Once they have the vision that they feel is best, they will work (often with others) to make it a reality. They are not afraid of getting their hands dirty nor are they afraid of taking a more difficult approach. Unlike other cardinal signs, Cancers tend to do well in collaborative relationships as long as they retain ultimate control. The Cancer child is happy to let others chat and dream about a project scheme while she hangs back quietly. But when the final decisions are made, she will want to be the one making them.

Although they excel at big-picture thinking, Cancer children can sometimes get bogged down or completely overwhelmed by details. This is where their love of rules comes into play. Little Crabs like and appreciate rules—and quite a few of them are drawn to careers in law—because rules provide a useful framework through which to deal with pesky details. Rules also help keep the Cancer child organized, a quality they very much appreciate but may need external support and encouragement to cultivate.

Cancer children may not like responsibility, but they accept it, and they know what their duties are when it comes to school. These children usually do well in school provided that they do not distract themselves with constant daydreaming. Cancer children tend to be especially gifted in the arts, math, history, and literature. Their intellectual intelligence is significant, but it is the Cancer child's emotional intelligence that really shines forth, and they can put that to good use when it comes to sophisticated reasoning and reading. The Cancer child does not like being told what to do but does appreciate a clear set of rules or directives as long as they are the same for everyone. If the Cancer child makes a mistake, they often will deny it or have a long story about why it is not their fault.

Likewise, Cancer children often don't take the initiative to do homework on their own, and they will thrive best in a situation where external structures support them in that and other activities. Gently and consistently teaching the Cancer child about the power of personal responsibility and initiative can be a powerful medicine that provides them with balance throughout their lives. Teachers and caregivers will need to keep a careful eye on their Cancer children to make sure that they do not distract themselves from the work at hand and that they stay focused. If the subject or project is one that the little Crab is interested in, then adults literally don't need to do a thing: the Cancer child will take the reins and run with it. But, if the assignment is busywork or pertains to a subject that the Cancer child is not a fan of, then teachers will need to make sure it really does get completed. These children can also be big-time procrastinators. For these reasons there can be a wide range of grades and assessments when it comes to the Cancer child's work, with some work being truly exceptional while other projects are decidedly lacking or hastily done. If caregivers start to see a dip in their Cancer child's schoolwork, a good idea is to have a conversation about why such work matters. Don't be afraid to share the big-picture vision with your Cancer child—they will respond to it beautifully.

As Cancer children mature and begin thinking about the next step in their education, they will often default to wanting to attend the same institutions and fields of study as family members. If the Cancer is truly interested in these places and studies, it's well and good, but if they're using family traditions to avoid considering the tough question of what they *really* want to do, there is a problem. Family and caregivers can support young adult Crabs by reminding them that it is okay for them to leave home, try something new, and diverge from the primary caregiver's footsteps. When left to their own devices, Cancer youths often find themselves interested in the professions of cooking, art and design, creative writing, and real estate ventures. They also make excellent financial investors and bankers.

Physical Activity

When it comes to physical activity, the Cancer child would often rather not engage, like a Sleeping Beauty. These children tend to like their comfort and activities that involve more sedentary positions. Those inclinations, paired with the Cancer child's love of food, can lead to serious issues around obesity. For this reason, it is a good idea to put Cancer children into some kind of physical activity. Activities that involve creative expression like dance and gymnastics are excellent choices. Sports that have a long tradition behind them and/or are considered "classics" are also good choices because the Cancer child responds well to history and tradition. And of course, the Moon-ruled children tend to like water sports such as swimming and water polo. Constitutionally, the Cancer child may tire easily, and a lower impact sport can be ideal for them. What these children lack in pure physical power they make up for with inspiration and vision. It will be the young Crab on the team or in the dance troupe that gives the inspiring speech, organizes the details, and makes sure that everyone has what they need to do the best possible job. The Cancer child may enjoy the camaraderie that comes with team experiences, but they also may still find reasons to evade or get out of physical activity. Parents and caregivers should make sure that their little Crabs are moving their bodies and working up a sweat instead of sitting on the bench dreaming about the next painting they want to do.

Art and Creativity

As we have seen, there may be resistance from the Cancer child when it comes to sports, but that is not the case with creative endeavors. Art and creativity are the realm of possibility—where one is free to engage in imaginative play and entertain all that is possible—and, as we learn from "Sleeping Beauty," the Cancer child flourishes in this realm. These little Crabs often seek creative outlets in art and music, so these classrooms are where they often feel most at home.

Cancer children have a wide variety of talents and can go in several different creative directions. Parents, teachers, and caregivers should look at the areas where their little Cancerian naturally excels and encourage them in those directions. While Cancer children are great at starting projects and artistic endeavors, they are not so hot at maintaining daily practice, which of course is required to achieve real mastery. For this reason, parents and caregivers need to establish a practice schedule early on and make sure their Cancer child is sticking to it. Like their element, Water, Cancer children will take the path of least resistance, so seeing projects to full completion or working until a skill has been mastered poses the biggest challenge for these creative souls. Their preference is to try something else when things get difficult, but with clear structure and encouragement from family and friends, Cancer children can gain amazing proficiency in their chosen skill or art. In turn, they may inspire others.

Extracurricular Activities

It is important to remember in the "Sleeping Beauty" story that the princess will one day become a queen—a wealthy woman responsible for the well-being of her entire realm. As the cardinal Water sign, Cancer children also feel similar tugs of responsibility; accruing rewards and influence is a necessity, not an option, as far as they are concerned.

One of the things that the Cancer child likes best is to simply be by themselves with their own imaginations—to be sovereign in their own domain. This means that even when it comes to activities that the

Cancer child is predisposed to like, such as art or music, they still may choose to opt out of them if given the choice. Parents and caregivers of Cancer children will need to strike a balance between honoring their child's very real need for solitude, quiet time, and rest and the need to encourage their child to develop meaningful friendships and dedicate extra time and energy to their areas of interest. *Encouragement* is the key word here. You won't get far with your little Crab if you try to force or shame them. They simply withdraw into their shells. But with gentle encouragement (and a few good rewards as incentives to sweeten the deal) the Cancer child can participate in a few extracurricular activities that they both benefit from and enjoy.

Technology

In "Sleeping Beauty," the realm disappears from the rest of the world behind giant hedges. Cancer children are not interested in trends like Gemini kids, and they tend to be some of the least technologically prone children of the Zodiac. They appreciate the way that technology can make complicated jobs easier and faster, so they will put technology to use in that very limited manner. However, these children are typically not interested in learning how a computer works, nor are they particularly moved by the computer games and videos on offer all the time. In fact, Cancer children often prefer analog tools to digital ones whenever given the choice, and they can find too much technology to be overstimulating and exhausting. For this reason, parents and caregivers would do well to monitor how tech is being employed at the Cancer child's school. If you notice a sudden drop in grades, participation, or classroom performance, one often-overlooked source of the problem is technology. Find out if a previously nondigital experience like reading has been turned into a digital one. That alone may explain any significant changes in the Cancer child's engagement at school. Along the same lines, Cancer children might be even more sensitive than other children to disruptions caused by electronic devices lit up and working in the bedroom.

Sleeping and Waking

The whole issue of sleeping and waking is one surrounded by magic for the Cancer child, as it is in our story "Sleeping Beauty." The Cancer child loves to sleep, and their dream life is of vital importance to them—and they need to feel magic to wake up. So it won't come as a surprise to people who know and love Cancer children that these little ones do not like getting out of bed. As much time and attention as the Cancer children dedicate to sleeping in their perfect bedrooms, they are inversely interested in getting up and getting dressed in the morning. Little Crabs are slow moving, fuzzy upon waking, and paradoxically both care and don't care about what they are wearing. For these reasons it is a good idea to give your Cancer child extra time in the morning, so bedtime will need to be adjusted accordingly. Play their favorite music to give them a little enchantment, like Sleeping Beauty awakened by a kiss from her true love. It's a good practice to work with the Cancer child to pick out an outfit (and maybe a backup) the night before school. That way they can bring their creative vision to the process and not be overwhelmed with making a choice about what they are wearing in the morning when they're still coming out of dreamland. Cancer children often need more sleep than others, so caregivers should make sure to honor that and recognize that bedtime is a special time for these little ones.

Discipline

In "Sleeping Beauty," the absence of the thirteenth fairy causes trouble for the whole realm. The Queen was not trying to offend the thirteenth fairy, it just did not seem like a big deal if her name was not on the invite list. But as we see, it was. It is easy to assume, after reading about these watery Cancer children, that they are pushovers and easy to manage. That assumption would be a mistake. Every Cancer child has an unforeseen thirteenth fairy. Cancer is a cardinal sign, which means that someone born under this sign is comfortable being a boss and *not* being bossed by anyone else. These little Crabs may completely withdraw if they feel that they are being told what to do, say, or feel—or they may become sneaky, secretive, and manipulative. Either way, you should know that they are not going to allow themselves to be managed. Their rebellion may be quiet and mostly unseen, but it is absolutely in full effect. A better way to work with the Cancer child is to invite them to direct themselves. Questions to ask: What do you think needs to happen now? What would you like to do next? What can we do about this problem? Inspire the Cancer child to take an active role in determining what is needed. Then they become the leaders, and as such they are much more willing to cooperate. Typically, Cancer children are not troublemakers. They don't act, interrupt, or call attention to themselves. They seldom bully, at least on a physical level. Cancer children can be experts at emotional manipulation, and though usually kindhearted and gentle, if they feel that manipulation is the only avenue by which to accomplish their ends, they will happily stroll down it. These children can also be passive-aggressive, usually in response to an outside stimulus that is difficult or challenging to them. If you see your Cancer child exhibiting either set of behaviors, it is a good idea to spend some one-on-one time connecting with them in order to figure out what is really going on. Also, because Cancer children tend to be mild, even shy, in temperament, these are children who could be bullied, so watch out for that.

How Best to Connect

The Cancer child responds to several different forms of connection. Art, music, imagination, and dream-sharing are vital ways to connect with the Cancer child. As the most family-centered of all the signs, simply having dedicated family time without interruption can make the Cancer child feel safe, protected, and loved. Cancer, being the sign of nourishment, usually loves to cook, so cooking together and then serving up a family dinner is one of the best ways to connect with your little Crab. It is worth remarking that the entire situation in the tale of Sleeping Beauty is caused by a banquet and the fussiness that such an event causes. Cancer is the sign of nourishment and food, and those born under this sign can be fussy when it comes to parties and banquets: the smart Cancer child learns early on not to fret about a missing gold plate and instead makes friends with the thirteenth fairy. Because bedtime is such an important time for these children in particular, it is a good idea to set aside this time as extra-special connection time. Light a candle, tell a story, snuggle down—these things will bring so much joy and happiness to your little Cancerian.

Polarity: Capricorn

Capricorn encourages Cancer to come out of its shell and get serious about being in the world, and to stop hiding and let its excellence shine out and inspire others. Capricorn reminds Cancer that work and family obligations are in a balance and ideally inform one another.

Cancer Ascendant

The child with Cancer at the Ascendant often has a round, moon-shaped face and a corresponding, ethereal moon glow about them. These children come off on the one hand as dreamy, imaginative, and maybe even slightly out of touch with reality. On the other hand, they're seen as competent, responsible, and devoted to family. Their work, in part, is to take their unique blend of talents and abilities and create poetry and sanctuary with them so that everyone can be nourished.

Cancer Moon

Children with their Moons in Cancer are ultrasensitive and imaginative. They often feel an affinity to the Moon itself, as well as to the seashore or tidal pools. Their dream life is often quite vivid, and they can have a hard time articulating that dream content in words—yet it can inspire art. Highly intuitive, these children are especially sensitive to their surroundings and are easily overwhelmed.

Activity
Moon Gazing

The Moon is the Ruling Planet for Cancer, so it only makes sense that these children would enjoy looking at it. Simply gazing at the Moon can make the Cancer child feel empowered and blessed. Making a point to catch the Moonrise on a daily basis gives the Cancer child a chance to see how the Moon (like their emotional lives) is constantly changing and how that is something beautiful to appreciate—about the Moon and about themselves!

Ritual
Dream Sharing

Dreams are important for all of us, but Cancer, like the other Water signs (Scorpio and Pisces), is especially sensitive to nighttime dreams and visions. So a good ritual for this sign is to get into the practice of dream sharing. When the Cancer child wakes up every morning, ask them about their night dreams, and then share yours in turn. This ritual, while simple, reinforces for the Cancer child that their dreams are legitimate and worth paying attention to.

Ritual for the Inner Cancer Child
Diving into Daydreams

When we adults turn our attention to healing our inner Cancer child, we discover that what these children often heard again and again was "Stop daydreaming!" Constantly chided for unrealistic expectations and having their heads in the clouds, Cancer children may never get a chance to share their imaginal realms before they are snuffed out by grown-ups. For Cancer, the most traditional way to express and celebrate the gifts of the imagination is through the art of poetry. It doesn't matter if you are a secretly budding poet or have never written anything more than a grocery list. When it comes to honoring the inner Cancer child the best thing to do is write a poem about something that matters to you.

CHAPTER 8

The Leo Child

"I aim to provide the public
with beneficial shocks."

**Alfred Hitchcock
(Leo, born August 13, 1899)**

BIRTHDAY: July 22–August 22

RULING PLANET: Sun

ELEMENT: Fire

QUALITY: Fixed

SYMBOL: Lion

HOUSE: Fifth House of Creation and Art

STATEMENT: I am here to create.

SEASON: High Summer

GUIDING STORY: "The Bamboo Princess"

*Blessed children, how brightly the fire shines and
how brightly your faces reflect it. Look up now and
find the constellation of Leo if you can. We see it
best during the month of April, and you may find
it by spying its brightest star, Regulus. Like that star,
one of our most essential tasks is to shine. There is
a story from China about a woman who shone like
the sun and was hidden in the unlikeliest of places.*

Once upon a time there was a poor man who was a woodcutter and
lived in a vast bamboo forest. Although the man was kind and good,
his wood always fetched the worst prices at market. Consequently,
he and his wife barely had enough to eat, and the only clothes they
owned were the ones they were wearing. Despite all of this, they were
happy with their life together in the forest and truly wished for only
one thing: a child to share it with.

Alas, no child came. Now one day, the woodcutter went deeper
into the forest than he had ever gone before to select which bamboo
stalks to cut down. He was just getting his bearings and judging the
different plants when he heard a sighing, beautiful voice. "Oh, help
me, please help me!" it cried. It seemed to come from everywhere and
nowhere all at the same time.

The woodcutter looked to the north and the south, to the east
and the west. The woodcutter looked down and up and all around,
but he could not locate where the voice was coming from. Then he
peered through the stalks of bamboo and saw that one was glowing
with a deep, beautiful, gold color. The voice seemed to be coming
from there, and sure enough it cried out again: "Oh help me, please,
help me!"

The woodcutter, knowing that some kind of magic was afoot,
immediately set to cutting down the stalk. Once his axe made the

final cut, the stalk disappeared, and in its place was the most beautiful young girl, who was shining with gold just like the stalk she had been trapped in.

She bowed in honor to the woodcutter and thanked him for saving her life. She explained that she was the daughter of the sun and moon and had been trapped by a dreaded enemy and placed in that bamboo stalk. Although she wanted to return to her heavenly home, she needed to regain her strength. The woodcutter immediately offered up his home to her. It was a humble dwelling to be sure, he told her, but one where she could rest and be completely safe. The young girl nodded happily, and so she went home with him to his delight and the delight of his wife.

The woodcutter did not know it at the time, but the young princess had blessed him. From that day forward, whenever he cut down bamboo stalks, he found piles of gold within the bamboo. This quickly made the woodcutter one of the most prosperous men in the land, but he still lived in his humble house in the woods, with his beloved wife and the young princess who was like a daughter to them.

Years passed and the princess grew in beauty and kindness. Many suitors came and asked for her hand, but she denied all of them, preferring to stay with her foster parents. One day, when the sun and the moon met in an eclipse, she explained gently to the woodcutter and his wife that it was time for her to ascend to the heavens, and they would never see her in this form again. They wept bitterly but they understood, and the woodcutter's wife made bean cakes for her to take on her journey. The princess told them before she took her leave that every time the moon shone on them it was her embracing them, and every time the sun shone upon them it was her kissing their cheek. And so she took her leave. The woodcutter and his wife were both very sad, but they watched the sun and the moon every day and found their joy once more, in their small hut, deep in the bamboo forest.

Leo Gifts		
Fun	Stylish	Popular
Enthusiastic	Openhearted	Playful
Theatrical	Luxurious	Joyful
Leo Challenges		
Vain	Self-centered	Petulant

THE LEO PERSONALITY

Like the Bamboo Princess, wherever the Leo child happens to be, everyone feels richer, happier, and more blessed. The Sun is the Planet that rules the sign of Leo, and Leo children exhibit so many qualities of their Ruling Planet that when we encounter them we can feel like we are standing in the presence of the Sun, too.

These children are fun, first and foremost. They like to have fun, and they like to do it with other people. Leo children take things lightly for the most part. They love jokes and laughter and thrilling adventures, and they love to play. They prioritize having fun in their own lives, and they have a knack for drawing those around them into fun play as well.

Leo children like to travel in groups just like their Lion counterparts do in nature. And, like a male Lion, the Leo child often wants to be seen as the leader of the pride. These children are friendly and sociable, chatty and generous, and they want to have a good time, but they also want to make sure everyone else is having a good time too. It is possible for Leo children to be shy (any child of any sign can be shy or loud or, most usually, a fascinating combination of both), but even shy Leo children still like to have fun and would still rather not be alone. They may prefer the company of their dog or cat to that of other children, but an entourage is a must for these little Lions.

In Astrology Leo has a bad reputation for being selfish. While this can be a quality of their character, it is, in my opinion, too emphasized, just as Gemini's unreliability is over-remarked upon. Less discussed is

Leo's incredible generosity. He is never alone because he is fun and also because he is free with his favors and his encouragement. Leo children are often wonderful advocates for children who have a harder time socially; they are usually not interested in excluding those who are different from them.

Leo children enjoy difference, and they love helping draw others out and into the spotlight. That spotlight showcases the Leo child's own creative abilities—usually in the performing arts and athletics—and also allows the Leo child to get creative in making space for other children to share their own creative natures. For the Leo child anything creative is fun, and anything fun should be creative. They are fine with rules as long as they can put their own signature flourish on them.

Leo children love the finer things in life and are especially drawn to shiny objects, jewelry, sparkles, and the color gold. They like luxury, but what luxury means will be different for each Leo child. They also like to share their little luxuries with other children and family members. Again, these children like full participation from everyone.

The little Lion is a natural performer, and so they are also naturally dramatic. Although the Leo child's penchant for drama is usually interpreted as a negative quality, it can actually be quite positive in the right situations. Leo children have wonderful facial expressions and often speak with their faces and their bodies as well as their actual words. In turn, they are able to pick up on what other people are really thinking and feeling based on expression and physical movement, making Leo children much more introspective and intelligent than they are sometimes given credit for being.

When the Leo child does not get her way, she can quickly become sullen, pouty, and angry. She will make unreasonable demands that she *knows* are unreasonable, and she will behave selfishly even with her closest friends. The Leo child can also be a bit on the vain side—wanting to be surrounded by the most beautiful or popular kids or wanting a specific item purely for the status it invokes. Supporting the Leo child's innate kindness, generosity, and warmth is the best way to counter these less fun attributes.

Friends and Play

Like the Bamboo Princess, Leo children cannot help but bring joy and happiness to all they touch. These children are often physically beautiful or dramatic in appearance—so even if they are shy, people are drawn to them and tend to seek them out.

For the Leo child the only question worth asking about friends and play is: Can you have too much of a good thing? The Leo child will assure you that you cannot. These little Lions love to play and have fun, and they are most happy when they are joined by a group of their peers. One-on-one engagements for the Leo child are not ideal. The child can find them boring and too restrained. A large- or medium-sized group of friends engaging in a fun activity, however, makes the Leo child's heart swell with joy. For this reason Leo children are the ones who typically attend every birthday and holiday party. They love parties—both hosting and being hosted. Leo children are usually socially adept and pretty popular. Their play is less conventional than some other children's play, and they usually add a performative and creative element to their playtime that is their unique signature. If it were left up to the Leo child, they would party all the time—which would result in a grouchy and sleepy Lion! So, it is important for parents and caregivers to give their Leo children good boundaries, especially around socializing, to make sure that these little ones also spend some time by themselves. Leo will never love being alone the way that a Pisces or Scorpio does, but learning to be by themselves is an important skill for these children. Because they are kind, warm, generous, and loving, Leo children tend to get along really well with their peers and are often quite popular.

Before they find their group of friends though, young Lions can be shy, retiring, and awkward. Leo children get into tangles with their friends, usually over behaviors that the other children see as selfish, although the Leo child might not agree. Leo children can also be seen as pushy, bossy, and grabby. They like to share but they also like to be the center of attention, and that can create conflict. Appealing to their generous natures is the best way to help them create strong and lasting friendships.

Because the Leo child is creative and likes novelty, she is usually very accepting and even embraces differences. She seeks out children who are not like her and is fascinated by the kids who do life differently than she does. Ultimately, she probably thinks she has the best approach to everything, but she appreciates a different point of view.

Academics

The Bamboo Princess possesses a natural and effortless shine, and like her, the Leo child's area of giftedness in academics shines most fully when they are given room to be creative. They have an enormous capacity to make the most routine assignments creatively their own. The Leo child tends to thrive in group activities and group settings when volume and noise control are not strictly enforced. They would like to have creative input in project development and do not appreciate or enjoy working by themselves at a single desk in a quiet and calm atmosphere. However, if teachers and caregivers make learning fun and creative, then Leo children are hooked, and they will often bring a lot of others along with them in their learning adventure.

These little Lions are smart, but they are often not the best students because they're more interested in having fun than they are in excelling at schoolwork. More to the point, these children don't typically see academics as very fun and therefore not incredibly important to them. A third strike against the Leo child in school is that academic assignments are often straightforward, cut-and-dried, and do not allow much room for creativity. As there is often not an opportunity for creative adaptation, the Leo child will do academically what comes easily to them in a half-hearted manner, and they will do their best to ignore or get away from the things that are harder to manage.

The Leo child is often the one who naturally puts much more thought into what he is going to wear to school as opposed to what he is going to do once he gets to school. School for him is less about learning the three "R"s and more about learning social dynamics, especially how to form social packs and run with them. Plus, Leo kids are cool, so even if they are quite nerdy, they often feel they have to keep that part hidden, unless they are given support to do otherwise. When it comes to subjects, Leo loves art, music, dance, and theater. They tend to be naturally gifted athletes—or they can be if they are not lazy lions—and they also tend to like history, especially biographies of important people to whom they relate. Anything that is too detail oriented is sure to lose the Leo child's attention, so they often need extra support in subjects like math and science. Even if they are naturally good in these subjects, they need support to stay engaged. Leo children also often have incredible memories, and memorizing poems, speeches, or the lines of a play come easily to these little ones. Because the Leo child is so social, in a conventional setting where the separation of individuals is rewarded, she may get in trouble for talking out of turn or disrupting her friends during class time.

As the Leo child matures, she may begin to take the performing arts even more seriously and consider a career track that places her at center stage. But even if the Leo young adult chooses a different field, they will pursue it with the sense that everyone is watching them and that they have to deliver a winning performance. This is true whether their interests take them into theatre or accounting. Like their fellow Fire sign Aries, Leo youths tend to want to get started with their actual work and careers. By the time high school is over they have had enough of learning in a classroom and are now ready to learn through experience, in the classroom of the world. Parents and caregivers can support their young Lions by being open to nontraditional education tracks and encouraging their child to learn by doing in whatever their chosen field might be.

Physical Activity

The Leo child can be either highly energetic or quite lazy when it comes to physical activity. Just as the woodcutter freed the Bamboo Princess from captivity, so the Leo child will be freed to shine by actively moving the body, to the extent caregivers are able to identify what the Leo child's particular physical giftedness is and what games they most enjoy. Usually these little ones excel in performing arts such as dance and gymnastics as well as in more conventional sports. Leo children are often preternaturally physically fit and know how to show their best angles from a young age. They are natural performers and prefer group endeavors to solitary sports like tennis or golf. If music, drama, and costumes are involved in their physical activity, then the Leo child is even more excited about it! However, there is another side to the little Lion: the lazy lion who would rather bask in the Sun and be gorgeous and waited on. Leo children often like to start a venture, only to find that once it gets a bit difficult they no longer want to continue. Leo children have a lot of enthusiasm and pluck, and parents and caregivers should call on those qualities while supporting their little ones to honor commitments and stick with activities—even through the boring, not-fun parts.

Giving the Leo child a team or group that depends on them showing up to do their part is a way to keep them committed to a physical activity long after the initial shine has worn off. Because Leo is a Fire sign—and the Fire signs all run their energy very fast and hot—it is a good idea for your little Lion to also have downtime and time to rest. A few well-chosen physical activities will be plenty for these golden children; if their calendar is too full, parents and caregivers will have a pouty, proud, and selfish child on their hands.

Art and Creativity

Leo rules the Fifth House of the Zodiac, the area of art and creativity, so these precocious kiddos are made for artistic and creative activities. What is interesting is that many Leo adults discover only in retrospect that they are quite creative. In school they may have missed the art room entirely because it always seemed like a quiet, calm place, and they were too busy chatting with their friends and building social connections. Parents and caregivers should keep this in mind and make sure that their little Leo children have a taste of art and creativity while they are school age. Until they do, they will feel like the princess from our story—imprisoned inside the bamboo shoots.

Leo children especially appreciate group projects such as plays, films, dance, orchestras, and large-scale visual-art projects that require many hands on deck. Music, performance, color, vibrancy, and high energy are all qualities that the little Lion is both drawn to and brings to any creative endeavor. These children like sparkle and shine, and this shows up in their visual art projects—please give Leo children all the glitter!—and also in their choices of musical instruments. Many a Leo loves a shiny, golden saxophone or trumpet. Drama and theater are often the areas where Leo children feel most at home. They know how to occupy the stage, and they love putting on different masks and playing with different personas. On stage the Leo child is able to let loose and share what she really thinks from the safety of a different character or story—this is often where she feels most safe and most seen. Leo children often also respond particularly well to photography, especially as they get older and can enjoy being both behind and in front of the camera.

Extracurricular Activities

Within the tale, the Bamboo Princess becomes a celebrity of sorts and is sought out by various eligible young men far and wide. If given their preference, Leo children will be with their group of friends socializing and doing something creative in their off hours. To adults it might look like they are just hanging out, but to the Leo child they are perfecting their social intelligence, which is a real and legitimate quality to nourish. That said, it is not a bad idea for parents and caregivers to make sure that Leo has some structured activities to participate in after school. Booking the Leo child with something every day is likely to create an angry and irritable child, but giving the Leo child a few structured activities that have social, creative, and physical elements is an excellent place to begin. And let the little Lion be with their pride! This is a natural part of the Leo child's talent, and these social abilities should be fostered within reason. Fortunately, the Leo child often has strong preferences about what they do or do not want to do, and they will make those preferences known to any who ask.

Technology

Leo children will find there are three areas that appeal to them: social media, technology that allows them room to shine, and anything involving detail-oriented work. Leo children tend to appreciate the fun, visual components of technology and will engage with technology if they can do it in a fun, creative way, especially if it allows them to be with their friends at the same time. They may not have the patience to learn how a specific piece of technology works and usually like someone else to set up their technical gadgets for them.

Though they appreciate the convenience of technology and can make good use of certain aspects of it—especially social media—they can be surprisingly analog in other ways, often preferring a handwritten note on a custom piece of stationery to an e-card. These little Lions are often visual learners, and they prefer face-to-face interactions whenever possible. Parents and caregivers don't need to worry much about the Leo child being on the screen for video games, but they should monitor a Leo's time spent on movie marathons and online shopping.

Sleeping and Waking

"The Bamboo Princess" ends in an ambiguous manner. The princess departs the earthly plane and dwells high in the heavens, and the listener is left with the impression that not only has she left an indelible mark on everyone she has come into contact with, but she also is preparing for her next adventure. So it is with the Leo child as well. From the vantage point of sleep and waking, this should be borne in mind, as the Leo child will be entering bedtime with the next adventure on her mind.

Leo children often inhabit the hours of the rock 'n' roll lifestyle long before they know what rock 'n' roll is. These little ones like to stay up late and may come home from school pretty jazzed up and on fire. If given free rein, they will spend all afternoon on the phone or screen with their friends, exchanging stories, advice, drama, and ideas. Given a preference, they'd stay up late socializing and then get up fairly late in the morning as well. Since that schedule does not really work with most schools, (and is probably not the healthiest even once the school years are over), parents and caregivers will need to have a moderating influence. The Leo child may be satisfied if they can stay up a little later than their peers and if going to bed is turned into a luxurious experience instead of a have-to. Nice pajamas, candles, and good smells make going to bed a fancy event that can get the Leo child primed and ready to hit the sheets.

All cats, wild or domestic, take bathing very seriously and give themselves full baths multiple times a day. The same is true for the Big Cat of the Zodiac. Make sure the Leo child has plenty of tub time and is squeaky clean before getting into bed—he will rest so much better.

Upon waking, the little Lion is often groggy and has a special case of "bed head." For these reasons, parents and caregivers should give their Leo children extra time for grooming in the morning. This is especially true because these little Lions can be quite high maintenance when it comes to fixing and styling their hair. Getting dressed and accessorized is another big area of concern and focus for Leo children of any gender, so understanding that wardrobe is a "thing" for these children can stop a lot of fights before they begin. Leo children are not going to pick out their outfits the night before because they don't know how they will feel until the next morning, and their feelings dictate many of their creative choices. Having multiple outfits and choices ready for the Leo child is a good idea, as is teaching the Leo child early on that while they can have a lot of choice in what they wear, not every choice will be available every day.

Discipline

Like the Bamboo Princess, Leo children are kind, warm-hearted, and loving. When they get into trouble it usually has to do with not paying attention, being overly chatty, or distracting other children from their work. In other words, their bad behaviors are not typically intentional. If the Leo child is unhappy, however, she can be petulant, bossy, and angry. At the most extreme end, the Leo child who is truly miserable can bully other children or put herself intentionally in situations where she is bullied. It is useful to remember that Leos are fixed signs, which means once they have decided something needs to be a certain way it is very hard to talk them down from that. Simply telling the Leo child to stop the undesired behavior is not going to go very far.

The Leo child responds better to pleasure than to punishment, and they also need to feel seen and heard, or they will simply continue doing whatever got them into trouble in the first place. When correcting the Leo child, it is useful to remember that these children thrive on attention and are not above using bad behavior to get that attention when all else fails. If the Leo child is acting up for these reasons, it is a good idea for parents or caregivers not to give them too much attention in relationship to the problematic behavior and instead ask where they could be paying more attention to them in a positive manner.

How Best to Connect

Traditionally, Leo is the sign of royalty. Leo children, like the Bamboo Princess, give off royal energy, even when they are simply dressed and come from less-than-royal circumstances. The gold nuggets that the Woodcutter began to discover after encountering the Princess allowed for a certain level of luxury in what had been a very simple lifestyle. This too is true of Leo children. They teach us to find what is luxurious and precious and to make space for it in our lives. Leo children are very loving when all is well in their world. They enjoy being with their families and tribal groups, and they especially enjoy it if there is also an opportunity for them to perform in some way for the pleasure of the group. Often Leo children are more vulnerable when they are in a family group than when they are in a one-on-one setting. Your little Lion also appreciates actions, so going to shows and performances, making art with them, or even rocking out on musical instruments with them are all really good ways of connecting.

Polarity: Aquarius

Aquarius points out that Leo has a prodigious intellect that should be included in all endeavors. Also, life is not always about the individual good—the community good or the good of the pack matters just as much, if not more, than one's own well-being.

Leo Ascendant

The child with Leo ascending has fabulous hair, a sparkling personality, and exudes confidence. They are drawn to bright, shiny objects, and events seem to be more dramatic when they show up. Part of the work of these children is to exude love and generosity, warming up everyone who comes into their path and reminding us that we are all worthy of the spotlight.

Leo Moon

Children with Leo Moon are comfortable in creative, expressive, and dramatic situations. They thrive in the setting of a play or orchestra. They are at ease with the public eye, public speaking, and social engagements. They are much less at home when they are alone or low on creative resources.

Activity
The Masks We Wear

Leo children are so loving and warmhearted that they often seem really happy all of the time. Although these children tend to be some of the sunniest in outlook, they experience the full range of emotions that other children do.

To explore this, you and your Leo child can make a variety of masks: some happy, some sad, some dramatic.

Talk with your child about what kinds of masks they would like to have and go from there. Make sure your Leo child assists you in the project—this is just the kind of creative work that Leo children love. Then, whenever your Leo child is going through something, ask them what mask best fits their feelings. From there you might even have them act out their experience. This can be a healing process for all Leo children and encourage close connection at the same time.

Ritual

Warm Heart

Each Zodiac Sign rules a part of the body, and Leo rules our hearts. Cultures all over the world and throughout time have recognized how important the heart and heart center of the body are, and they have many different ways of honoring it. For your big-hearted Leo child, a gentle massage with a favorite lotion or oil at the heart center before bed is a great way to inspire any conversation or connection that needs to happen. Massage also calms the little Lion before sleep. As Leo children get older, this ritual is one they can do for themselves, and it reminds them to take care of their hearts—in all ways.

Ritual for the Inner Leo Child

Taking Center Stage

"Get out of the way!" is a phrase that adults honoring their inner Leo child often heard again and again in different forms. They always seem to be right at center stage, sometimes through their own devising but other times through simple happenstance. Leo children are meant to occupy the spotlight; it is part of the medicine that they have to share with the world. So, for adults who are tending to their inner Leo child, the hurdle to cross is the choice to deliberately *not* get out of the way—to stay put and to take up space. The ritual for this is simple. The next time you are in a social situation and you feel the desire to shrink back and become a proverbial wallflower, instead try standing center stage. Talk, laugh, be your charming self, and don't move an inch. Take up that spotlight. It will encourage others to do the same.

CHAPTER 9

The Virgo Child

"The miracle is not that we do this work,
but that we are happy to do it."

Mother Teresa
(Virgo, born August 26, 1910)

BIRTHDAY: August 22–September 22

RULING PLANET: Mercury

ELEMENT: Earth

QUALITY: Mutable

SYMBOL: The Virgin

HOUSE: Sixth House of Health and Devotion

STATEMENT: I am here to serve.

SEASON: Late Summer

GUIDING STORY: "Dancing at the Sipapu"

*Come now children, the night is deeper and colder,
which is the best time for seeing the stars. Look up
and try to find Virgo, the celestial Virgin. You see her
most easily during the month of May, and her brightest
star, Spica, may serve as your guide. Watch her as she
dances through the sky. Why do we dance? You might
wonder. There are so many reasons, but let me tell you
about one ancient dance that is done to call down the
rains that nourish the earth and bring people together.
This is a tale that comes from the Pojoaque Pueblo
of the Tano-Tewa tribe in Northern New Mexico.*

Once upon a time, Earth had a big stone at her navel, the *sipapu*, where all of the creatures of the world first came from. The Bear People, the Bushy-Tailed Ones, the Spider People, the Dragonfly People, the Deer People and the Snake People all came from this center.

Plants grew too. The Prickly Pear cactus with its tender fruits, the Chamisa and White Sage, the Juniper and Piñon, and of course Maize, the Corn People. There were the Red Corn People and Blue Corn People, Yellow Corn People and White Corn People. They all grew together and were beautiful, and Earth loved them very much for they were her children.

So it went for a long time with Earth's children living on her, and she was happy. One day though, a cold and mischievous wind blew from the West. The wind shook all of the creatures so hard, and then it scattered them, taking them in many different directions.

Some of the creatures who had previously gotten along with one another began to fight each other. Everything was scattered in every direction—especially the Corn People. They had been scattered the farthest apart, separated by that wind so that if by some miracle their paths crossed, they would not recognize each other. Without her children, the land of Earth's body began to dry up and grow brittle. She wanted to weep but did not have enough water to do even that.

She called out to her children, hoping that her far-away and weakened voice would be loud enough for at least some of them to hear. She called out to the Ones who had gone North, to the Ones who had gone South, to the Ones who had gone East, to the Ones who had gone West, and to all of the Ones in between.

A few from each direction did hear her, and they began dancing. They danced to put themselves back together, to remember who they were and where they were from and what they loved. Then they danced to return to their Mother, to help her, and to heal her. From every direction they came dancing back to the center, back to the sipapu, back together. It was then that Earth laughed in joy and the rains began to fall. And the land and the creatures were safe and nourished once more.

Virgo Gifts		
Mature	Pure	Put together
Organized	Full of integrity	Ethical
Cautious	Caring	Devoted
Virgo Challenges		
Critical	Demanding	Martyr

THE VIRGO PERSONALITY

In the story, "Dancing at the Sipapu," Earth is the oldest character, and it is from her that everything springs. Her ancient quality is contrasted with her role as Mother and an affinity for all of the young creatures that spring from her body. Although she is both ancient and wise, as the story illustrates, Earth is still vulnerable, and this is true for our Virgo children as well. Mercury rules two Zodiac Signs: Gemini and Virgo. Gemini children often appear younger than they are and take a longer time to mature. Virgo children often appear older than they are—not so much in physical appearance but in mannerism, speech, and behavior. Sometimes they seem to have emerged from the womb fully matured. This is part of the craftiness of Mercury and points to one of the most important things to remember about Virgo: despite their mature attitudes and abilities, these children are still children and should not be forced to be "adult" too early in their lives. Virgo children are usually physically quite lovely and always put together. One of the ancient meanings of the "Virgin," for which Virgo is named, is "Sovereign"—indicating that this sign is complete within itself. This deep quality can exacerbate the idea that Virgo children are just adults in miniature.

These little ones like to match, often have a preferred color scheme and style choice, and like classics of all types: books, lines, looks, movies, and music. There is often something timeless about Virgos that makes adults treat them with respect and at the same time makes other children look at them a bit sideways. The Virgo child is the one who keeps his room neat and tidy—*and* his desk, *and* his backpack. It is not that he doesn't like a messy space, it is that he literally feels depleted by messes and disorganization. These are the children who can play on the playground all day long and come home without a hair out of place: it is one of their secret superpowers.

Within every Virgo child there is a creative—dare we say messy?—artist waiting to be seen. This wildly creative side of Virgo children is usually kept under wraps, but it is there. If the Virgo child is given the right support and encouragement, they will allow themselves to be creative without second-guessing their right to do so.

There is also, in every Virgo child, a propensity for devotion to something greater and higher. This can be a religious calling, a spiritual pursuit, or something more practical like the practice of medicine: Virgo rules the sector of the Zodiac that deals with health. Left unchecked, Virgo's desire to devote themselves to something great can lead them in the direction of cults or zealotry, but when in alignment the Virgo child is able to show how the spiritual and practical can complement each other.

The Virgo child's challenges center around their drive for perfection; these children may expect perfection from others and their external circumstances, but they definitely expect perfection from themselves. In light of this, these little Sovereigns are often critical of themselves and others, always finding the one thing that isn't quite right. They can be demanding and expect everything and everyone to measure up to their (sometimes unrealistically high) standards—starting with themselves. The Virgo child may be seen by other children as being overly nitpicking, but she is often forgiven for this because it is so obvious to everyone that the person she expects the most from is herself. Parents and caregivers have to watch this Virgo tendency of tearing the self down in order to build it up in a better way.

Finally, the Virgo child can sometimes pitch themselves as martyrs and victims. This usually occurs when Virgo children are exhausted, have tried to make people happy (and feel they have failed), or have gone to great lengths and feel unappreciated. Because Virgo children are so good at so many things, they often create close-to-perfect situations and then hang back in the background without receiving proper acknowledgment or thanks. When this occurs, the Virgo child will take on the role of the silently suffering martyr, doing everything for everyone but making sure everyone feels really guilty about it all at the same time. The best way to address this is to make sure that the Virgo child does feel seen and is appreciated for their efforts.

Friends and Play

Virgo's relationship to friends and play follows the character of Earth in our story. Although Virgo children are a bit shy at first and are happy observing what their peers are up to, they are still and solid like the earth itself. However, once they begin to feel comfortable, Virgo children can reveal their chatty, funny, and thoughtful sides and become quite popular. Remember, Virgos are ruled by charming Mercury, so just as Earth produced a wide variety of life, these little Sovereigns can have a variety of friends. Because Virgo children are often incredibly well put together and have a strong sense of style, they are often followed by others who want to imitate or be inspired by their looks. Virgo children tend to be physically beautiful and healthy, and these qualities also set them up to be popular and well liked. These children do not necessarily thrive in one-on-one settings—they actually tend to be get a little nervous and hyperactive in such scenarios. But they also don't thrive off of big-group energy the way Aries or Leo children do. Instead, a smaller, curated group of friends to play with makes the Virgo child happy. Play can be a confusing thing for adults to watch when it comes to their Virgo children. On the one hand, Virgo children often love to be outside, and they love nature and green growing things. On the other hand, Virgo children do not like to make messes or get messed up, so playing outside is something they may both enjoy and not enjoy at the same time.

At times the Virgo child really likes playing and the creativity it allows them to express, but at other times the Virgo child has a definite idea of who should play and *how* they should play—and they will quickly find that their friends are not willing to cooperate. Virgo children can also get in trouble with their friends when they see them as projects to help fix or improve: think of the Jane Austen novel *Emma* for an illustration of how this can backfire. The Virgo child does not mean any harm or disrespect; she wants to help her friends and believes that everyone is as dedicated to being their best as the Virgo child herself is. Part of this child's lesson is that not every problem needs to be solved, at least not by them. Those thorny issues aside, Virgo children do beautifully with their friends and often are still close to their childhood friends as adults.

Academics

From the sipapu in our story, all things issue from their proper place and time. This could be a Virgo mantra: everything in its place and a place for everything.

The Virgo child is the straight-A student and teacher's pet all rolled into one—but only as long as the teacher is doing what the Virgo child expects them to do. Virgo children tend to do very well in school.

Their detail-oriented, careful, and measured approach to learning ensures that they are likely to get good grades, and their observance of classroom rules means that teachers and other caregivers appreciate them and, as they get older, often depend on them. Virgo children are especially drawn to math, science, and writing as these are areas where they have natural ability and gifts.

A Virgo's stylish appearance can really hide an inner nerd who delights in learning and acing the tests. Even though Virgo children are secretly creative, they often struggle with creative projects, especially when they are young, and they may find that creative thinking is the part of school that most flummoxes them.

Although sociable, Virgo children tend to be quiet and restrained in class, so teachers and caregivers may need to work closely with them, especially when it comes to verbalizing their knowledge. Along the same lines, though they appreciate their friends, these little Sovereigns sometimes do better academically when working solo as opposed to working with others. In group settings the Virgo kids are often the workhorses who make sure everything gets done and then get upset when everybody else gets all the credit. The Virgo child will have to learn in school the importance of mistakes and shift their mindset from one of never wanting to make a mistake to one of recognizing that mistakes are actually necessary for learning.

Finally, the Virgo child may run into issues at school because they take too long to complete projects. This tendency comes from their need to double- and triple-check their work to make sure everything is just perfect. Academic work that requires care and attention is the kind of work that these children are made for.

As the Virgo child matures, he will want to have a plan for what happens after high school. Although we might assume that Virgo children would naturally want to continue learning in traditional college or university settings, this is not always the case. Recall that the strongest impulse for the Virgo child and adult centers around service—Virgo wants to be of service and to help. So it is not uncommon for these signs to seek out avenues that allow them to start serving and making a quiet impact immediately. Many Virgo children are drawn to the health and science fields, which combine their natural love of health, purity, and details with the ability to be of service in the healing of humankind. Virgo young adults who are not interested in health or science careers often find themselves gravitating toward writing, editing, and publishing. Like all good Earth signs, Virgo young adults want to know what practical benefits any training will bring them and how it will impact their bottom line financially.

Physical Activity

Dancing is key to the happy ending in "Dancing at the Sipapu," and this might lead us to suspect that motion and physical activity are especially important for Virgo children. Indeed they are. As an Earth sign, Virgo children join all the Earth signs with being tempted to be still, chill out, and relax instead of moving their bodies. Virgo children, however, are less likely to succumb to sedentary behavior than other kids because these Mercury-ruled children love to move and also because their drive to perfection includes their physical bodies. Organized sports are a great place for Virgo children to get their daily dose of physical activity, and they tend to enjoy tennis, golf, lacrosse, ballet, and gymnastics. Similar to their play preferences, Virgo children like being on a team, though a smaller team is ideal. Virgo children have an appreciation of physical style, so sports with classic-looking equipment and gear often appeal to them on an aesthetic level. While Virgo children are typically not the strongest or the most physically gifted, they often make great strategists and can keep other teammates focused on the work at hand. Some Virgo children eschew team sports and prefer to be outside in nature. For these little Sovereigns, horseback riding, hiking, and cross-country skiing are ideal physical pursuits.

Working hard is one way that Virgo children shine. These kids will work on something until they achieve excellence, giving Virgo athletes an extra boost. Even though they may not come in with all the natural talent, they are among the most likely to make full and complete use of what they have. One word of caution: Virgo children like to focus, and often adults with this sign are accused of being obsessive. It is Virgo's dedication to excellence that brings about such intense focus, but when it comes to physical activity, this tendency can have the Virgo child ready to throw all in for one single sport or physical activity instead of being open to trying several different activities. Help keep your little Virgo flexible by introducing them to a wide variety of activities when they first begin participating in such events. Doing so will help them discover the genuine order their heart so desires.

Art and Creativity

In our story, "Dancing at the Sipapu," there is nothing more creative in the universe than Earth. The order she so loves is in alliance with her power to create. The way things are regenerated is through dance. Dance helps all beings remember who they are and where they should be. Within every Virgo child there is Earth looking to call her children home by means of a great dance.

Virgo children have a paradoxical relationship with art and creativity. On one hand, Virgo children often seem to be the least likely to want to throw paint on a canvas or clay on a wheel. These children are stylish, clean, neat, organized, and not messy. It seems, so the reasoning goes, that anything that is messy or that could be messy would be abhorrent to Virgo children. Plus, these kids often don't seem creative to onlookers. They follow rules, turn in their work on time, and their hair is never out of place. And yet, once we get to know the Virgo child, we realize that he is intensely creative and especially gifted at the art of composition. Arranging, organizing, and composing—whether via visual art, music, or performing arts—are some of the areas where these little Sovereigns truly excel. This is a specific aspect of art and creativity. It is very possible that if a Virgo child goes to a normal, after-school art class, she is not going to enjoy herself and might walk away thinking she hates art. Not so. Take the same child to a museum and let her follow her eye to the exhibits that most attract her, or take her to an orchestra concert so she can hear the power of numerous different instruments coming together in harmony. Suddenly we find that the Virgo child loves art, loves creativity, loves the different possible arrangements in the arts. Therefore, the Virgo child's art classes and forays into creative work should emphasize the principles of composition across all mediums. This will speak to the Virgo on a deep level, and she will no longer suffer under the wrong idea that she is not creative. Virgo children are also natural writers and editors, so any creative activity that allows them to explore the written word is one they will very much enjoy!

Extracurricular Activities

In "Dancing at the Sipapu," Earth holds space for all of her children to move about, grow and change. She is still, but her stillness allows for all of the activity to occur. A similar dynamic can be found in the Virgo child's approach to extracurricular activities. These little Sovereigns do not want to be a bother to the adults around them. They know about being responsible for everyone and making sure that everyone has what they need—and they also know that this can be *exhausting*. What does this have to do with extracurricular activities? Well, the Virgo child might be really interested in doing one (or more!) activities but decide not to even ask about them because they don't want to stress out the adults in their lives. Virgo children are nothing if not considerate. This means that parents and caregivers need to be proactive in finding out what their little Virgo would like to explore and making sure that they have the resources to do just that. One pursuit the Virgo child might love—which appeals to her sense of higher order and a higher calling—is the care of animals, such as volunteering at pet adoption centers or learning to groom horses.

Technology

Often equated with the new, technology can sometimes be seen as intrusive, like the West Wind in our story. Mercury-ruled Virgo children tend to be binary when it comes to technology. They are either very analog and old school, preferring classic modes of connection and communication like writing with a fountain pen on beautiful stationery. Or, they are interested in technology purely from a pragmatic viewpoint. Virgo children often see technology first and foremost as a tool for work. This doesn't mean that they can't or won't get sucked into the entertainment side of technology (video games, social networking, movies, etc.), but it does mean that their primary relationship with technology will always be business or getting work done. For the Virgo child who does make use of technology, parents and caregivers will have to be on the lookout to make sure that these little ones do not get too overwhelmed or burned out after staring at a screen. These young Sovereigns, as Earth signs, tend to be more negatively impacted by prolonged exposure to tech gadgets than other children. Pair that with their desire to get the job done and do it perfectly, and you can have a Virgo kid who is spending way too much time on the computer and feeling drained, exhausted, and depleted as a result.

Sleeping and Waking

Virgo children tend to be fairly easy to put to bed, and the one thing to really watch out for with these low-maintenance children is that parents and caregivers take care to spend time with the Virgo child before bed and to tuck them in. Some Virgo children like to go to bed a bit earlier and may happily head off to their bedrooms of their own accord. Virgo children definitely need to bathe or shower before bedtime as cleanliness is important to them. Their rooms, night clothes, and bodies need to be clean in order for them to truly be able to rest. Without this cleanliness, the Virgo child can feel like the restless Earth in our story: dried up and lost. Virgo children also tend to wake up fairly early, and though they may be a bit slow to start, once they are up, they're up. These children can be clotheshorses like Leo kids, but in a different way. Matching is very important to the Virgo child, so make sure that a couple of matching outfits, including shoes and accessories, are ready in order to save a lot of time and drama in the morning.

Discipline

It is often assumed that because of their goody-goody vibe, Virgo kids love to follow rules. This is not necessarily the case. They will happily follow the rules if the rules are sensible. However, if a Virgo child is confronted with a set of rules that does not make common sense, or worse, that they see as an ethical lapse, then they will refuse to follow those rules, and they'll have a logically flawless presentation about why they aren't following the rules and why no one else should either.

A Virgo child is one who rarely needs to be disciplined. Typically quite well behaved, she really strives to make things easier for everyone and is usually quite accommodating. When the Virgo child gets into conflict, it is usually because he is feeling unseen and unappreciated or he is surrounded by chaos, which is energetically draining. This is the moment in the story when Earth goes wandering out of all bounds, restlessly searching for a solution to her crisis. In either situation the Virgo may respond in a passive-aggressive manner and make it seem as if he is a martyr having to always put his desires last.

Virgo children typically respond really well to praise and appreciation. Punitive measures don't work well on them because chances are they are being harder on themselves than parents or caregivers could be. The best ways to correct problematic behaviors include praising the Virgo child by emphasizing what they have done well and how their efforts are appreciated, giving them a nice gift (Virgo kids love presents!), and refusing to buy into stories of martyrdom.

How Best to Connect

The Virgo child loves to connect through daily work and routine or through an activity like shopping or gardening. It's not so much that these children always have to be busy—though the rulership of Mercury on the sign does indicate preference for a certain level of activity—it is more that Virgo children love to work or to be engaged in something that is meaningful to them. They cannot stand just being idle. Therefore we connect best with the Virgo child when we meet them on their level and join them in work. They often like it when you help them clean, straighten up, or organize. The Virgo child is an expert in devotion, so activities where this child can be focused and serious (shopping, gardening, cooking) are also good places to connect. The conversations will occur as the activity progresses—and Virgo children *will* talk, they just need to warm up first. A final place of connection? The car. Virgo children often enjoy going for long rides and can share a lot when they are in the vehicle with their people.

Polarity: Pisces

Pisces and Virgo are in polarity with one another. Pisces teaches Virgo about the deeper meaning of order—that expanded definition of perfection—in which it is okay to make a mess. Pisces also points out that making art is a legitimate way of making meaning. Life often involves imperfection at earlier and/or later stages. Finally, Pisces gently whispers in Virgo's ear that she should pay attention to her dreams and give them more credence.

Virgo Ascendant

Children with Virgo ascending present themselves as put together, quiet, unassuming, organized, and smart. They often have a serious facade and are able to work in a diligent and efficient manner. These children are often quite healthy and have an aura of good health and purity around them. Part of their work is to take their unique abilities, find what it is they are most devoted to, and follow that path.

Virgo Moon

Children with their Moon in Virgo tend to communicate through touch and tactile experiences more than words. They are very aware of the spaces they occupy and need those spaces to be clean and simple. These children are often quietly devout in nature, and their spiritual life matters to them. They are neither comfortable nor do well in chaotic surroundings. Emotionally they are calm and even-keeled with a tendency to feel sorry for themselves and to be passive-aggressive when stressed.

Activity
Clean Sweep

Virgo children are very observant and tend to hold a lot inside—these little ones are actually a lot more emotional than people think. A nice practice to help the Virgo child process those emotions is to do a ritual sweeping every day when they get home or any time they feel anxious. Take a broom and sweep from the back of the home all the way to the front and then out the front door. When the Virgo child is very little, give them their own small broom. When they get bigger they can use the household broom. Explain that as you are sweeping, you are removing any thoughts, feelings, stories, or ideas that no longer need to be part of their space and lives. This activity will often help the Virgo child share anything that has been on their mind as they literally sweep it out the door.

Ritual
Arranging an Altar

Every Virgo I know—child and adult alike—enjoys making altars. They may not know that's what they are doing (in their minds they are often just arranging things), but in fact they are creating little sacred spaces filled with specific objects. Parents and caregivers can connect with their Virgo children by taking this one step further and encouraging (and working with them) to create intentional altars.

The altars can be about anything—a thought, feeling, or worry—and they can change as needed. This is a great way to encourage the Virgo child's natural abilities when it comes to design, aesthetic, and devotion.

Ritual for the Inner Virgo Child
Words of Gratitude

"Thank you" are words that the adult honoring their inner Virgo child really needs to hear but all too often doesn't. So write yourself a letter thanking yourself for all the amazing things you do and you are. Frame the letter and put it on a wall where you can see it every day. It is hard to encourage other people to appreciate us if we don't first show that we appreciate ourselves.

CHAPTER 10

The Libra Child

"The good man is the
friend of all living things."

**Mahatma Gandhi
(Libra, born October 2, 1869)**

BIRTHDAY: September 22–October 22

RULING PLANET: Venus

ELEMENT: Air

QUALITY: Cardinal

SYMBOL: Scales/Balance

HOUSE: Seventh House of Relationships and Balance

STATEMENT: I am here to relate.

SEASON: Early Autumn

GUIDING STORY: "The Lion's Whisker"

Children, have you learned yet how when you gather together you stay warmer? Together look up now and find the constellation of Libra. We see it best in June, and it is bordered by the constellations Virgo, Scorpio, and Lupus among others. Just as you stay warmer when you come together, we learn that many things are made better where there are at least two of us. We cannot go through any dark night completely by ourselves, and yet sometimes it feels as if we must. Our next story comes from the beautiful land of Africa and tells us what is required to have true togetherness.

In a village long ago there lived a husband and wife. They had been married for only a few years but were deeply unhappy. The wife never smiled or laughed, and her eyes did not have the glimmer that other women had in theirs. Her husband, who had not that long ago fought in a great battle with another tribe, seemed to be always angry—yelling for no reason and nervous. He would jump even when there was nothing there. He woke up in the middle of the night with terrible dreams, but when his wife tried to comfort him by placing her hand on his strong back, he only turned away. He worked and provided well for the family, but it was clear to the wife that things could not continue as they had been.

She went to the Medicine Man in the village for help. He listened to her story and then nodded yes, he could help her. He had just the potion to heal the marriage, but he needed one last, essential ingredient. Would she be able to get it? She would. The wife promised that she would do whatever was needed. The Medicine Man nodded then and told her what she must get: a whisker from a fully grown male lion that was given to her willingly by the creature itself. The woman's heart sank, for surely this was an impossible task, but when she saw her husband's cold face that night, she relented and decided she would indeed do anything at all to save her marriage.

The next day the woman got a big piece of bloody meat and went to the local watering hole. She set down the meat and waited, and the biggest lion she had ever seen came sauntering down the path and devoured the meat in one go. She remained hidden the entire time, shaking with fear.

The next day she did the same, but right before the lion left, she stepped out from behind the bushes. He looked at her with mild interest and then turned and stalked off. This went on for many weeks. The woman showed herself and got a little closer to the lion each time he fed.

Finally, months later, the woman sat right beside the lion as he ate the meat. He watched her warily out of his gorgeous golden eyes, and when he was finished, he yawned, sat on his haunches, and began washing himself as all cats do after eating. Gently the woman reached out a hand and caressed his face, and the lion, in the way of all cats, leaned in for more caressing. As the woman stroked his gorgeous mane, the Lion spoke to her casually.

"Sister," his deep voice rumbled, "you have brought me good meat every day for months. What is it that you need?"

The woman bowed to him in honor and explained that she needed a single whisker to heal her husband. The lion asked the woman her name, and she told him. He gave her the whisker, and in return she promised she would still feed him, for they were friends now.

The woman went to the Medicine Man in triumph, waving her whisker with excitement. He smiled and said, "Excellent! The curse on your marriage is now broken!" The woman was confused—he had not even taken the lion's whisker and added it to the potion.

The Medicine Man sat her down gently and spoke in a quiet voice. "Have you not noticed, sister, that since you have been watching the lion, you have been less worried about your husband? Have you not noticed that your eyes sparkle in anticipation of seeing the creature, that your braids are tighter and glisten with good oil, and that the food you cook tastes better than ever? Your husband has noticed. And have you not found that in your own self you have great bravery, courage, cleverness, and patience—enough to become friends with a lion? If you can do that, then you know exactly how to make friends with the lion inside your husband."

He then made the woman a charm bag with the lion's whisker tucked safely inside—not because she needed magic but because she needed to remember. She found that he was right, and she went home to where her husband was waiting for her. He embraced her tenderly and began to weep as she held him, knowing all would be well once more.

Libra Gifts		
Fair	Balanced	Cultured
Diplomatic	Charming	Smart
Relational	Loving	Just
Libra Challenges		
Indecisive	Overly dependent	Bossy

THE LIBRA PERSONALITY

The traditional African folk tale of "The Lion's Whisker" holds a paradox at its heart. The motivation for the heroine of the story is the need to save her failing marriage, but the solution to her problem is to learn how to be happy and fully herself, even while her central relationship is damaged. This is the work of all Librans, and it begins in childhood.

Libra is the seventh sign of the Zodiac and marks a significant step in soul development. Up until the sign of Libra the focus has been on the individual and the things the individual needs (money, pleasure, learning, connection, food, housing, family, fun, good health, and aspirations). But now, as we enter the seventh sign, the focus changes to our relationships with others and what they need and want. With this sign and House we become aware of reciprocity, fair exchanges, and balance.

As cardinal Air signs, Libra children have no issue taking charge, but because one of their most important values is fairness, they try to share both the responsibilities and the accolades with others. Born under the sign of the Scales, the Libra child tries to be balanced herself. She often strikes a middle ground between being talkative and friendly and quiet and thoughtful. She typically does not like to be by herself, and even if she does enjoy being alone from time to time, she is concerned with what other people are saying and thinking about her.

The Libra child has an innate social grace. He is there to stop an argument before it gets started. And if it starts anyway, he is there afterward to offer a box of Kleenex and a listening ear if someone is upset. Libran children are charming to other kids, their parents, and teachers, so they easily influence people and have plenty of allies.

Above all, Libran children are loving. They love harmony, happiness, and peace. They seek out loving people and prioritize relationships, including close friendships, sometimes above all else.

Finally, the Venus-ruled, Air-sign Libra has an eye for what is beautiful, popular, and on trend. That can be useful, but sometimes these little ones can also be a bit shallow, wanting only to associate with the cool kids or emphasizing looks over character. The Libra child can easily be taken in by a pretty picture or the just-right words and can betray themselves and their friends in the pursuit of something shallow if they are not careful.

Friends and Play

Libra children, like the heroine of the story, are relationship focused. Perhaps the most exciting part of the story is the fact that the woman finally becomes real friends with a lion.

The Libra child can and does become friends with all kinds of unlikely people and creatures. Relationships, after all, are key, and love is love.

This child is the one whom everyone likes—at least at first. These kids are well loved and easy to get along with. Typically, Libran children are friendly, enthusiastic, good-natured, and pleasant. These Venus-ruled kiddos love being friendly and social, and they especially enjoy making room for those who would otherwise not fit in easily.

Libra children tend to be floaters. That is, they move from one group of friends to another group of friends with relative ease and typically have a handful of friends that they are closer to, with one primary friendship being the most important. The Libra child really *does* the best-friend thing. Often, in the case of the Libra child, their best friend may be a member of the opposite sex. Libra children are ruled by ultra-feminine Venus and aligned with the masculine element of Air, which means they all have a bit of androgyny about them. Libra girls tend to be comfortable being truly just friends with boys, and vice versa. If left to her own devices, the Libra child will have the same best friend all through her school days, and if and when that friendship hits a bump, the little Scale takes it very hard. For it is often only with her best friend that the Libra child truly shares herself and confides what she really thinks.

Because they are friendly with so many different people, Libra children often find that when several groups of friends come together there is conflict, which can stress them out. Parents and caregivers can help their Libra child think through what combinations of friends make sense and what combinations might create fireworks. In so doing, they save their child a lot of stress.

For all of their friendliness and charm, Libra children can sometimes start out as shy and awkward. So, when first meeting potential friends, they may need encouragement and support from parents/ caregivers to extend themselves socially. The Libra child values play that emphasizes relationships. Practically, this means that the Libra child doesn't really care what the game is as long as it allows for connection and communication. Libra children often like to play house or "getting married" (or some iteration thereof), and they often like to play games where they are in command or issuing orders—for they are natural leaders and like to be in charge. Typically when the Libra child hits a snag in their friendships it is not because of them. These bright children are easy to get along with and often go out of their way to make sure that their friends are comfortable and happy. Sometimes they annoy their friends with their dependency, but more often a special friend might start spending time with someone else, and the Libra child will discover an inner dragon of jealousy. When that happens the Libra child can turn cold and aloof, deciding, in essence, that if their friend is not as committed to the relationship as they are, then there really is no relationship to speak of.

This brings up another potential challenge for the Libra child: overdependence on relationships. Different Libran children resolve this challenge in different ways. Some Libra children meet this problem by having a large and relatively shallow group of friends. They are social and charming, but they do not let anyone get too close. Other little Scales tend to keep the number of close friends fairly small, ignore larger groups, and learn to be by themselves when their few friends are not available. Some Libran kids will really latch on to a single friend, and as long as things are going well, all is fine. If there is a hiccup in the friendship, however, the Libra child can go into a quick tailspin. This is not codependence so much as overdependence, and the core issue is that often the Libra child is using their friendships to help them figure out who they are. The Libra child is the one who likes whatever her friend likes and doesn't like whatever her friend doesn't like. Part of this child's work is to discover who they are independent of their other relationships. The same rules hold true for the Libra child's primary familial relationships.

Academics

The heroine in the story of "The Lion's Whisker" has to be smart, patient, and focused just like Libra children. This translates well in terms of both academic and social intelligence. They know how to read a room and gauge motivations with ease, and they also know how to rock a test and get high marks from teachers.

This intelligence can cut both ways, however, as Libra children can sometimes think something to death. They see situations not from one or two angles but from many different sides and angles, which can lead to one of the most oft-cited negative Libran qualities: indecision. It's not so much that the Libra child doesn't know what she wants, it's that she has a thorough and legalistic mind that wants to exhaust all avenues of possibility before making a decision, because once she decides, she wants it to be the *right* choice.

The little Scales do have challenges in school though. Libran children tend to forget to double-check their work, make careless mistakes, and rush to finish their assignments too quickly. (Libra, like the other cardinal signs, likes to be first.)

Just as the Taurus child likes to talk about money, the Libra child enjoys conversing about politics and current events. This can throw off parents and caregivers, but engaging your Libra child in thoughtful political analysis and commentary is much better than trying to get them to stop talking politics. They'll just wait until you are out of the room, only to start up again! The Libra child may have times when he is quiet and times when he is more vocal. But when he speaks, it is usually to a rapt audience. This is because Libra children are naturally some of the most articulate little ones in the Zodiac. They have a natural way with words and can be very diplomatic and persuasive. But be careful here, sometimes the Libra child is just trying on an argument or a point of view, and they may not want to be held to it later. When it comes to academics, Libra children can also be quite competitive and a bit clueless as to how their classroom behavior affects others—it is often a Libra who messes up the curve for everyone else and then doesn't understand why their friends are so unhappy with them!

The Libra child often finds school and learning to be a haven and a place where they can truly spread their wings. The more their school involves political ideas, culture, and art, the happier the little Libra child is.

Young-adult Libras considering what comes next after finishing high school often find themselves drawn to unique college experiences. The Libra youth is likely to be drawn to subjects like philosophy, political science, and law. Many Librans end up focusing on a career in law and do well to study subjects in their undergraduate years that prepare them for law school. Libras may also be drawn to social groups like sororities or fraternities and the sense of belonging such groups can confer. Relationships are always important to these children, so parents and caregivers would do well to make sure that their Libra child is paying attention to school and not losing themselves in a romantic relationship. On the other hand, if the Libra child comes home from college with their beloved in tow and is ready to get married or make a life-long commitment, get ready to be supportive. Once these marriage-loving youths have set their mind on wedding vows, there is little that can be done to persuade them to change their minds.

Physical Activity

In the story, "The Lion's Whisker," the heroine's action is motivated by the external need to seek a remedy for her relationship—and so her energetic search begins. Librans have lots of enthusiasm and a good amount of energy, but they typically lack endurance, so when it comes to physical activities, endurance is something they need to build. Aerial activities like tumbling, gymnastics, and cheerleading often appeal to these little Scales, as do performing arts that involve physical movement like dance. Because of its emphasis on balance and holding tension creatively, yoga is often very popular with Libra children—as is aerobics, ballet, or any kind of dance fitness.

The Libra child is willing to try most team sports, especially if they have a good friend or two who are playing the sport. However, as they get older, Libra children may find that some team sports seem less cultured than other activities and will decide not to pursue a specific sport, not because they don't enjoy it, but because they have a principled disagreement with it. For example, they might dislike the commercialism associated with a sport or the fact that women's teams are not funded as well as men's teams.

When it comes to team sports they approve of, the Libra child is often in a leadership position and helps the team come together in meaningful ways. These children can be counted on for a rousing pep talk or a fast critical assessment and suggested change of strategy. Because these Venus-ruled kiddos like to be comfortable, the Libra child might choose not to do a physical activity or will only half-heartedly engage in one, so this is an area where parents and caregivers will need to provide extra support.

Art and Creativity

In "The Lion's Whisker," our heroine learns that the whisker is not the cure she needs, but rather inherent qualities she already possesses but hasn't recognized. The great power of art is that it is exercised for its own sake—for its own enjoyment—and this experience of pure joy is medicine to Libra's purpose-oriented nature. Art also tends to be healing and peacemaking, which is a deep interest of Libra. Art and culture is an area that their sign rules, and if they are aware, it will be something they treasure and prioritize for this reason. However, that does not translate to the Libran wanting to get down and dirty in art class. Often the Libra child's abilities lie less in the visual arts and more in the direction of performing arts like dance, theater, gymnastics, choir, or band. Another area of creative work that these little Scales often respond very well to is writing. These cardinal Air signs love to communicate through the written word just like their fellow Gemini Air signs do.

Finally, Libra children often love speaking contests—public speaking, oratory, and extemporaneous speaking are all areas in which the Libra child can excel. Debate is another area that the Libra child does well in, as these children love composing arguments and trying them out. Any creative act that can be turned into both a collaboration and competition gets extra points in the Libra child's book.

Extracurricular Activities

In "The Lion's Whisker" there is a backstory for the husband's unhappiness that is never fully fleshed out, but it seems to deal with war or conflict of some kind. The Libra child has an eye for spotting imbalance and injustice—and a talent for working swiftly to correct them. He also has an eye for seeing people who have been affected by war or other atrocities and will work to help those individuals return to a point of balance. While it is true that most North American children don't see armed conflict, it is also true that many little ones come from homes and neighborhoods that can feel like battle zones. The Libran wants to fix that or at least bring some harmony and balance into the situation.

The Libra child's extracurricular activities can be guided, with these things in mind, toward a sense of balance and peacemaking. Parents and caregivers will need to help the Libra child select a balanced group of extracurricular activities. Making sure that the Libra child really likes or is engaged in an activity—not just doing it because their friends are—is a good place to begin. While some children benefit from leaning into their areas of specialization and expertise, the Libra child does best with a truly balanced assortment of activities—some physical and some more mental or creative in nature. A stressed-out Libra child with too many activities to balance tends to shut down socially and be very anxious and nervous, and obviously won't perform their best. Beyond these considerations, an area of extracurricular interest might include helping out at animal shelters, feeding the homeless, painting Little Free Library boxes, or participating in any community volunteer program that excites your Libra child's interest in restoring balance and healing conflicts.

Please note that the Libra child's eyes are much bigger than his stomach! This is especially true when it comes to all extracurricular activities. If it were up to him, he would do *all* the activities. Libra children don't like to decide before they test the waters. They want to be with their friends, and they like to be involved in everything. That means that picking just a few activities is really difficult for them.

Technology

Most of us feel the mesmerizing effect that technology holds over us, but children are especially affected. In "The Lion's Whisker," the heroine discovers that what she needs she already possesses—not the magical medicine bag but her own personal powers of courage and wisdom.

Similarly, the Libra child is well positioned to keep technology in perspective as a tool, but not as an end in itself, as if it were a solution to Libra's relationship problems.

It shouldn't come as a surprise that the Libra child likes to use technology for the purposes of connecting to others. Social media is a happy place for many Libran children because they can talk to their friends, see what their friends are up to, and generally feel connected and able to communicate. Social media comes with certain challenges, of course, so the Libra child's technology habits need to be monitored closely. Also, Libra children tend to get easily stressed out around technology. While *every* child should have their screen time monitored, this is especially true for Libran kiddos who often feel exhausted after hours of looking at a screen.

Sleeping and Waking

The little Scales are great lovers of dreams. Their interest is not the intoxication of dreaming, but rather they love the way dreams can seem to bring messages to them, messages of healing and justice. Dreams can involve them in great missions and searches like the one told in "The Lion's Whisker."

Libra children, on the other hand, are not heavy sleepers—they tend to be early to bed and early to rise. Connecting with their people before bedtime is really important to these children, and going to bed in the middle of a fight or disagreement is one of the worst things to do as far as they are concerned. They will get no rest until things are resolved. For the Libra child this often means talking things out until they are satisfied, and that can take a while. Reading or talking before bed is a great activity to help Librans wind down and sleep peacefully.

These children usually find it easy to get up in the morning, but organization may be hard for them, so this is another Zodiac Sign where a little preplanning the night before really helps. This includes pulling outfits for the Libra child to wear. These little ones can be very fashion conscious *and* indecisive about what they want to wear on a given day, so having a few choices really helps. Also, Libra children tend not to think about food, but when they do, they often have specific requests. In the interest of saving time in the morning, have a few favorite breakfast items on hand, and make sure your child snags something nutritious on their way out the door.

Libras often love morning time the best: it is when they get their best thinking done and when they are at their peak performance, so parents and caregivers can keep this in mind when creating schedules and plans.

Discipline

The Libra child can be so motivated by a sense of right and by the need for healing injustices—as our heroine in the story is—that they rarely need to be disciplined. Along with Virgos and Capricorns, these children are often some of the best-behaved kids in school and at home. Libra children do not like it when people get upset or angry, especially when those people are upset or angry with them. If the Libra child does get into trouble, it is usually because she is talking too much or socializing with friends and distracting others from their work.

Libra children can also be a bit duplicitous, usually for the sake of keeping the peace—so they can get into trouble for that too. Once the Libra child is in trouble, correcting his behavior is often fairly easy because he is a natural people pleaser and does not want to do anything that creates stress or unhappiness. The only time teachers and caregivers really need to worry is in a situation where the Libra child feels that something is unfair or someone is being treated unfairly. In those cases, the Libra child loses all concern for other people's feelings and instead expects the wrong to be addressed and made right. They will shout, argue, disagree, and happily stage a sit-in until they feel that fairness and justice have been restored.

How Best to Connect

As we have seen, our story's heroine thinks the medicine she needs is the lion's whisker, but what is really needed are all the qualities she demonstrated in order to get the whisker. In other words, all that was required was for her to be fully present for her self and her love. On the question of how best to connect with Libran children, they must also discover that often much less is needed than they think, and what is really needed is for them to be fully present in whatever they are doing and with whomever they are doing it.

Libra children are Air signs, which means that they value ideas, thoughts, speech, and words. The best way to connect with the Libra child is to be fully present with them and to exchange ideas, words, and stories. This kind of connection energizes the Libra child, reinforces the relationship that they have with you, and leaves them feeling safe, loved, and in right relationship.

Polarity: Aries

Aries teaches Libra the valuable lesson of knowing oneself and one's own particular feelings, desires, and preferences before considering what works best for everyone else. Aries also reminds Libra that it is not enough to take an intellectual stand against unfairness or injustice; actions may need to be taken as well.

Libra Ascendant

Libra ascending children are often walking fashion plates, always aware of the latest trends, and always in style. They are fashion conscious and like to make a charming first impression. They often have dazzling smiles and a charming personality, and they can be chatty. The child with Libra at the Ascendant is most happy when doing work that promotes peace, justice, harmony, and beauty.

Libra Moon

Children with their Moon in Libra are very comfortable when everyone is happy. Conflict makes them nervous and can depress them as well. These children are fair in their tempers, getting angry only when a situation really warrants it. They are true romantics, and love and partnerships are very important to them and can take a toll on their emotional health if they are imbalanced. Style and fashion are also areas where these children are quite gifted and discerning.

Activity
Art Walk and Talk

Take the Libra child to an art museum or art gallery and slowly walk through the exhibit, encouraging the child to take their time at each piece of art. Then go out to lunch or have a picnic and discuss what the Libra child saw and felt as they experienced the art. This will leave them feeling deeply refreshed, relaxed, and satisfied.

Ritual
Balance Pose

Encourage your Libra child to actually embody the feeling of balance that they often seek out. Any pose or exercise that has the child balancing works. Start by having them walk a balance beam at the playground. Yoga postures like Tree Pose will teach them vital ways to embody the ideal of balance. This also teaches harmony-loving Libra that tension is actually necessary in order to achieve true balance.

Ritual for the Inner Libra Child
Decision Making, Done!

The Libran inner child is often wounded through constant haranguing: "Make a decision!" For Libra, a cardinal sign who often finds herself in charge, one of the most luxurious things is to outsource plans and decision-making to some-one else. For this ritual we give our inner Libran children permission to do just that. Call up a friend or talk to your partner. Tell them that you are doing some work around healing old wounds and that you would like them to plan a day outing or experience for you. (You can promise to return the favor later if you want.) During this time you do not have to make a single decision, simply allow yourself to flow along with the decisions someone else is making for you and enjoy receiving and not being in charge.

CHAPTER 11

The Scorpio Child

"Every act of creation is
first an act of destruction."

Pablo Picasso
(Scorpio, born October 25, 1881)

BIRTHDAY: October 22–November 21

RULING PLANET: Mars, Pluto

ELEMENT: Water

QUALITY: Fixed

SYMBOL: Grey Lizard/Scorpion/Eagle

HOUSE: Eighth House of Magic and Mystery

STATEMENT: I am here to empower.

SEASON: High Autumn

GUIDING STORY: "Santa Muerte: The Tale of
Mictecacihuatl"

Ah my sweetlings, how I love to see you hold each other close, eyes wide and bright, as the night grows ever deeper. Look now and find the constellation of Scorpius; it is most visible in July and holds many deep-sky objects, which is appropriate given its nature. Stories, like stars, have their own secrets, twists, and turns; they also have unexpected moments. Tilt them a bit this way and they have a happy ending; tilt them a bit the other way and the ending is not so happy, and maybe horrific. Sometimes though, the stories that scare us the most are the ones that are not complete. In these cases, we must investigate until we discover what will round them out. The story of Mictecacihuatl (mik.te:. ka.ˈsí.wa:tɬ)—who is known as Santa Muerte here where I live in San Antonio and also in Mexico where this tale is originally from—is such a story and perfect for the sign of the Scorpion, who is not afraid of the dark places.

Now they say today that Santa Muerte was sacrificed as a baby, and that is how she came to her position. But any mother who listens to her story knows that this is not true. She was not sacrificed. Rather, she was born—deeply beloved for her bright, dark beauty—and then, as is the way sometimes with the very young, she caught ill and died, all before turning one year old.

Her little soul, skeleton glowing gold and emerald and azure, made its way down to the Underworld where all of the dead went. There she was cared for, so that as she grew her radiant bones and her bright eyes became ever more lovely.

The Lord of the Dead was captivated by her beauty and declared that she would be his Queen forever more.

Now they say that Santa Muerte was tasked with the sacred job of tending the bones, but the truth is that she asked for this job. She knew the power of bones, the songs and stories and dreams they contained. She knew the mysteries that poured flesh and muscle onto bone, skin onto flesh, hair and nail and bright eye all coming into being. She loved this best, the taking of the bones and calling them back up to life.

Now they say that she made a mistake. One day, as she was carrying a bundle of bones from the depths of the Underworld back to the surface world of sun and lake and tree, Santa Muerte stumbled. Maybe she wasn't paying attention—who knows for sure?— but what we do know is that the bones all got mixed up, and life up here has been a little chaotic ever since then. This is the way the story goes.

But leave Santa Muerte an offering of sugar, apples, copal incense; leave her an offering of something good to drink, and she will tell you something different. She will tell you how, really, it was boring. Everyone being the same, looking the same, talking the same, staying in their little *nichos*—no moving around, no getting into trouble. She will remind you that, having grown up from infancy in the Underworld and talking to many, many, people who died, she knew a little something about what made life interesting. It was not a mistake. She "slipped." The bones fell out pell-mell every which way. And we people have been encountering each other in all of our splendid differences ever since. This was Santa Muerte's way of making life a little bit sweeter, and it is why today this most beloved Lady of the Dead is sought out and honored especially by those who feel isolated, alone, and different from everyone else.

Scorpio Gifts		
Powerful	Intense	Alluring
Magical	Mysterious	Loyal
Psychic	Realistic	Wise
Scorpio Challenges		
Vengeful	Secretive	Destructive

THE SCORPIO PERSONALITY

"Santa Muerte: The Tale of Mictecacihuatl" speaks to the life and personality of the Scorpio child. Like Santa Muerte, the Scorpio child is easily spotted as one who seems to be comfortable with the uncomfortable and difficult aspects of life. These children may have had traumatic beginnings themselves, or they may have perfectly "normal" childhoods; nevertheless, they recognize the roles that pain and suffering play in human life.

The Scorpio child exudes a kind of innate power in their personality and in the sheer force of their will. Scorpio children are competitive like Aries and Libra, focused like Taurus, and smart like Gemini. Along with the power they exude and the intensity they bring to their endeavors, Scorpio children are alluring. They can use that power for good by encouraging other children in the exact ways they most need encouragement and by making even the shyest and most retiring child feel seen and heard. Or, they can use that power for ill, creating peer pressure and influencing their peers to do all manner of mischief. A challenge emerges here because often the Scorpio child does not realize how much influence she really has over others.

Whether in the classroom, with friends in a social setting, playing a sport, or making art, the Scorpio child brings a level of intensity to everything they do that sets them apart from others. One of the places where the Scorpio child's intensity can most easily be seen is in the things they like to discuss. The Scorpio child is happy to talk about money, finances, and intense subjects like death and religion all day long.

Friends and Play

Santa Muerte ("Saint Death" in Spanish) has a lot of names, including Little Saint Death and Lady Death. She comes across to most people at first as dark, morbid, and even scary, but when you get down to the root, she is a protector of abundance and life and rejuvenation. Scorpio children may be viewed in much the same way as Santa

Muerte, but what they really are is intense and keyed into the Sacred in an incredibly deep manner. Scorpio children do not come across as friendly at first glance. These are often the children who hang back, brood, and seem to always be glowering. That's all surface, though, and the intrepid children who are patient and persistent enough to get through the exterior walls will find that they could not ask for a more loyal or devoted friend than their Scorpio sidekick.

Often the children who make the biggest impact on the these little Scorpions are their apparent polar opposite: those kids who are chatty, bright, social, charming, fun, funny, and friendly. The Scorpio child rarely asserts herself in a friendship or seeks out a friend—she doesn't have to because she is naturally so alluring and interesting. Instead, potential friends find *her*, draw her out, and take the initial lead in forming the friendship. Once comfortable with a friend or a few friends, the Scorpio child reveals a whip-smart mind, wicked sense of humor, and daring sense of adventure that makes friendships intense and long lasting.

Scorpio children do best with either one-on-one or small-group socializing. Large groups stress them out and deplete them energetically, but if large-group socializing serves some deeper purpose then the Scorpio child can do it—they just won't enjoy it.

As they get older, the Scorpio child can become quite socially adept. These children have something of the psychic in them, so they know what to say as well as when and how to say it. Older Scorpio children can often be found among the popular kids, even though no matter how many people seem to like them, a part of them will always believe they are fundamentally different, weird, and out of place.

Scorpio children are extremely loyal, and they are also devoted friends. The issues in their friendships emerge if Scorpio feels betrayed (and sensitive Scorpio children can take even small slights as betrayals), when the Scorpio child feels angry, or when the Scorpio child feels they're being forced to do or be something they don't want to be or do. As the Scorpio child gets older, issues of sex and sexual competition can also be potential wedges in friendships. The key for the friends of

Scorpio children is to accept their broody friends for who they are, and the key for the Scorpio child is to quit waiting for their closest friends to disappoint them.

As she gets older, the Scorpio child is also going to think about and talk about sex and sexuality—a lot. While Libra is the sign of love and marriage, Scorpio is the sign of intimacy and sex, and Scorpio children are often the first to experiment with sex and desire. Frank, honest conversations about these topics (that are age appropriate) will go a long way in garnering the Scorpio child's respect and confidence.

Academics

Children born under the sign of the Scorpion are, like the child in our tale, often quite comfortable with the most intense subjects, including death and what happens to us after we die. And so while the Scorpio child can be incredibly intellectual, where they really shine is in their emotional intelligence and street smarts. Just because the Scorpio child is intelligent, though, does not necessarily mean they will do well in school. The Scorpio child is not motivated to make other people happy or to get the A+ or gold stars. These children need to feel that something is actually riding on their grades and work in order for them to do their best and truly make an effort. Otherwise they are likely to see the routine of schoolwork as something less than important and not worth their time or their attention.

The Scorpio child may also get bored in school and so looks for ways to distract herself (and sometimes other children as well). One way to make the Scorpio child sit up, pay attention, and do their best is through games and competitions. Scorpio was originally ruled by the Planet Mars and so, like Aries, the other Mars-ruled sign, Scorpio children love contests and competitions of all kinds. In fact, it is often through competitions that teachers and caregivers first realize how truly smart the Scorpio child is. It might take these little Scorpions longer to make connections, write down answers, and complete assignments. This has nothing to do with their intelligence and everything to do with the fact that they have a profound ability to focus and concentrate, and they are thorough in everything that they do. If these children come from families that value education and place emphasis on the importance of school, and especially if the Scorpio child understands the relationship between academic performance and career options later in life, then they will happily buckle down and do the work requested of them with excellence to spare.

Subjects that the Scorpio child tends to excel at include math, history, writing, and health. Scorpio children are often drawn to healing and the healing arts, and as they get older many Scorpio kids find themselves interested in the "soft" social sciences like economics, anthropology, and psychology. Scorpio children often have a strong affiliation with math and money the way that Taurus children do because their sign is also associated with finances and especially with investments. If there are clubs at the child's school that teach how to invest, then enroll these kids—they will love it!

For Scorpio children to have true academic success, they need to respect both the projects they're assigned and the teachers who are handing out the assignments. If these children are not doing well in school, parents and caregivers should first find out if they are feeling bored, secondly determine how they feel about their teachers and classes, and then thirdly determine if there has been any friend drama that has interrupted their ability to concentrate and focus.

As they mature and begin thinking about life after high school, Scorpio children will be interested in college and continuing their education if they can see how that choice will financially help them. Scorpio is a financially motivated sign that is not afraid to talk money, so the fields of business, finance, and accounting are all good areas for them to explore as potential career tracks. Born as they are with an affinity for the shadows and legalistic minds, Scorpios also often go into the fields of criminal justice and law. Whatever field the young Scorpio pursues, parents and caregivers should be ready for them to approach it with their typical intensity and single-minded focus.

Physical Activity

Santa Muerte's tale of growing up in the Underworld, marrying the God of Death, and then spilling the bones so that the topside world is full of endless variety, are all actions that any little Scorpion would recognize as both familiar and fitting. Consequently, the Scorpio child has a rich inner and fantasy life, which can often lead to resistance against physical activity. My advice? Don't let it. It is important for all children to be given opportunities for exercise, but it is especially important for the Scorpio child to learn early on to love and respect their physical bodies. If they do not, then later it becomes especially easy for these kids to abuse their bodies through drinking, drugs, and unsafe sex.

Fortunately, a lot of physical activities are team sports, so the Scorpio child can find many ways to satisfy their desire for competitions and opportunities to prove themselves. These children may at first prefer more solitary sports like running, swimming, tennis, or golf, but with encouragement they will join larger teams and become important members of those teams. Scorpio children are not usually the strongest physically, but they can be aggressive, passionate, and excellent strategists for their team. Scorpio children who are drawn to activities like dance, gymnastics, and cheerleading are often the ones who bring a seductive element to routines.

Parents and caregivers should celebrate this aspect of their children and not allow their kids to be branded in ways that are shaming or disrespectful. A seductive and alluring quality is part and parcel of the Scorpio giftedness, and others need to accept that. Both Middle Eastern and American "tribal-style" belly dance are art forms that combine sensual movement with concentration and physical rigor. This is one wonderful way for the Scorpio child to explore her sensual side in an age-appropriate manner while also learning precision and a physically challenging discipline. (There are classes for all age groups and genders.) Middle Eastern drumming is another art form that is very physical and celebrates many of the same qualities.

With proper encouragement and support, Scorpio children will do well with their chosen physical activities and bring a level of intensity to their games unmatched by all but Capricorn kids. However, if there is infighting among teammates, or if the Scorpio child feels that one teammate has done something wrong or lacks integrity, then they will often want to just quit the team. Likewise, if another player is very good at what they do, they might inspire envy in the Scorpio child, which, if left unchecked, can create lots of drama within the team. Parents and caregivers should watch for this and make sure that their Scorpio child truly feels connected to their other teammates.

As they get older, it is not unusual for Scorpio kids to take up less conventional physical activities like modern dance or squash. Parents and caregivers can get a leg up on that tendency by scouting out what unusual modes of movement practices are available in their areas.

Art and Creativity

When it comes to the underworld—the realm of the glowing bones of Santa Muerte and magical transformation—the Scorpio child finds himself in familiar territory. He is comfortable dealing with the unseen, the shadow sides of life that no one wants to talk about, and traumatic experiences that need to be processed in order to heal. However, no matter what is found there, the return to the here and now—to the everyday world—with the insights and inspiration of the underworld is necessary. He cannot stay there. And there's the rub. There's no place where our little Scorpion would rather be than in a region he is most comfortable in—the region where extremes touch one another and adrenaline is pumping.

This is where the arts of any kind come into play for the Scorpio child. The arts have the power to give form and expression to Scorpio's underworld experience, proffering its rich gifts to the everyday world above. Art and creativity in any form is a vehicle for the Scorpio child to help moderate and balance some of his more extreme and possibly self-destructive tendencies. The unifying factor in creative work and art-making for all Scorpio children is that through their art they express and process their feelings. Through their creative work they are able to speak to the presence of pain and suffering in the world that they are always aware of.

Scorpio children are naturally creative and gifted kids who often don't realize how gifted they are. Which is to say that your Scorpio child might need encouragement to explore the various creative avenues that are open to him. Scorpio children really do range in their creative abilities, with some taking to canvas and paint, others to plastic arts like sculpture, some to the art of writing and/or storytelling, others to music, and still others to performing arts where they can bring their smoldering energy to the stage or screen.

Therefore, while it may take time to find the right mode of creative expression for the Scorpio child, it is important that effort be applied here because they do need to be able to express themselves creatively. There is another area of art that the Scorpio child may find themselves especially drawn to: the magical or Sacred Arts. Scorpio children often love to ritualize things, and they are drawn to the ideas of hidden knowledge or anything esoteric, even in the major world religions. Parents and caregivers need not fear these tendencies but instead can embrace them and support the Scorpio child in their creative spiritual questing.

Extracurricular Activities

Like Santa Muerte, the Scorpio child often goes where angels fear to tread, but in so doing becomes a different kind of angel altogether. For all of their daring, the Scorpio child is often content not to load themselves up with extracurricular activities. They like unstructured time when they can just be. However, it is important that these children have a robust appreciation of extracurricular activities because if they are allowed to just hang out, they often end up feeling bored—and a bored Scorpio kid is much more likely to get into trouble. As always it is good to strike a balance, but what the right balance looks like for Scorpio is enough activities, and enough different activities, to keep them engaged and interested. Competitions and contests should figure into the Scorpio child's schedule regularly, as should means of creative expression. Attending church, temple, mosque, or whatever spiritual service is observed by the family is also an important activity for the young Scorpion. These children are naturally spiritual, and that aspect of their natures should be cultivated and honored.

Technology

In our story, Santa Muerte inhabits dark and fearful regions. You can expect the Scorpio child (or a child with Scorpio influence) to uncover some of the more unsavory and dangerous parts of technology. Parental controls might offer some immediate relief, but the Scorpio child's curiosity will be strong, and possibly even intensified, when they become aware of the blocks set in their way. Sooner or later, they will come face to face with the things we try to keep them away from. The question is, what can be done to prepare them for that day?

I find the story of Santa Muerte useful when thinking about Scorpio kids because it reminds me that despite her appearance and her home in the Underworld, Santa Muerte possesses the life-affirming ability to rejuvenate the bones. What would happen if, in our guidance of Scorpio-influenced children, we learn what it means to trust their particular instincts?

These little Scorpions can have strong addictive tendencies. But what is the gift of those tendencies? A positive thing parents and caregivers can do is to help foster counter-experiences to technology addiction and help the Scorpio child unlock their particular gift of intensity.

Technology has a passive, consumptive side and an active, creative side. Instead of letting children be always on the side of passive consumption, we could give them ongoing support in experiences with creation or production. Encourage Scorpio children to learn the science and mechanics of the various technical gadgets available by giving them the tools and material support they need to make these discoveries for themselves. They are, after all, natural investigators! Technology is also a good opportunity to foster needed artistic creation. There are some wonderful new techno-tools for creating music and visual arts, and these could be introduced to the Scorpio child.

As Scorpio children get older, if parents and caregivers are not able to talk frankly, respectfully, and lovingly about sex, Scorpio children will likely head to the internet to get their information and may develop habits around pornography. The same holds true for the Sacred Arts and magic: if the Scorpio child is not able to talk freely about their spiritual questions and interests, they will find places where they can.

Scorpio children often enjoy the entertainment aspects of technology and can be quite good at learning different programing languages or understanding intuitively how the mechanics of tech gear work. Any game that features a contest, especially if it can be played with friends, draws the Scorpio child's attention. Bonus points if the game has elements of crime and crime detection, as Scorpio children have a naturally investigative mind and are often fascinated by the subject of crime and punishment.

Sleeping and Waking

Death—both literal and metaphorical—is part of the terrain that the Scorpio child considers to be native, but it is not the whole of it. Healing, love and deep intimacy, and the ability to put whatever resources are at their disposal to the best possible use is also part of the Scorpio tale. Scorpio-influenced youths love the power of dreams, but as they get older they are often night owls who feel most comfortable in the hours from midnight to 3:00 a.m. Obviously this kind of a schedule does not work for most children! Parents and caregivers can honor the Scorpio child's love of late nights by letting them stay up a little later than their friends get to, but they still need a reasonable bedtime. Scorpio children can function well on less sleep for a while, but when parents, teachers, or caregivers start noticing that these children are getting snappy, aggressive for no reason, or angry, they should know that the sleep schedule needs to be adjusted because the Scorpio child is exhausted.

While they love late nights, little Scorpions are not typically morning people so they need extra time—a couple of predefined rituals wouldn't hurt—in order to get up and get with it. Scorpio children can be a bit obsessive when it comes to cleaning their rooms, getting ready for school, and making sure that they have everything they need. Reminders about what they should take to be equipped for school can be helpful, but don't try to pick out their clothes—they will hate every choice made for them and have to make their own choices all over again. Like their polarity Taurus, Scorpios may have a set "uniform" that they default to on a daily basis. The best practice is just to make sure these kids have extra time in the morning and to give them discrete amounts of time to complete projects (e.g., "You have twenty minutes to get your clothes on").

Discipline

As you might imagine, given our story, children influenced by Scorpio energies often find themselves on the wrong side of the law. This could be seen as ironic, since Scorpio carries forward Libra's ingrained love and respect for rules. But there is a certain giftedness in the breaking of rules, and the Scorpio child senses this. Scorpio children are especially keen on sniffing out counterfeit surfaces and fake appearances—and that also goes for what they perceive as phony rules that powerful people make to keep their power intact. Breaking rules doesn't necessarily mean Scorpio children are unruly or don't respect rules. It can also mean they deeply love the highest and most genuine laws, and they keenly feel the need for those laws.

The problem is that Scorpio gets bored and restless very easily, as his heightened sensitivity detects superficial behavior ten miles away. Often, in his effort to outrun his boredom or a shallow discussion, he ends up rebelling in some dramatic manner.

As young children, this often looks like the proverbial acting out: little Scorpions refusing to sit still, do what they are supposed to, and most especially say what they are supposed to say. Even a young Scorpio child can have quite a sharp tongue! As they get older, these behaviors can morph into attention-getting and law-crossing antics that can, at the most extreme end of the spectrum, result in a Scorpio-influenced kid's placement in juvenile detention. Scorpio, like Taurus, is a fixed sign, which means that the best chance for correcting problematic behavior with children influenced by Scorpio is to get in front of it before it starts. This is especially true with the Scorpio child because they are hard to move or shift once they have made up their minds on a course of action; these children also play their cards close to their chest and they may have been brooding over/planning a certain set of behaviors for a long time before actually expressing them. Scorpio children can reform their behavior when given the proper incentives: financial ones are often the best. They also improve their behavior when they are asked to take on leadership positions and positions of service. Though all of our kids are rewarded by volunteering, this is especially the case with Scorpio children, who often feel that it is only through meaningful service that they can address the harsher elements of the world that they are all too aware of.

How Best to Connect

If you've been following the course of this chapter, from the moment you listened to "Santa Muerte," you will not be surprised to hear that little Scorpions are intense. They are intensely aware, intensely feeling, intensely sensitive, and intense about their connections with their people. The best way to connect with the Scorpio child is to not be afraid of their intensity. Don't try to water it down, sugarcoat the truth, or pretend like you cannot hear their thorny, difficult questions. They know you can hear them just fine. Instead, be honest with them, answer their questions, and when you don't know the answers find them out together. Scorpio children love to investigate. Don't be afraid to discuss and help them think about even really hard stuff. Scorpio children are soothed and educated by stories. It is one of their favorite ways to learn, so tell them stories, especially those in the fantasy genre.

Finally, these children are drawn to the Sacred Arts. Make magic with them. Teach them little divination games. These are the things that will leave them feeling heard, seen, and most importantly, understood.

Polarity: Taurus

Taurus reminds ever-intense Scorpio that not everything has to be a deep and dramatic voyage to the realms of the inner psyche. It's okay to relax and enjoy life! Taurus also points out that Scorpio can afford to be more gentle and kind in their approach and behavior. Finally, Taurus reminds Scorpio that money is not an end but a means, so hoarding is not a helpful behavior.

Scorpio Ascendant

Children with Scorpio at the Ascendant tend to present themselves as intense, focused, driven, and melancholic in nature. They may prefer dressing in somber colors or wear lots of black or have a Goth aesthetic. These children often seem mysterious and enigmatic to others and can also appear to be slightly manipulative. The child with Scorpio at the Ascendant thrives when they are able to delve deeply into psychic and psychological shadows and find healing through transformation.

Scorpio Moon

Scorpio Moon children are deeply intuitive and truly come across as natural psychics. They often have nightmares or complicated dreams when young, and they benefit from talking through those night visions with adults. These children feel emotions in great crashing waves and need to learn to regulate their emotional states. Breathing exercises, prayer, and meditation are good supports. A feeling of being over-whelmed can easily set in for these little ones, and when it does they will seek out various ways to self-medicate if they do not have other coping methods.

Upping the Offerings

As mentioned, Scorpio children love all things related to
magic and Sacred Arts, so a great practice that allows them
to explore those areas in a safe and beneficial way is an
offering. The best way to start is with everyday items that
the Scorpio child has an ongoing relationship with. They
can make an offering of cool, clear water to their favorite
tree or an offering of birdseed to the birds. When the child
makes the offering, they may bless it or offer it up in any
way they like. This intentional practice puts Scorpio children in mind of service, which is a huge strength for them.

Creating an Ancestor Altar

Scorpio children are often naturally comfortable around death
and dying, and they sometimes get the reputation of being
morbid because they seek out stories and experiences around
these subjects. Moreover, they experience a lot of resistance
when adults in their lives want to shush them up or not talk
about these very real and very present aspects of life. So
instead, why not celebrate our Dearly Beloved Dead with an
Ancestor altar? These are altars that are traditionally worked
with across the world at various times of the year. Get your
little Scorpio involved by first enlisting their help on a research
project that will determine what Ancestor-honoring practices
are worked within their culture, and then create the altar itself.
As you do so, be sure to tell stories about the beloved, dead
family members you are honoring. If you are really flailing for
a place to begin, you can always start with a picture of one
Ancestor (maybe someone the young Scorpio knew in life),
some fresh flowers, and a glass of water as a simple offering.

Ritual for the Inner Scorpio Child
Intensified Service

Adults who are in the process of healing their inner
Scorpio child often hear the criticism that they are "too
intense!" This ritual is a way of honoring that natural intensity and putting it to good use. For this practice, the adult
should decide on an issue they are very focused on and
care very much about, for example, populations in locked
institutions, disabled veterans, or abused animals. Then
they should seek out service or volunteer opportunities
in those areas. They can take this ritual act a step further
by dedicating the merits of their good work to the cause
closest to their hearts.

CHAPTER 12

The Sagittarius Child

"We have all a better guide in ourselves, if we would
attend to it, than any other person can be."

Jane Austen
(Sagittarius, born December 16, 1775)

BIRTHDAY: November 21–December 21

RULING PLANET: Jupiter

ELEMENT: Fire

QUALITY: Mutable

SYMBOL: Centaur

HOUSE: Ninth House of Adventure and Wisdom

STATEMENT: I am here to teach.

SEASON: Late Autumn

GUIDING STORY: "The Crane Wife"

We are entering the deepest part of the night now. See if you can find in the starry sky the sign of Sagittarius, the Celestial Centaur and Archer. This sign is best seen in the month of August and can be found by honing in on the "teapot" group of stars where the Milky Way appears to be steam emerging from the pot's spout! As the moon shines down on us, the shadows begin to appear. Looking off into the distance, my sweet ones, you might think you see a deer or a rabbit or even the fleeting shape of a bird across the moon. Usually it is an illusion, but not always as we learn in this next tale from Japan.

In the mountains, under the moon, and deep in the snow walked a poor, lone fisherman with rough hands and empty nets. He was making his way back to his simple home as he did every night after spending the day casting his nets. Tonight, though, was different, and the fisherman could feel it, but he didn't know why it felt different. Until, that is, he saw the bird lying in the white snow under the white moon with its great white wings and delicate black legs.

There, in the snow, he could see the splatter of crimson blood, where an arrow had pieced the bird's wing. His own heart was pierced. He gathered up the warm and trembling creature in his arms and saw it look upon him with eyes that seemed almost trusting and almost human.

The fisherman tended to the bird that night, and in the morning was both surprised and not surprised to see a beautiful woman lying where the bird had been before. The woman went to the fisherman who had saved her and held out her hand. He understood that from this day forward she would be his very own, his Crane Wife.

Now the fisherman was joy-filled at his beautiful wife, but his worries were compounded because he was still quite poor. The Crane Wife assured her husband that she could bring great fortune to him through her excellent weaving. And true to her word, the Crane Wife wove beautiful clothes, and he took them to market and did indeed see that they fetched a great price.

The fisherman went back to his lovely wife and demanded she weave more so that they could have even more money. He either did not see, or chose to ignore, the disappointment that flashed in her eyes, and he took more fine cloth to market the next day, making ever more and more money.

This went on, and the fisherman was glad because he was rich but he did not touch his wife any longer—not to even to kiss or embrace her—and so one day when he went to her weaving room, he was shocked to see her standing outside of the room instead of sitting at her loom. She told him that she was leaving, and her words fell like white feathers, like the snow had fallen on the night that he had first encountered her. She would no longer, she explained, be trapped in a dark room before a loom that cut her fingers and dimmed her eyes. She would fly once again. She would be free. The fisherman fell to his knees, destroyed by his own foolishness and greed. He begged her to reconsider and asked for forgiveness, but it was too late—he was left with a pile of fabric that would fetch another great price at market and the image of a beautiful white crane taking flight into the wide-open sky.

Sagittarius Gifts

Joyful	Gregarious	Philosophical
Cosmopolitan	Honest	Open-minded
Accepting	Adventurous	Free

Sagittarius Challenges

Noncommittal	Blunt	Cultish

THE SAGITTARIUS PERSONALITY

The tale of the Crane Wife brings home a truth that the Sagittarius child knows all too well: freedom is of paramount importance. This sign, after all, is represented by the mythical figure of the Centaurs, beings who were half-man, half-horse and known to be gifted warriors, teachers, and healers who valued their freedom above all else.

Sagittarius is ruled by the Planet Jupiter, which is considered by both ancient and modern astrologers to be a Planet of prosperity, good luck, glad tidings, and generosity. True to their Jupiter-ruled natures, the Sagittarius child does seem to be a magnet for good luck and exciting possibility, and the fact that they are so generous and giving with pretty much everyone also means that they are well-liked by other children.

Sagittarius children enter a room and often seem to take up all the space in it—their presence is larger than life. Sometimes this translates into talking a lot or being loud, but often it is more of an energetic quality rather than a practical behavior. Once the Sagittarius child has turned her mind to whatever is being taught that day (something she typically does with ease as Sagittarius loves to learn), she demonstrates a deeply philosophical nature, often glossing past the surface facts and figures and immediately honing in on the more existential questions of whatever subject is at hand. This philosophical bent can make the Sagittarius child seem wise—and he is absolutely interested in seeking out wisdom as all good philosophers are. But it can also make him seem a bit abstract or vague in his thinking. An easy way to think of it is that the Sagittarius child is likely to struggle with multiple-choice questions but often excels in the essay portion of tests.

Often it is the mutable signs (Gemini, Virgo, Sagittarius, and Pisces) that hold the most paradoxical tendencies. For the Sagittarius child, their propensity to be abstract in their thinking is paired with their habit of speaking in a truthful and clean manner. Sagittarius children are absolutely honest. They will tell you what they think and, with a bit more coaxing, what they feel. Then they let the chips fall where they may. It is often this exact pairing of forthright honesty with intellectual depth that makes the little Centaur the poster child for the kid who is wise beyond their years.

That apparent wisdom is only deepened by the native love Sagittarius children have for everything foreign and different. These children, along with Libra and Leo, are some of the most accepting of differences and actually feel nourished by learning about different places, people, culture, food, and lifestyles. They love to travel and be on the move, and they tend to have a much more open mind when it comes to everything from learning rote subjects to trying out different kinds of food. As Sagittarius-influenced children get older, they often develop strong affinities with specific foreign nations or people, and they have a cultured and well-traveled globetrotting air about them—even if they have not gone very far in their actual travels.

Friends and Play

Like the Crane Wife's luminous beauty, there is often something luminous and liminal about the Sagittarius child, who has more than a whiff of the wild and wondrous about them. Sagittarius-influenced children light up a room when they walk in, for when all is well in these children's worlds, they are full of joy, and that joy is infectious. These children have a naturally sunny and optimistic disposition, but adults should not let that outward mode fool them. Sagittarian children are not afraid to get deep, and they can say the wisest things at the most unexpected moments.

Sagittarius children are often sought out, popular, and generally well liked by most of their peers. The issue is that the little Centaur is actually quite selective about whom they develop strong and close friendships with. These children know how to socially carry themselves, and their love of adventure and keen intelligence paired with their Jupiter-given love of social events, parties, and festivals ensures that they are always on the invitation list. They will show up, have a great time, and encourage others to have a great time as well. They will just as quickly vanish or head out with a smaller cadre of friends to go do something truly exciting and/or exclusive. In their younger years, Sagittarius-influenced children can play easily with a number of different kinds of children and enjoy themselves. Troubles can occur, however, when the Sagittarius child has one good friend on Monday, a different one on Tuesday, and yet another new friend on Wednesday. This behavior arises from the Sagittarius child's love of freedom and also their ability to be completely present and fully engaged in the connections that are the most interesting at the present moment.

The biggest challenges for the Sagittarius child come first in the form of not being able to commit. This becomes an issue in teenage and early adult years with respect to relationships of all kinds, especially romantic relationships: the Sagittarian kid wants to be free and cares deeply about their relationship, yet doesn't see why those two qualities might seem to cancel each other out. Parents and caregivers often see the younger Sagittarius child's desire to remain sovereign and independent translated by other children as either the Sagittarian not caring much about a friendship or, worse, betraying the friendship altogether. The little Centaur's desire for freedom and independence must be respected while also honoring their need to be aware of other people's feelings and desires.

If the Sagittarius is not properly taught to take other people's feelings into account—and honestly even in some cases when they *are* well taught—their quality of overly blunt truth-telling can get them into trouble. Sagittarius is one of the most honest signs, but it is not necessarily one of the more eloquent. In other words, the Sagittarius child will tell you the truth, but often it's not so much *what* they say but *how* they say it that sticks and stings. This bluntness can obviously lead to hurt feelings and disrupted relationships—and it could leave the truth-telling Archer feeling quite confused.

Finally, the Sagittarius child's refusal to commit completely to friends, projects, and various endeavors, paired with their abstract thinking and spiritual interests, can lead these children to project an air of flakiness and unreliability that frustrates parents, teachers, and caregivers. The Sagittarius is the child who swears up and down they want a big party and then, on the day of the party, throws a temper tantrum or seems bewildered and explains that they have changed their minds and really just want to hang out with two friends. They may also declare one week that Susie is their best friend only to tell you the next week that they feel connected most to Jamal. Parents, teachers, and caregivers can help a Sagittarius child be reliable *and* experience freedom by channeling their need for freedom down specific avenues.

Sagittarius-influenced kids, like all Fire signs, love physical play. They like to *do* things with their friends, and it's a bonus if those things can be turned into mini-adventures or quests. These children also love movement and traveling, so friendships that bring in those qualities are sure to succeed. Finally, the Sagittarius child is the one who is most happy to befriend any foreign or new students at school; they are not afraid of what is different or "other" but are actually energized by it. Blessed by Jupiter's great endurance and strength, one of the challenges other children will face with the Sagittarius child is the need to keep up.

Academics

Like the Crane Wife in our story, one of the tests that these little Centaurs face is how to integrate their natural gifts and wisdom into the world that they have been born into. Academics and school is a natural vehicle for this process.

When it comes to learning, teachers could hardly ask for a more engaged student than the Sagittarius-influenced child *if* that child is creatively stimulated along their learning journey. Sagittarius rules higher education, and while some of the themes of higher ed do not apply to primary education, others do, and the Sagittarius child focuses on them. Although they love learning, these children may not initially thrive in school because they can sometimes think too hard and too deeply about matters that are actually more surface level, and they can seem to be abstract or vague in that thinking.

The Sagittarius child is the one who enthusiastically raises his hand, asks a question, and has the teacher (and class) veering off topic but getting to some really juicy information and opinions. But Sagittarius's mental gifts often do not emerge in early childhood, and they may come off as average students. As they get older, courses become more varied and intellectual pursuits more nuanced and serious, and the Sagittarius child thrives and often does quite well—starting in middle school and going all the way through college. Attending a college, university, or trade school of some kind is important to the Sagittarius child.

Because these children prefer to be hassle–free and low maintenance, they may not make a big deal about struggles they face in school. They might not even bring up the subject of secondary education if they know that it stresses out their parents or caregivers, but rest assured that they care about their grades *and* their future. A young Centaur who does not have an opportunity to continue their education but immediately goes into the workplace is often an individual who doesn't feel fully complete, and they may seek out further education at a later time in life.

Parents, teachers, and caregivers can best support the Sagittarius child by explaining to them that while asking deeper, philosophical questions is good, it is also important to do the work the teacher asks for and to stay on topic during classes. In other words, a little encouragement to focus goes a long way for these children!

When the Sagittarius child gets older and their attention turns to what happens after high school, they may be interested in colleges and universities that have strong philosophy, religion, or comparative literature departments. Archaeology and anthropology are also areas of interest, especially when paired with world travel. Often Sagittarians are drawn to careers where teaching will make up at least part of their day-to-day work. That can include careers centered around teaching, such as being an academic lecturer, or careers where the teaching is less formalized but nonetheless present, such as mentorship in business programs.

Physical Activity

The Sagittarius child often performs a physical action, like the Crane Wife performs weaving, so that they can better process their thoughts and their feelings. However, they are capable of doing their best thinking while they are in motion. Movement, exercise, sports, and the performing arts all appeal to children born under the sign of the Centaur. Often they get very literal and enjoy archery or any sport in which taking aim is an important skill to hone. Sagittarius-influenced children like to move, need to move, and typically know that about themselves. These kids tend to love nature and to be outside doing physical activities that allow them to engage with nature. Hiking, skiing, archery, trail-biking, or running are especially appropriate.

Consistency in physical activity can be challenging for the Sagittarius child. Parents might put these children in one sport for years, only to find that when they reach middle school or high school, they quit the basketball team and decide they are really all about track and field. This of course can frustrate coaches and team members, so it is a best practice to give the Sagittarius child many different options for physical activity and make sure that they understand that they don't have to choose any one thing. But if and when they *do* choose to get more intense about a specific activity, they will be expected to follow through with that commitment.

Art and Creativity

Like the Crane Wife, Sagittarius children tend to be generous beyond measure and incredibly talented. Yet so often this mundane world feels foreign in some way to Sagittarius children, just as the Crane Wife is out of place in the Fisherman's world. This is one reason many of these children strongly identify with foreign cultures, places, people, and the arts. Creativity can satisfy their need for adventure, so Sagittarius children love creative practices and naturally seek them out.

They may find that they are not the most skilled artisans (although some definitely are), but it doesn't matter. They feel alive and tuned in when they are doing something creative. For the Sagittarius child it is possible that the art or creative act will be more spiritual in nature. They may feel called to learn about the Sacred Arts or to take up a child-friendly form of divination. They may also feel called to bright colors and lively mediums, and the general bohemian aesthetic that is often found in the arts makes these little Fire signs feel right at home and like they are finally understood. Art is akin to play for these little Centaurs, so parents and caregivers will do best by not forcing these children into concentrating on just one form of art or creative work and instead encouraging them to explore all of their options and to play. The only time art and creativity does not appeal to the Sagittarius child is when it feels like they're not allowed to play or when it becomes too high maintenance. Sagittarius children, for instance, often eschew creative endeavors in which special costumes or stage makeup are required—that just feels too fussy for them.

Extracurricular Activities

The Sagittarius child is a dedicated adventure seeker. These children love going on all kinds of adventures and quests, and they do everything better—from learning to hiking—when the process is turned into an adventure. The questing nature of the Sagittarius child is also felt within. These children are often seekers in every sense of the word, and that includes spiritually. Sagittarius children value freedom above pretty much everything else, so they're not typically people who settle well into institutionalized forms of religion or learning. They are always yearning to discover new depths and uncharted territory in these areas, however, so exposing the Sagittarius child to many different kinds of religious observance and spiritual practice can be a great gift to them. Often the Sagittarius child pairs her wisdom with spiritual points or pursuits and will be seen by other children as joyful, deep, and unconventional.

Little Centaurs like to keep things moving, and they like to have new experiences all of the time. As we might imagine, this can lead to an ever-revolving door of extracurricular activities and experiments. The key to success here is to change up the Sagittarius child's extracurricular activities on a somewhat regular basis *and* support them in honoring commitments they have made. Remember that the Sagittarius child is a thinker, so although they want to be involved in many different social events, they also need downtime to think and give their minds a time-out. The last thing we want is a scattered, burned-out child! Sagittarius will also benefit from having a parent or caregiver provide external structure around an activity. They often become overwhelmed by practical concerns and need external support in making sure they are prepared and on schedule.

Technology

Like the Crane Wife, these children tend to be self-sufficient and rarely ask for things. Sagittarius children find their happy place in nature and the great outdoors, so technology can at first feel really alien and isolating to them. Like Virgo kids, Sagittarius children sometimes prefer the analog to the digital and choose a real book over an e-book. There is a classic quality about them. However, as they get older, the Sagittarius child will value technology most of all because through it they can learn so much. Researching, discovering, and investigating new ideas, questions, and information are all catnip to the Sagittarius child, and they will appreciate and quickly learn to use any technology that helps make that possible.

However, the Sagittarius child values freedom and sovereignty, which eventually results in a love/hate relationship with technology. They will appreciate the ease and freedom that it creates in their lives, but they will also resent it to some degree, especially as they become more dependent on it. As far as entertainment goes, movies, video games, and shows in which there is a questing element will be the Sagittarius child's favorites. Even so, the Sagittarius child can hang awhile with a screen, but soon they need to stretch their legs, go outside, and do something physical, mental—or both.

Sleeping and Waking

The Planet Jupiter is known for its blessings, benevolence, and extravagance. This last quality comes into play with the Sagittarius child's sleeping and waking habits. Often the little Centaur needs a good eight to ten hours of sleep a night. They may not know that they have this need, but they do. These children may find they have a hard time shutting down their minds and calming themselves in order to fall asleep. For this reason, it is a good idea to have a set bedtime ritual, ideally one that involves some kind of blessing or prayer, as those actions appeal to these children. Even if the Sagittarius child swears up and down that they are fine, make sure that they get enough rest and that they have eaten well before bedtime—these kids often have a big appetite. Assuming that the Sagittarius kid has slept well and for long enough, getting up should not be a problem. Sagittarius children can be ready to roll out the door in record time. These little Centaurs are often happy wearing the same clothes two days in a row, and they are fine if there is some kind of school uniform and they don't have to think about what they wear at all. In fact, with the Sagittarius child, guidance from parents and caregivers will be less about asking them to pick out clothes and more about encouraging them to put some consideration into their appearance.

Discipline

The Crane Wife and the Fisherman suffer a disconnect for a long time, until it is too late. He exploits her gifts thoughtlessly, without regard to the potential riches that could unfold in their relationship. Sagittarius children have a great capacity for relationships, as we have seen above, but their constant activity can make them overlook the value of relationships. Lacking a proper outlet for communicating thoughts and feelings combined with physical exhaustion from continuous action can have the Sagittarius child moving from low intensity to exploding in a short period of time. Sagittarius children get into trouble when their need for freedom gets in the way of the duties and responsibilities that they need to pay attention to and take seriously. These children do not find themselves in the penalty box often, but when they do, they typically work hard to redeem themselves and correct whatever created the situation in the first place.

However, if the Sagittarius child feels they have been treated unfairly or dishonestly or that their integrity is being questioned, then watch out, because a firestorm is coming. Teachers and caregivers can get the Sagittarius child to correct their behavior by speaking to them intelligently, philosophically, and rationally. Don't let these children's sometimes flaky or inconsistent ways fool you. They are some of the sharpest in the class. The Sagittarius child has very little interest in doing something because an authority told them to, but if they see that their behavior improves the greater good, then they are willing to reform it.

How Best to Connect

These children tend to value adventures in wisdom and spiritual matters above all else, and they need people in their lives who understand and support that. If not, then in a very real way they might fly away, just as the Crane Wife does. Sagittarius-influenced children feel most connected to their people when they are outside: walking, horseback riding, or checking out the local Chinatown neighborhood. These children connect while engaging in activities, and favorites for the Sagittarius child include outdoorsy activities or learning about new cultures and places. Ideally the activity has built-in pauses for idea sharing and thoughtful conversation: for these are the elements that make Sagittarius children feel truly seen and valued.

Polarity: Gemini

Gemini reminds overly philosophical Sagittarius that in order to be a teacher one must also commit to being a lifelong learner, and that knowledge is nothing without meaningful connection. Gemini also encourages overly blunt Sagittarius to watch their words and speak the truth, but to do it with care and kindness.

Sagittarius Ascendant

Children with Sagittarius at the Ascendant are often larger both physically and energetically. They come off as friendly, fun, and funny, and they also give off an air of being blessed no matter what their material circumstances are. These children flourish when they point their talents in the direction of freedom and wisdom.

Sagittarius Moon

Children with a Sagittarius Moon are comfortable with "out there" mystical experiences, travel, and encountering the Other in whatever form that takes. They are globalists in their outlook and love learning from and participating in other cultures. These children often have an affinity toward magic, mysticism, and shamanism as they weave their love of nature into their understanding of traditions from around the world. Emotionally they are mostly unflappable and low maintenance. They are not comfortable when confined and tend to be claustrophobic.

Activity
Chasing the New

The Sagittarius child loves to learn about new places, new cultures, and new ways of doing things. Even if you don't have the time or resources to be a globetrotter, make it a point to take your little Sagittarius out for adventures on the town. Learn where ethnic centers and neighborhoods are in your area, and take the Sagittarius child out for a show, demonstration of a culturally specific craft, a class, or a delicious meal. These little ones always love learning something new!

Ritual
Wish Papers

Sagittarius children love magic, mysticism, and freedom; fortunately there is a ritual that honors all of these while also calling on their native element of Fire. That ritual involves Wish Paper, which you can find online or at many gift stores. You can also just buy rice paper yourself, and it will work the same way.

Take the piece of paper and have the Sagittarius child write, draw, or inscribe their wish in whatever ways work best for them. Then, roll the paper into a cylinder and place it on a heat-proof plate. Light the cylinder on fire, and watch the ashes magically rise up into the air! Bonus points if you time this project to coincide with a New or Full Moon.

Ritual for the Inner Sagittarius Child
Breaking the Chains

The inner Sagittarius child is wounded from constantly being told, "Be responsible!" As an adult, they may feel like their relationship to freedom has been lost or eclipsed by various duties and obligations. This ritual can heal those feelings.

Start by brainstorming a list of the various things that keep you from feeling free. Go over that list and select which qualities you want to keep present in your life—even though they don't allow for total freedom—and which qualities you would like to truly be released from. Make a second list with these latter qualities all written down.

Get, find, or make an inexpensive metal chain. It doesn't matter what kind of metal, but it needs to be breakable. Anoint it with your saliva, then place the chain on the second list you made and let it sit there for at least three days.

On the third day go outside your home and break the chain! Take the two pieces and bury or hang half the chain on the north side of your city or town; then bury the other half on the south side of town. The idea is to get the two pieces as far apart as possible, so that you break up whatever keeps you from feeling free..

CHAPTER 13

The Capricorn Child

"Well done is better than well said."

Benjamin Franklin
(Capricorn, born January 17, 1706)

BIRTHDAY: December 21–January 19

RULING PLANET: Saturn

ELEMENT: Earth

QUALITY: Cardinal

SYMBOL: Sea Goat

HOUSE: Tenth House of Work and Mastery

STATEMENT: I am here to master.

SEASON: Early Winter

GUIDING STORY: "The Elves and the Shoemaker"

*Now as the clouds move and cover the moon, see, sweet
children, if you can spy the constellation of Capricornus.
Though Deneb Algedi is its brightest star, it shines rather faintly.
You can see this Sea Goat best during the month of September.
I know it grows cold, so put your hands in your pockets and
curl your toes deep into your shoes. How fortunate we are
to have such things as pockets and coats and shoes! Stop
and think of it for a moment my little ones—each one of
these things is designed and made by someone. Consider all
of the planning and work and skill that goes into fashioning
something like a jacket or a shoe. And now, we shall hear a
story from Germany about a man who made such things.*

Once upon a time there was a shoemaker who lived in a shining
kingdom in a cozy, thatched cottage. And within that cottage he resided
mostly in the spacious workroom where he could be found morning,
noon, and night bent over a long and scarred worktable. Here the air
smelled of oil and wood, leather, and silk—all speaking to the man's pro-
fession. He was a shoemaker of great ability and was widely sought out.

The shoemaker loved his craft, loved making shoes for others, and
took great pride in his fine work. However, his wife fretted over him,
for he was always at work and never took a break to walk with her in
the woods or buy something frivolous at the village market. He made
a good living, this shoemaker, and he was delighted on the day when
his wife told him that they were expecting a child.

His delight, however, turned to dismay when he came upon his
wife a few days later and saw her weeping bitterly.

"My love!" he exclaimed. "My heart! Why do you weep so?"

"I weep, husband," she said through her tears, "because I know that
I shall raise this child all by myself, and you shall never see it, for you
will be working as always you have and always you will."

Well, the shoemaker was at a loss. He did not want to lose his wife, but a huge order had just come in, and he knew he would be working three times as hard. Sighing heavily, he went into his workshop and poured milk into a wee bowl that sat in the corner of the shop—an old tradition his mother taught him, one that she said was for the fairies, who would repay him in kind when he was in great need.

After pouring the milk, he blew out the oil lamps and went to bed to comfort his wife. He hardly slept for worrying about his workload. The next morning, he woke up and barely said a word to his beloved before he went to his workshop. When he opened the door and lit the lamps, he was shocked at what he saw: every single pair of shoes from the order had been beautifully crafted and was sitting on his workbench, ready to be delivered. He wondered at how this was possible while he took the shoes and delivered them to the very pleased customers. In fact, the customers were so delighted that they ordered *more* shoes!

The poor shoemaker went home with an even greater order than before, and when his wife saw it they got into an argument. The shoemaker tried to explain to her the magic that had happened, but between the shouting and yelling there was no time. Finally, they embraced and went to bed, and once again the shoemaker left an open order on his table. And yet again, in the morning when he opened up the workshop, he saw that the shoes had been beautifully crafted and were ready to be delivered. The same course of events occurred, and he came home with pockets full of money and the biggest order for shoes yet. He told his wife he was going to stay up and work, and she accepted that because he had spent the last two evenings by her side. But the shoemaker actually stayed up to watch what was happening in his workshop. Once the last lamp had been blown out and the milk had been poured into the dish, to his utter amazement he saw tiny little men and women come out—Elves, hurrying about here and there, working with great diligence and skill like master cobblers.

The shoemaker was so grateful for the Elves' help that the next day he sat at his bench and fashioned each of them a beautiful pair of shoes. When the Elves saw their gifts that night, they were ever so grateful and delighted. From then on, the Elves and the Shoemaker worked together so the Shoemaker could spend more time with his family and the Elves always had the most beautiful shoes.

Capricorn Gifts		
Adult	Industrious	Masterful
Enduring	Ambitious	Timely
Aware	Protective	Practical
Capricorn Challenges		
Competitive	Exclusive	Lethargic

THE CAPRICORN PERSONALITY

The story "The Elves and the Shoemaker" is both a celebration and cautionary tale about work—and work is what both adult and child Capricorns like to do best. It is the action that defines them.

Capricorn children are exceptionally grounded and able to navigate deep thoughts. What else would you expect from the sign that is represented not by a mere Goat as some have claimed, but rather by a Sea Goat, a mythical creature that is part Goat with the tail of a Fish or Mermaid? Sea Goats move slowly but thoroughly, and very little shakes them from their appointed task or pursuit. These children excel at single-minded focus. If teachers are looking for the adult in the classroom, their eyes will probably land on the Capricorn child, who has an innate maturity about them that makes them feel older and more aware than everyone else. This quality of maturity and adult-like bearing is one that most Capricorn children have both on the surface and at deeper levels.

Work and industriousness are hallmark signatures of Capricorns, both young and old. Their habit of working harder and longer than everyone else usually begins for most Capricorns when they are still quite young. The Capricorn child is industrious—they make sure they complete their given tasks on time and that they have made every effort to do their best. And they are also masterful at what they do.

Part of the little Sea Goat's unique ability to work so hard and do so well has to do with their strength. These cardinal Earth signs are often some of the strongest children in terms of both physical strength and endurance, as well as in terms of mental strength. Capricorn children may not be the quickest (that prize often goes to Gemini), but they are the tortoises who finish the race, and they don't stop until they have both completed their assignment and completed it well.

These children are deeply concerned with mastering skills and being excellent in all that they do. In many cases they make it a competition, and they need to be taught that the person they're truly competing against is themselves.

The Capricorn child is a case study in articulating ambition clearly. They know what they want and what they don't, and they speak their minds clearly. (Libra children are often in awe of this!) They will get clear on what they want and then, in the organized manner of an Earth sign, go about achieving that goal. Their dedication is often a source of inspiration, not just to children but also to the adults around them.

With so many admirable, amazing qualities it is easy to overlook the more negative tendencies of the Capricorn child, but do pay attention to these as they are indicators that the Capricorn child is out of balance in some manner. The first area to look at is the Sea Goat's competitive nature.

Several of our Star Children—Aries, Libra, and Scorpio—are especially competitive. Good-natured competition that encourages children to meet and exceed their personal best can be an incredibly instructive tool. For the Capricorn, however, competition can take on the edge of "winning no matter the cost." These children can and will exhibit low-integrity behavior and may even put themselves in harm's way for the sake of winning. To be clear, this is not all Capricorn children all of the time. Rather, it is the Capricorn child who has been pressured, usually by external figures, to succeed no matter what. Although not all Capricorn children will engage in competition at dangerously high intensity levels, most of them are extremely competitive, and this quality can be both beneficial and harmful.

Capricorn children work incredibly hard, are devoted to their people, and want nothing but the best—and this is all really exhausting! The stressed-out Capricorn who is always falling behind or who feels too mature to enjoy funny jokes or time on the playground may become withdrawn and lethargic. In this case, we see almost the opposite of the typical Capricorn behavior. Here there is little effort, less engagement, and a shoulder shrug when teachers or parents encourage the child to take things more seriously or to try harder. This quality usually comes from a sense of loneliness that many Capricorn children experience—some of the more childlike behaviors feel foreign and strange to them, and they may have a hard time relating to other children. If that occurs and is not corrected, the Capricorn child can become quite passive. Supporting our Capricorn children and letting them be kids without worries or concerns is the best way to meet this challenge.

Friends and Play

In the tale "The Elves and the Shoemaker," it becomes clear that the shoemaker's relationships suffer. Even the thing that is supposed to bring him ultimate joy—the impending birth of his child—is cause for stress. This is often how Capricorn children feel too. On one hand, their relationships to peers, teachers, and caregivers is relatively even-keeled. Adults especially appreciate these children who typically have more maturity in their little finger than most kids have in their entire body. However, the Capricorn child can feel stressed by this because it puts them under pressure to always be the best, the grown-up, the "good" one.

Capricorn children do not experience ease around friendships and especially around play. But this difficulty doesn't mean they cannot be supported in these areas! Friendships can be a bit easier as long as parents and caretakers understand that the Capricorn child will be overwhelmed by large social gatherings (at least in their early years) and thrives best in situations that involve one-on-one or small-group interactions.

A well-balanced Capricorn child is selective in whom he befriends and spends time with. He wants to be surrounded by friends he gets along with and understands, and he doesn't want to waste time with superficial small talk or vapid (to him) social situations. This conscious cultivating of friends and peers who really "get you" can be a good thing. However, the shadow side of this behavior is the Capricorn child who is exclusive in her friendships, not based on whether she is surrounded by authentic friends but determined by more superficial qualities like whether her friends wear the right clothes, belong to the right clubs, or live in the right neighborhoods. In this case the Capricorn child closes herself off to friends who might be more authentic and resonant with her because they don't meet her criteria, and so she misses out. Proper encouragement from parents and caregivers about clarity around what really matters will support the Capricorn child in being selective but not exclusive.

The Sea Goat child who is looking for authentic friends (instead of friends who all "look" the right way) usually has a pretty apt idea about who she will and will not get along with and will end up choosing her friends quite well. Friends are most likely to have a falling-out with the Capricorn child if they perceive that the child does not actually like to play, is too bossy (a perennial challenge for cardinal signs), or is too definite in their opinions.

Capricorn children are serious, mature, and goal oriented. These qualities, though admirable, do not lend themselves easily to play, which is something Capricorn children often have to learn how to do. Games that appeal to these children tend to be realistic and goal oriented, as opposed to the products of fantasy. If there is a reward for first place, all the better as the Capricorn child has a penchant for rewards and winning.

Physical play that allows a Capricorn child to work with their prodigious strength, and/or solving puzzles are activities Capricorn children often excel at. Most Capricorn children will go through periods of intense loneliness. This is the cost of being ruled by the Planet Saturn and having so much maturity and wisdom: sometimes these children don't feel like they "get" other kids—or that other kids don't "get" them. Fortunately for these little Sea Goats, the older they grow, the less lonely they will feel.

Academics

Like the Shoemaker in our story, Capricorn children often become known early on as hard, dedicated workers who produce excellent results. As we might imagine, Capricorn children tend to do really well in school. This is not necessarily because they are the best and the brightest—though many are!—but rather because they work for it. Capricorn children often take their time completing tasks and assignments (unless there is a timed element to the task at hand) because they want to make sure they have done the best possible job. If teachers, parents, or caregivers encounter a Capricorn who is not interested in school, then these rules still apply: they will be industrious, excellent, and masterful at whatever task they have set their minds to—whether it is socially acceptable or not. They work for good grades and for the respect and prestige that go along with them. Also, Capricorn children often like school because they have a resonance with institutions of all kinds.

These children may experience some challenges when it comes to cooperative activities like group projects because they will either try to take control and boss everyone else around or try to do all of the work—or both. Capricorn children can also suffer setbacks both emotionally and mentally in classrooms that are poorly organized or that emphasize process over results. These children need clean, clear guidelines and surroundings to do their best work, and although they are thorough workers, they sometimes get stuck on creative problem-solving, usually because they mistakenly don't see themselves as creative people.

Capricorn children do well with traditional learning styles and techniques, and they're often interested in the areas of history, math, economics, and business. At the most negative, the Capricorn child can be seen as an insincere grade grubber. At the best end of the spectrum, where most Capricorn children naturally hang out, these kids and their love of excellence serve as a galvanizing force of inspiration for everyone else.

Capricorn children are planners, so they often think about college and what happens during high school long before they even enter high school. For these Sea Goats, money and craftsmanship need to go hand in hand, and they are often drawn to jobs at well-heeled legal or financial institutions. Some Capricorns opt for careers in the arts, and fashion design seems to be especially beloved by those who are greatly influenced by this sign. When it comes to colleges and universities, a prestigious reputation does matter to the Capricorn child, and branding is important, not something to shrug aside. Parents and caregivers can support their Sea Goat by helping them think about college and university in terms not just of outward prestige, but also in terms of programs that really will build and develop their preferred skill sets. Yet not all Capricorns are drawn to continuing their education, and many of them want to immediately begin working and making money. For these youths, going to a trade school in order to learn a specific skill and to begin applying it can be deeply satisfying.

Physical Activity

Possessing all the qualities of the shoemaker's work ethic, the Capricorn child is often celebrated by their teachers, parents, and caregivers. Unless something is really wrong, the Capricorn child can never be accused of not making an effort. As we saw earlier, physical play allows the Capricorn-influenced child to work with their prodigious strength. Capricorn children need a lot of physical activity. These children are strong, are often bigger boned or taller than other children, and have incredible endurance. They also tend to be slower and not as flexible.

Because Capricorn children have a great deal of physical strength and endurance, those qualities need to be exercised and put to good use so that the Capricorn child does not get lazy or indolent. A child who is in pursuit of excellence in all that they are and all that they do is already noteworthy, but the Capricorn child takes it a step farther because they are often forthright about their ambitions. In many ways, Capricorn children are a bit paradoxical, for Capricorn is the sign that rules maturity, adulthood, careers, and work in the world—all very adult concerns. These areas get translated, of course, for children, but the Capricorn child shares many qualities with adult contemporaries, which often makes even adults feel especially comfortable with them.

These little Sea Goats may decide they don't really need to do a lot of physical activity, and they're smart enough to argue that studying extra hard or taking an afterschool class makes their schedule too full to squeeze in any kind of athletic activity. However, there is also the opposite type: Capricorn kids who live and breathe sports, especially for the shiny medals and trophies that come at the end of a season. Either way, it is important for the Capricorn child to have plenty of opportunities to move their bodies, develop their natural strength and ath-letic abilities, and engage in healthy competitions. The Capricorn child is often drawn to team sports such as football, lacrosse, tennis, and basketball. If a Capricorn child shows no interest in organized sports, they may be the type that loves outdoor adventures and extreme chal-lenges like hiking, cross-country skiing, and triathlons.

Art and Creativity

Capricorn children and adults suffer from a common misconcep-tion: that they are not creative people. These cardinal Earth signs are serious, ambitious, mature, and concerned with excellence, yes, but hey are also highly creative, especially in the tactile arts. "The Elves and the Shoemaker" is an especially appropriate tale for Capricorn children, and not just because many fashion designers today have Capricorn prominently placed in their charts!

A certain amount of messiness and imperfection is part of any creative process. Creative people have to throw things at the wall, sometimes over and over again, before they discover what will stick. Capricorn children do not like to make mistakes and to some extent do not like to go out of their preferred comfort zones. All of this is to say that Capricorn children should absolutely be supported in experiencing their creative sides, and they should go into creative settings with the understanding that the only way to attain excellence is to make a bunch of mistakes. Once they move past that initial feeling of fear and resistance they will be astounded—as will others—at the art they can bring into the world. For these reasons it is useful to give Capricorn children art supplies early on and, as they get older, to support them in joining age-appropriate fine-art courses.

Extracurricular Activities

Often little Sea Goats find that they do not, or cannot, take simple pleasure in events or activities that delight other children, and their maturity and focus on work can make them feel as isolated as the shoemaker was in his workshop.

The Capricorn-influenced child needs to be monitored when it comes to extracurricular activities. A thriving Capricorn, left to her own devices, will schedule herself morning to night with all sorts of activities. These are the kids who become class presidents, team captains, and all-school volunteer coordinators. They organize bake sales to fight climate change and carve out time in between their ridiculous class load to tutor younger kids. They sincerely enjoy doing all of these activities, but they also know that a steady stream of busyness makes them more attractive candidates for colleges and, later on, workplaces. The trade-off is that the Capricorn child may have a very real feeling that she is missing out on her childhood or teenage years. She is not completely wrong! A Capricorn kid who is not thriving may go the opposite direction: being unambitious about extracurricular activities and preferring to laze about. Striking a balance looks different for each person. For the Capricorn child, balance looks like a mix of creative, physical, and academic activities but with the willingness to focus on the areas where the child shows the most promise. Capricorn children like digging into and ever expanding their natural talents, and this inclination should be encouraged.

Technology

If given a choice between analog or digital technology, these little Sea Goats, like all Earth signs, tend to choose analog. Children born under the influence of Capricorn energies especially like using classic items, from fine watches to leather-bound paper planners, to keep up with time. When Capricorn children do engage with technology, they like their gadgets to be sleek, efficient, and top of the line. They will especially respond to the time- and energy-saving aspect of technology, like the shoemaker's elvish helpers in our story.

The exclusive corners of the internet are the most appealing to them. Social media can appeal to Capricorn-influenced children, but they often will stress about what to make public and what to hide. As Capricorn children age, the way they are perceived by the general public becomes more and more important to them. As they develop their relationship with technology, Capricorn children will use tech for organizational, health, household, and academic efficiency and to keep up with the latest styles. But the most popular social-media streams will probably feel too crowded to them, and they will always prefer a real book to anything digital.

Sleeping and Waking

Another wonderful element of the Capricorn child is their sense of time, timing, and timeliness. Saturn, the Planet that rules Capricorn, is strongly associated with the quality of time, as can be seen from Saturn's Greek name, Chronos, and in instruments associated with time. (A chronometer, for instance, is a fancy way of saying "watch.") Capricorn children have a built-in sense of what is appropriate and also *when* something is appropriate. Their intuition tells them when it is the right time to make an argument, a pitch, or a strategic move—and also when the timing is wrong. They are comfortable taking their time, especially if it allows them to do their best. A stressed-out Capricorn child is easy to spot because he often feels he has no time or is running out of time. This leads into the issue of getting enough sleep at night.

Capricorn children tend to be night owls, with their preferred time of day being midnight. Given that penchant, parents and caregivers might think that waking up the Capricorn child in the morning would be tough, but often these children are ready to go—they just call on their reserve of strength. If the Capricorn child starts to become lazy or indolent, parents and caregivers can know that they are not getting enough sleep and can adjust accordingly. If these little Sea Goats seem to be restless or not sleeping well, it is often because they are suffering from anxiety. The Capricorn child sleeps best in clean, well-organized spaces and will need a hearty breakfast upon waking.

Discipline

Elves and fairies who appear as characters in tales often mark the paths that take us back to our first relationship—with the Earth itself. For these cardinal Earth-sign children, this is a relationship that should always be tended because it keeps these little Sea Goats grounded and centered.

Capricorn children are not typically ones for acting out. If they do start consistently misbehaving, it is almost always a sign that they are dealing with something at home or in their personal lives that is causing them distress. Capricorn children respond to rewards much better than punishments, so parents, caregivers, and teachers who wish to reform their behavior should come up with rewards—the shinier the better—that reinforce positive behaviors as opposed to focusing on negative behaviors. One aspect of the Capricorn child's behavior that can be particularly difficult to navigate is that of their exclusive tastes hurting the feelings of other children and peers. In these cases, the little Sea Goat needs to understand on an emotional level how their behavior is affecting others. Only after that will they be able to reform their behavior, and usually when they are ready, they can do it quite quickly.

How Best to Connect

In our story, the elves are the answer to the shoemaker's problem, and this too speaks to a lesser known but very present quality in Capricorn: their deep association with nature and the ways that nature and the natural world can soothe, de-stress, and center them.

Capricorn children are not just aware of time and the greater role it plays, they are also aware of everything else. These children have an eye for the way that they appear and are excellent at scrutinizing how others appear, including noting what is off and what is not off. They are aware of how they seem to adults, and they know what they need to do and say in order to achieve their ambitions or meet their goals. For these reasons, the Capricorn child may be the most gifted at strategic thinking. Capricorns are not friends with everyone, but the people they consider their own receive a deep devotion and a potent protectiveness from them. Even Capricorn children exhibit this protective quality toward those they love.

Like the other Earth signs, these little Sea Goats feel most deeply connected when doing something with their loved ones. Capricorn children are often less picky about the activity. It could be a hike, making dinner together, or watching a game of basketball, but they feel connected in doing the activity itself. It is also especially important for these children to know that they are loved unconditionally and that they do not have to be or do anything in particular to "deserve" that love. It is just there for them. These children also thrive through physical touch and often express themselves more in that manner than they do verbally.

Polarity: Cancer

Cancer reminds overly serious Capricorn to allow their work to be informed by dreams, imagination, and vision. Cancer also challenges Capricorn to take some of its workaholic energy and focus that on friends, home, and family.

Capricorn Ascendant

Children with Capricorn ascending often present themselves as serious, mature, and businesslike. They often look older than other children and have a maturity about them that sets them apart. Their style is often classic, and they like shiny metal accessories. They exude excellence in everything they do. The child with Capricorn at the Ascendant is fulfilled when they take their interests, home in on them, and develop true mastery. They are rarely satisfied with anything less.

Capricorn Moon

Children with their Moon in Capricorn are often quiet, shy, and serious. They are comfortable outside: in the woods, in a garden, or with plants or animals. They can also be quite comfortable in businesslike settings, and they love learning about what their parents do. These young people are emotionally steady but deep and often will think and feel into something for days before talking about it. They are also quite competitive and always want to have and be the best.

Activity
Forest Bathing

Capricorn kids can carry around more stress than some adults. There are many ways to address that stress, but one of the easiest fixes for the Capricorn child is to go outside into a wildish place and simply be among trees, plants, and creatures. This practice is known as *shinrin-yoku* in Japan and has been recommended there by therapists and physicians as one of the best and most comprehensive ways to treat stress and to return to a state of grounded insight and wisdom.

Ritual
Wishing Seeds

Capricorn children love nothing so much as a concrete practice. This one allows them to state what they want clearly, without shame or excuse, and to get a bit whimsical. You need a good-sized seed, such as a pumpkin or bean seed, to wish on. Provide the child with a marker so that they can write a single word or draw a small image on the seed that represents their wish. Help them plant the seed, water it, nurture it, and watch their wish become reality.

Ritual for the Inner Capricorn Child
Investing in Adulthood

Adults who are tending to their inner Capricorn child often carry wounds from being told that they are "boring." Really, they are mature and grown-up, even as children, and when they are children, those qualities are often seen as faults and not appreciated. However, the inner Capricorn child *likes* being a grown-up. They appreciate maturity, responsibility, and the ability to make their own choices. So let's honor the inner child by also honoring the inner adult! Take some time to think about what object says "grown-up" to you. It might be a specific kind of handbag or watch, a pair of shoes, a book or pen, or a plant in your backyard. Whatever it is, identify it and then procure it. If it is out of your price range, create a plan and start saving for it. This object will become your talisman that speaks to and honors the adult within.

CHAPTER 14

The Aquarius Child

"What important is man should live in
righteousness, in natural love for mankind."

Bob Marley
(Aquarius, born February 6, 1945)

BIRTHDAY: January 19–February 18

RULING PLANET: Saturn, Uranus

ELEMENT: Air

QUALITY: Fixed

SYMBOL: Human/Water Bearer/Angel

HOUSE: Eleventh House of Expansion and Activism

STATEMENT: I am here to envision.

SEASON: High Winter

GUIDING STORY: "Morozko and the Maiden"

*We are now in the deepest part of the night and so,
little ones, look up to the stars and see if you can spy
Aquarius, the constellation of the Water Bearer. It is
easiest to see at the end of October and was called
The Great One by the ancient Babylonian star watchers.
Now, in the dark nights of the deep winter, it is a known
truth that the young and the old must not go into the
wild wood, no matter how beautiful and enchanting
it looks and no matter how hungry they might be. For
the cold will cast a spell over anyone who dares to do
so, and they shall begin to find themselves exceedingly
tired, curling up in the snow for what they believe
will be a short nap—only to find that they never wake
again. For to curl up in the snow on nights like this
is to die. Even knowing this, though, does not stop
some—especially certain young people—from traveling
into the woods. Here is a story from Russia about what
might happen and who we might encounter when we do.*

Once upon a time there was a wretched girl who had been cast
out of her great house by a wicked stepmother. She was in the middle
of the woods, making her way to a chicken-footed house that had a
propensity to move about without giving proper notice. This girl was
courageous and beautiful, but neither beauty nor courage warmed her
thin bones in the cruelly cold night. As she found herself in the deepest part of the wood, where the skeleton branches of the trees grew
in so close that the moon became only thick ribbons of light, she felt
an icy death-wind blow across her cheek, and she knew that the King
of Winter, Morozko, had found her. Oh, what a delicious morsel she
must look to him, she knew. But she resolved that she would not fall
victim to his icy advances.

"Morozko," she called out. "King of Winter! I know you are here, and I know what you want!"

The icy death-wind blew ever stronger and carried a cruel and sniggering laugh upon it.

"I am here, fair maiden. And how do you find this weather? Is it warm enough for you?"

The girl, no fool, sighed and pretended to fan herself as if very hot.

"I actually find it a bit warm. I'd love it to be just a touch cooler."

Morozko bristled at the challenge. The wind grew even stronger, and all of the animals in the wood hid their faces in fear, bright eyes fiercely shut. The girl refused to shiver and stood her ground calmly, but her nails bit so deeply into her palms that crimson drops of blood fell onto the snowy ground.

"And *now* fair maiden—how do you find it?"

The young girl laughed and clapped her hands together.

"It is lovely, the perfect temperature. Well . . . almost. It could be just a bit cooler."

At this the icy death-wind grew still, and the girl knew she was in real trouble as the temperature plummeted and a great blizzard appeared from nowhere. A ringing voice called out over the ice and snow.

"And now, my sweet?"

The young girl sighed in delight through her chattering teeth. "Ah, now *this* is perfect weather, my Lord! How might I thank you for your hospitality?"

Morozko snorted in derision, amusement, and admiration at the girl's precocious and foolish courage. Mortals. This foolish courage was their saving grace.

The young girl felt strong arms wrapped in the warmest of furs surround her and lay her down at the base of a tree. Hot spiced wine was served to her, and though she could see the moon and stars and falling snow, she felt warm, safe, and at peace.

The next morning, as the sun dared to show her pale face over the mountains, the young girl woke up. She saw that she was in the forest, covered in warm furs, with a great fire crackling. She had new boots, a new cloak, and a new pair of gloves laid out for her as nicely as could be. There was also a golden chest full of priceless jewels. Some say she also had the never-dying love of the Winter King, but that is another tale for another night.

Aquarius Gifts		
Rebellious	Brilliant	Inspired
Future-focused	Connected	Expansive
Communal	Original	Inventive
Aquarius Challenges		
Aloof	Guarded	Detached

THE AQUARIUS PERSONALITY

Like the young woman in "Morozko and the Maiden," the Aquarius child is precocious, and this is part of her unique giftedness, a saving grace. She is the punk rocker of the Zodiac, the misfit. Some would point to the fact that the Aquarian child doesn't even have a typical Zodiacal creature assignment; Aquarius is conceived of as the Human, the Water Bearer, or sometimes an Angel—the one who brings life and vital information. The Aquarian child is, in a way, as much out of time as the Capricorn child is in it. She will dress in a way that makes no sense today, but in six months or six years she will be on point and on trend. She is weird and lovable exactly because of her weirdness. And she is a rebel. For the Aquarian child, being told that something must be done or should happen in a precise way is a guaranteed formula that will have her figuring out a hundred other ways that are better, prettier, make more sense, and are more creative than what was previously demanded.

These children may be shy and awkward, put-together and self-confident, or loud and brash, but the common denominator is that they are fundamentally unable to do what they are told. They can try, and if they like you they *will* try, but even their best attempts fall flat. They have to put their own signature and gloss on everything; they have to spice it up with a little rebellion. For our purposes though, rebellion is a positive quality, and in the hands of these children it usually is.

Rebellion—when handed to us by an Aquarius—looks like the next crucial step, the possibility that has not been recognized until now, the needed action. This is because, in part, the Aquarian child is brilliant. He may do terribly in school—all those rules and expectations!—but he is uniquely gifted not just in what he thinks but *how* he thinks. The Aquarius child is not only brilliant but inspiring. These children are trailblazers. They are not cardinal signs, so they don't so much lead the way as *show* the way that everyone should have been traveling in the first place.

They are often very aware of injustice. They are politically minded and able to galvanize and inspire large numbers of people when they put their minds to it. These little Water Bearers are especially inspiring to other children because they show that there is always another way. Aquarian children are visionaries, particularly about the future. Often these children have an incredibly strong sense of what is to come, what is possible, and what the world will be like when they are adults.

Typically, young Aquarians come into the world thinking that everyone has these thoughts and this awareness, but then they realize just how many children and peers don't, and they start to feel very isolated and awkward. Parents can support their little Aquarians early on by arranging playdates and fostering early friendships with children who seem compatible and like-minded.

Fortunately, the Aquarius child is also a master at making connections, both in terms of people and friends and also in terms of ideas.

Aquarius children often go from being very quiet to being very, very loud, and they are often drawn to loud noises and music. These children are dipping their toes into one of the most powerful qualities, the ability to amplify and broadcast ideas, opinions, thoughts, stories, and art forms of all kinds to a much larger audience than they would normally reach.

Many of these children have such a diverse network of connections that they are able to broadcast and expand information quickly and efficiently, connecting people who would otherwise never hear about each other. Like all of our Star Children, the little Water Bearer has a contrasting nature in some respects. On one hand he sees things, especially the future, in such an original way that he may well feel like an alien or robot looking down on Earth—and he feels the loneliness of that. On the other hand, he is very dedicated to his friends and community minded.

We might describe such a figure as aloof or detached, and these are qualities that are also assigned to Aquarius children. It is true that these children can sometimes seem to lack basic awareness about how their actions affect other people and also about how feelings, as opposed to only thoughts, are part of most people's experiences. It's not that the Aquarius child doesn't care about how they affect other people, it's simply that they have a very rich vision of what is possible and the brilliance to create what is needed for that future. So, they are often quite busy and lost in their own thoughts!

Friends and Play

"Morozko and the Maiden" is one of several high-winter tales that feature the elements of cold, ice, and freezing at their center. This is particularly fitting for the Aquarius child, who sometimes feels so alien to the rest of the world and other children she knows.

The child who has been able to moderate the influence of Aquarius has overcome the feeling of isolation. She will have a large group of friends, who are all totally different, and a large number of ideas that constellate around a common theme that often can only be understood by her. The Aquarius child cannot help but make these connections and associations, which is good because no matter how alien they sometimes feel, those friendships often prove to be the much-needed anchor for the Aquarius child. These children are not just connected—they are also sources of expansion.

Aquarius children often have a hard time making friends when they are younger. Between sometimes being labeled (along with Aries and

Scorpio) as the "bad" kids, being off the wall in their ideas, super smart, and socially a bit detached, these are the children who the *other* kids don't know what to do with . . . until they do. As the young Water Bearer gets older and their peers also start paying attention to things like social-justice issues, cool yet not mainstream music or art, and the bravery of rebels, they become drawn to the Aquarius. Parents and caregivers may notice that even while their child is surrounded by many others, they still sometimes feel alone. Though the Aquarius child will always have a motley crew of people around them, their deepest and truest friendships will be singular and rare and will develop over years. Aquarian children definitely play the long game. Wounds around friendships affect these children on a deeper level than they affect others, so parents and caregivers will need to watch out for that and be able to roll with the Aquarian child's mercurial moods. One minute these kids will want to have a big party with *all* of their people, the next they will lock themselves into their closet and have a panic attack because there are too many people! Aquarius is one of the signs that rules friendships, but that doesn't mean that this part comes easy. Often the area that a Zodiac Sign is strongly affiliated with over is the same area that sign has to work hardest to fully inhabit.

Academics

The maiden in our story has something of the Sight. She knows that complaining or admitting to the Frost Demon that the weather is too cold means she will die. The Aquarius child is also gifted with Sight and often has a preternatural sense of what the future will be. It is not unusual to see these children go into the fields of futurism or cutting-edge technologies.

Aquarius children are incredibly intelligent—brilliant even—but that is no guarantee they will do well in school. Under the right conditions and in the right circumstances they can. These little Water Bearers are often labeled "gifted and talented" and placed in honors or advanced classes given their natural abilities. The stumbling block for many Aquarius children is their need for rebellion, originality, and inventiveness. If these kids are told to zig right, they are going to zag left—guaranteed. The only other sign that carries this level of rebelliousness is actually the next one, Pisces, though they are better able to keep it under wraps. Aquarius children are allergic to rules, guidelines, and blueprints. They do not understand why *anyone* would want to do something the same way as everyone else. Obviously, in educational settings this can create problems. Aquarius children often do best in school settings that prize creative thinking and inventive problem-solving, and where rules are kept to a minimum but there is also definite structure. They are often incredibly smart children but are frequently bad test takers. Part of the Aquarius child's work is to discover that it is acceptable in some instances to follow the rules, that not all laws are shams, and that many people do things the same way because it is the best way. In other words, these children have to learn to pick their moments of rebellion and not be ready to rebel at all times. In school settings, Aquarian children may start out shy but can become loud and articulate at the same time. These mutable Air signs are often gifted writers and speakers, and they tend to like science, technology, and creative writing.

Aquarian children often have a hard time in high school and are ready to get out and move on to the next thing. Some Water Bearers are decidedly not keen on the idea of more education and may decide to live on their own terms through their artistic or musical skills. Some of them are drawn to politics and will volunteer for political campaigns or organize protests. Aquarian youths who do go to college or university often find that they are unable to stay there, even though a part of them loves learning, because the institutions may be too staid, stuffy, or lacking in vision. These Aquarians, especially if they have technical skills, may follow the American story of tinkering in their garage and come up with a billion-dollar idea. The young Water Bearer may not have a completely clear idea of what they want to do, but if all else fails they can always do a very Aquarian thing: run off and join a circus!

Physical Activity

Every Aquarius child will relate to the idea of consistent acts of rebellion, for broad-thinking and future-seeing Aquarius sometimes feels emotionally frozen from what they experience in the world, and the only way to kindle the heat, warm themselves, and stave off death is to rebel in small ways over and over again. This tendency does not lend itself to organized sports. The Aquarius child is a heady child, and their head is full of awesome ideas. Who can blame them for wanting to stay there? Moreover, these children tend not to be the strongest or most athletically gifted, and they see there are lots of rules associated with many sports and physical endeavors, which doesn't sound very appealing to them. For all of these reasons, the Aquarius child might want to skip physical activities altogether. But of course this is not a good idea. Instead, these children should be pointed to physical activities that come with few rules, lots of creativity, and even a sense of the rebellious. Team sports can actually be a great outlet for the little Water Bearer's more aggressive, rock 'n' roll side, if they can handle the rules and regulations. Circus arts, aerial yoga, mountain biking, and skydiving are all activities the Aquarius child might really get into and enjoy.

Art and Creativity

Many Aquarius children do not discover their affinity for art and creativity until they are much older, or they repress their artistic and creative urges as they age because the other areas they are interested in—science, math, tech—seem to have no connection to art-making. So it is possible that when they are younger, the Aquarius child is either rushing to the art studio or feels like they do not belong there. The truth is that all little Water Bearers are creatively gifted, and many of them benefit greatly when the ideas in their heads receive an outlet through their hands. Music and painting or drawing are two areas where the Aquarius child can particularly flourish because both require the honing of technical skills, which Aquarian children love to focus on. Art takes on a new level of interest for the Aquarius child as they get older, especially when they begin to see how it can speak to politics. Aquarius-influenced children are the ones who go where angels fear to tread and then come back and write a story about their adventure.

The Aquarius child's love of originality is reflected in their interest in science and technology. For the Aquarius, science is a creative pursuit, and inventions fascinate them. It is not unusual for these children to want to be inventors and to learn all they can about great inventors of the past. When we think about an inventor at work in their lab, we might reflect on how the scientist who is hard at work does not think about others and seems pretty unaware of the other people around her. This illustrates the paradoxical nature of all Aquarians—loving larger groups on the one hand but also desperately needing alone time on the other.

Extracurricular Activities

Aquarius children often run into problems because they are focused on the collective and the community to the exclusion of their personal needs, desires, and interests. The Aquarius child is known for acts of rebellion, big and small, yet they are also incredibly original. This is another defining characteristic of Aquarian children. They will always come up with an idea, scheme, strategy, or method of implementation that is completely unique and their own. Other children will try to duplicate the Aquarius approach, especially when they see how well it works, but the Aquarius child has already moved miles ahead and is now thinking about a completely new possibility.

The Aquarius child is happy being busy and socially engaged, so their calendars are often quite full. These children will naturally seek out a variety of extracurricular activities so that on Mondays they might have theater arts, followed by robotics on Tuesdays and jazz band on Wednesdays. They will have different sets of friends in each activity and often the one thing all of these friends have in common is—you guessed it!—the Aquarius child. However, these little Water Bearers are so mentally active all the time that they can tire out pretty quickly.

This means parents and caregivers need to watch their Aquarian child to make sure they do not completely overload themselves with activities beyond school. Time to rest and play is essential.

Technology

Aquarian children possess the maiden's ability to see the future. They have a natural affinity for the futuristic aspects of technology, and they view technology as a way to create a better world and future for those who come after us. These kids do well with every aspect of tech, from social media to computer programming. They are interested not just in enjoying technology and learning about how it works but also in the philosophy of technology, which captures the Aquarian child's imagination and sense of possibility. These children are often futurists: they are interested in learning how technology can help both them and the collective create a better tomorrow. Parents and caregivers should expect their little Aquarians to spend a lot of time in front of screens and not be surprised to stumble over various computer parts when they enter an Aquarius child's room.

Sleeping and Waking

Aquarian children tend to have erratic sleep schedules that make getting the proper amount of rest difficult. These children may stay up late, wake up super early, or do a combination of both. The struggle is usually turning off their minds so that they are able to get a full night's rest. For the Aquarius child talking or reading is actually not the best bedtime activity because it keeps them mentally active and engaged. Instead, tell calming stories or simply lie down together so you have physical contact; these are much better ways to soothe the active Aquarius child and enable them to rest well and deeply. Other things that will assist the Aquarius child include tools like weighted blankets, meditation practices, and aromatherapy.

Aquarian children tend to rest much better in a room that is clean and organized, but they tend to be messy themselves, so younger children especially will need help maintaining a clean space. The good news is that once Aquarians are up, they're up! It doesn't take these children long to wake up and get ready, although it is common that the outfits they put together will raise an eyebrow or two. Because Aquarian children tend to be disorganized—especially about things they deem nonessential—make sure they have all their schoolwork and needed supplies before they walk out the door.

Discipline

In "Morozko and the Maiden," the smart young woman finds reward, not punishment, for her rebellion. This is the way for the Aquarius child too. When Aquarians rebel, they do it in the way that we *all* need them to, and they often find their rewards on the other side of those rebellious acts.

How does one discipline a rebel, get results, and avoid breaking their rebellious spirit entirely? This is the question that plagues the parents, teachers, and caregivers of the Aquarian child. The answer is actually quite simple: everyone needs purpose, but the Aquarius child needs an honest-to-goodness cause. A bored Water Bearer gets into trouble; an Aquarius without direction does the same. But give the Aquarian child something they can think about, learn from, and, perhaps most importantly, agitate for, and you have a happy child who is too busy organizing the food drive, protest, or school election to get into trouble. In other words, we cannot and should not try to get rid of the Aquarian child's natural need to rebel. Instead, we just need to redirect that energy into an area that is going to help them become more thoughtful, satisfy them, and keep them engaged.

How Best to Connect

In the story, Morozko is the personification of Cold itself. He does not warm up to the maiden until she has proven to be both interesting and brave. Once he does connect with her, he leaves her wealthy and blessed beyond her wildest dreams. Little Water Bearers operate in much the same way; they often come across as aloof. They do not immediately know what to say or what to do to make themselves likable and approachable, and they usually have had some experiences, even in early life, of feeling completely misunderstood. This leads the Aquarius child to feel especially guarded, and they typically do not lower their defenses or let specific people "in" until those people have made quite an effort to get to know them. As community-minded as the Aquarian child is, they do not always have the easiest time finding their own real community.

The Aquarius-influenced child can feel as isolated and alone as the maiden is in her wide, snowy wood. They too can succumb to a cold aloofness that reinforces the alienation from humanity that they already sometimes feel. It is not that Aquarian children are disdainful of others, rather it is that they often feel they are on the outside looking in at people they truly care for, but they have a difficult time finding the words and accessing the feelings that let someone know they are loved.

Aquarians are thinkers, but they are also active thinkers who like to do things while they think. Hanging out with the Aquarius in their homemade lab, talking with them while they lay down a sick drumtrack for their bespoke punk album, or going with them to protest war or volunteer at a food bank is the best way to connect with these brilliant souls. They come alive when they are serving others and working toward a common good and better future.

Polarity: Leo

Leo reminds cool-headed Aquarius to bring their heart and passion into the situation. Leo also points out that not every act has to be one of self-aware community consciousness raising, and that perhaps the best thing every now and then is to step out on stage and take up the spotlight. Be warm! Be generous! Let people in! These are the words Leo starts cheering whenever they see Aquarius saunter by.

Aquarius Ascendant

The child with Aquarius ascending shows up as completely unique and original. No one else is like her. She is high tech and high concept. She dresses differently, speaks differently, and asks questions that seem to emerge not just from left field but maybe from another dimension. She is unconventional. These children find success when they're able to take their interests in the direction of serving the community and speaking to the future.

Aquarius Moon

The child with Aquarius Moon is good natured and happy unless their thoughts run away with them, in which case they get nervous, anxious, and start to talk a lot. These children are always asking questions and telling us how things work. They are comfortable with science, science fiction, outer space, and time travel. They like knowing how things work from the inside out. They are not comfortable with sloppy expressions of emotion, sentimentality, or being told that they cannot ask questions. They need to be allowed to be weird.

Activity
Scent Smarts

Aquarian children, like all Air signs, are very sensitive to scent. Different scents can put them into completely different moods. For this activity, bust out the scents—essential oils, perfumes, candles, incense—whatever you have on hand, and start to discover what the Aquarius child likes and doesn't like. Encourage them to use words in describing how the scents affect them. Ideally, make an oil or perfume blend for when they are feeling alone and isolated, one to pump up their energy, and one to help soothe and calm them, especially before bed. They can add these special blends to salt and make bath-time scrubbing potions—an excellent way to honor the water-bearing part of the Aquarius nature.

Ritual
Prayer Ribbons

It can be a hugely beneficial act for the Aquarian child to articulate their big dreams, desires, and needs for themselves and their Holy Helpers (the divine, sacred, and even famous cultural heroes who speak to each one of us). Aquarius children can be skeptical when it comes to matters of faith, but they are also more open-minded than most children. If introduced properly to the act of prayer as something that spans place, time, and spiritual paths—and something that can be deeply creative—then they can easily get on board.

Make a prayer ribbon by taking a piece of ribbon, deciding what prayer you want to make for it, and then writing or drawing that prayer onto the ribbon. You can then anoint the ribbon with oil or soak it in sacred waters before hanging it in a tree for the wind to carry the prayers up. The Aquarian child will especially love this because it engages them with their natural element of Air.

Ritual for the Inner Aquarius Child
A Touchstone for the Weird

Adults who are working on nurturing their inner Aquarius child often heard, over and over again, one word that described them when they were growing up. That word was "weird." For many Aquarian children, being weird started out as a wound and then turned into a badge of honor, and yet many adults still feel the sting of this designation. So instead of running away from Weird, make a touchstone for it. Find, make, or buy a pocket-sized object that is just weird and strange. Place it in your pocket and carry it with you, letting it remind you that your strangeness and your blessedness are actually the same thing.

CHAPTER 15

The Pisces Child

"I saw the angel in the marble and
carved until I set him free."

Michelangelo
(Pisces, born March 6, 1475)

BIRTHDAY: February 18–March 20

RULING PLANET: Jupiter, Neptune

ELEMENT: Water

SYMBOL: Fish

QUALITY: Mutable

HOUSE: Twelfth House of Healing and Beauty

STATEMENT: I am here to heal.

SEASON: Late Winter

GUIDING STORY: "The Fisher King"

Dawn is breaking now over the horizon, but perhaps
there is still enough darkness to see our final constellation,
that of the celestial Fish, Pisces. It is most easy to spot in
November. The Babylonians recognized this constellation
as the Great Swallow, and the Greeks associated it with the
Goddess Aphrodite and her beloved son, Eros. Interestingly,
many of the stories associated with the heavenly Fish deal
with the themes of wounds that need to be healed and loss
that is redeemed. Our final story deals with such material
as well. It is called by many names, but here we will refer
to it simply as "The Fisher King," and it comes to us from
ancient England. Close your eyes now and listen . . .

There was once a round table where no man could claim he was better or lesser than any other who sat by his side. This table had been created by a king who knew that in order to truly rule, he must serve and care for his entire realm. And around this table were knights of old: loyal and brave and true. The knights and their king had been on many quests, but there was one that was unceasing, and that was the quest for the Grail. Part of the problem was that no one knew exactly what the Grail was. Was it a magical cup that would confer immortality upon whomever drank from it? Was it a stone with miraculous properties of healing? Was it something else entirely? Many knights had quested after this holy and healing object, and one had come remarkably close to finding it, but it slipped through his fingers. And yet, here he was, trying once more to redeem what had been lost.

The knight was known as Parcival. He was not shining like the sun, though once he had been. Many battles—some won, some lost—had left their mark upon him. A great failure of nerve haunted him all his days and nights, and his beloved wife was far away from him, a distance he counted in years.

Parcival was strong and brave as a knight should be, but he was also soft in curious places, and his eyes held what might be something like wisdom. This was his last chance to find the Grail. The land he had wandered through for year after year was a broken land. The rivers refused to run, and the water was too foul to drink. The birds did not sing, and their eggs lay empty. The roses had been overtaken by poisonous weeds, and the trees silently screamed as they died, one after the other. The women did not bear children easily, and when they did, the children often did not survive.

Parcival, you see, was not a knight fighting for the favor of a woman or the honor of a king. Parcival had been tasked to fight—for life itself. By some miracle he made his way to the castle, one he had known from a previous visit.

In front of the castle was a dark lake, and at the edge of the lake was a grey-faced man in a fine hat and cloak who gently kept his fishing rod above the water. The stench coming from him was something terrible, so bad, in fact, that it was the source of the poison that had caused such disease in this land. He bore a wound that would not heal, no matter how many healing herbs and salves were applied to it.

Parcival had seen him before and knew him well. He knew that the man would be dead if it were not for the treasure that he kept, the sacred Grail. He knew also that no regular medicine could save the man's life. The only medicine that would suffice would come in the form of just right words said at the just right time. Parcival had had an opportunity once before to utter those words, and he had failed. This time would be different. Parcival waited. He bided his time. He sat awhile with the Fisher King. Finally, the King turned to him.

"You have come for the treasure of the Grail."

"I have come to heal your wound," Parcival said, correcting him gently.

"It is not possible."

"It is," said the tired knight in his lackluster armor, sighing with both depth and weariness. "So let me ask you, good sir, who is served by the Grail?"

It was the question the ancient Fisher King had waited for, year upon year, for so many eons that he had lost count. He spoke softly and in shocked tones as his wound began to close up, to heal.

"It was never a who."

Parcival asked him to speak up.

"It was never a *who*, good knight. It was a *what*. What is served by the grail? *What*? I'm asking you, Quester, so tell me."

Parcival spoke as if in a trance, words falling like healing rain from his lips.

"It is life, good King. Life and all that makes life possible. That is what the Grail protects; that is what the Grail serves."

The change was immediate. The Fisher King lost years from his face, his hair became lustrous once more, and something of his old strength returned. The land was suffused with the scent of a thousand spring blooms all rioting at once. A simple stone, the Grail itself, was given into Parcival's waiting hands, and when he turned, he saw his beautiful wife and the two sons he had never laid eyes on. As he went to her embrace, he heard the skies full of birdsong once more. He caught the flash of verdant green out of the side of his eye and the crimson bloom of the rose in her grandeur once more. Once again in his beloved's arms, he wept.

He was home.

Pisces Gifts

| Artistic | Compassionate | Sensitive |

Unconditionally loving — Psychic

Liminal — Spiritual — Healing

Salvific (power to heal or save)

Pisces Challenges

Isolated — Addictive Personalities — Self-sabotaging

THE PISCES PERSONALITY

Piscean children and adults are often told that they are sensitive, but those making such pronouncements rarely think about what that actually means. It means that the Pisces child often sees the world as it appears in the beginning of "The Fisher King." Though the grass may look green and the sky blue—though people say the right words and children do the right actions—the Pisces child sees something different: pollution, suffering animals, air that is not fit to breathe, the supposedly kind words and kind actions that sometimes mask something quite cruel. For these reasons, the world often seems too much for the little Pisces child. Like Parcival in the tale, Pisces children often feel that their entire life is a quest that has as its goal healing and wholeness for the world and everyone in it. If that seems like a lot of pressure for a child to put on themself that's because it is! And yet, many Pisces children experience these feelings. Just as Parcival's ability to heal the Fisher King also brings about his own healing through a reunion with his wife, so it is that the Pisces child senses that if they can heal what is broken in the world, they can also heal what feels broken in themselves. This quality speaks to a deep impulse within the Pisces child, which is to be a source of redemption and restoration, to heal and take away the "sins of the world."

Pisces is the sign of the Fish, and these children, like their namesake, often go quite deep. They are not afraid of depth and tend to seek it out, even to the point of sometimes conferring depth on a person or question to which it does not belong.

"Creative" is a word used to describe the Pisces child almost as often as "sensitive." These children are often gifted in several creative areas (e.g., music *and* visual art, sculpting *and* theater, violin *and* ballet). Doing something artistic and creative is native ground for the Pisces, and they often do it so effortlessly that the other children feel there is some kind of magic involved.

Pisceans often feel alone and misunderstood, but when they do something creative they feel like all is right in their world and that it makes sense. In these moments they know who they are and what they are about.

The Pisces child is easy to spot as the one most aware of how everyone else feels. Unlike the Libra child, who is very aware of other people for the sake of keeping the peace, or the Gemini child who is aware of how everyone feels because they are socially so gifted, the Pisces child is aware of how everyone feels because they genuinely care and they want to help. These are the children who have the tissue box ready before a classmate starts to cry and the ones who volunteer to escort a friend to the nurse's station. This quality of compassion is one of the Pisces child's biggest hallmarks, and it goes so deep that the Pisces child often feels something akin to what the person they are assisting feels.

Along the same lines, Pisces children are unconditional in giving their love. Once they feel that they love someone, that is *it*. It may take a long time for a Pisces to let a friend in, but once they do, the friendship is deeply treasured. Even when the friend is not so nice, the Pisces child is likely to forgive and forget. This ability to unconditionally love is both a strength and a potential vulnerability, so discernment must be carefully exercised and nurtured here. Fortunately, the Pisces child also has a good filter because they are indeed sensitive, and they are often quite adept at reading what is behind people's words and deeds. They can read not only between the lines but also into the invisible ink of the page. This sensitivity means that the Pisces child tends to take things very personally, so at a young age they must learn to develop thick skin to protect themselves.

Once they do that, this natural sensitivity can become the Pisces child's greatest asset, allowing them to see what people are really about and helping them avoid many deceptions. In fact, this sensitivity in Pisces children often goes beyond being something that is merely about sensitivity and becomes a kind of intuitive power. These little Fish often are very gifted intuitively, and they can develop those gifts as they get older if they choose to. As a child though, the Pisces needs to discover how to take their abilities in stride—not ignoring or neglecting them but also not overemphasizing them. If they don't learn this, they can become very severe and demanding with themselves and others.

Friends and Play

The Pisces child can initially have a rough time making friends and engaging in play. Like Parcival in our story, their sensitivity and their creativity sets them apart. They may feel isolated, but at the same time feel overwhelmed by innocent overtures of friendship or fun. However, as the Pisces child learns to soothe their anxiety, they discover more ways to connect with others and they find a social group of similar and usually creative people. Once that occurs, the friendships can form quickly and are usually lasting unless the friend tries to make the Pisces child do or be something that they are not. Then these little Fish will swim away in the opposite direction.

Pisces children are usually quite gifted at play, but they have to feel safe and secure in order to let themselves get lost in it. Again, these skills will come later, and parents and caregivers should not worry overly much if their Pisces children are shy and retiring when they are very young and just beginning school. However, parents and caregivers should also make sure they encourage their Pisces child to reach out to others and to make playdates with friends happen, as the Pisces child typically relates best to their friends after school and one on one.

As we might imagine, these deep, introspective qualities can make it difficult for the Pisces child to clearly articulate what they think and feel. They can easily take small slights and blow them out of proportion, and they must learn that not everyone is in need of help and healing. Once they do that, they will discover that they have the potential to make deep, true, and lasting friendships. A dangerous area that the Pisces child will need to watch out for, especially as they get older, is addiction. Pisces are one of the most addiction prone of all the signs because they are so sensitive and too often come to a place where they feel overwhelmed by the world. With the potential for a Pisces's addiction to sugar and TV during childhood and to drugs, sex, and alcohol later on, parents, caregivers, and teachers all need to pay special attention to changes in core behavior and attitude of their Piscean kids to make sure they're not falling into the trap of addictive behavior.

Finally, the Pisces child can be a gifted saboteur. No, they are not secretly cutting the cables that hold up the stage lights, but these children can sabotage themselves. They often do this through unkind, uncompassionate self-talk where they tear themselves down. Sometimes this behavior manifests in more extreme forms, and they might, for instance, destroy a work of art or instrument due to their unhappiness—usually with themselves. The remedy is for the Pisces child to be reminded that their work is remarkable and that mistakes are actually a good thing.

Academics

In our story, Parcival is not a knight who gains his wisdom by achieving victory after victory. Parcival is a knight who wins the greatest prize by making mistakes and errors, but who continues with his quest anyway. This journey is one that the school-age Pisces may find very familiar. The Pisces child is deep and intelligent. But like the Aquarius child, that does not necessarily mean they will do well in school. Sometimes these children do poorly because they are bored. They can be quite gifted at getting out of hard work and excusing themselves from challenges. They may also be careless, forgetting to double-check their work and neglecting to make sure they did what was necessary to complete their assignments. Often this flows from the fact that they are paying attention to things on the periphery. Just as Parcival's heart turned to matters greater and higher than what knights are normally supposed to seek, so our Pisces child may find the goals of ordinary academic life lackluster and seek a higher calling.

With proper support from parents and caregivers, the Pisces child can do really well in school, and their natural intelligence and curiosity can carry them far. Parents need to make sure their Pisces child is being challenged and not bored to tears. Any creative element to academic projects and assignments is an added plus, and here the Pisces child easily shines. These children are often drawn to literature, philosophy, and history as well as creative subjects and foreign languages. Another potential problem to watch for is negative self-talk. Pisces children often think they have done much worse on school projects and assignments than they actually have, and they may also engage in negative self-talk fixating on how "dumb" they are. Parents and caregivers can get in front of this and help their Pisces children understand that everyone talks to themselves this way from time to time, but it is never helpful.

As the Pisces child grows up and considers the question of "what comes next" they may find themselves overwhelmed by the variety of choices *or* they may feel that they have very few choices. As noted above, for all of their deep wisdom, these children do not always have the best academic track records. On the other hand, I have met quite a few Pisces adults who were sure they did poorly in school only to look at their academic records years later and find out they did really well. The point is that a young-adult Pisces needs both support and guidance from parents and caregivers as they consider their futures. If the Fish child is gifted in the arts, as many are, they may decide not to continue their formal education and go straight into working in their chosen field. However, performing arts colleges, musical conservatories, and art and design schools can be very nourishing places for these youths, especially if the courses in artistry are paired with a practical-minded curriculum that teaches the Pisces youth to be aware of the financial and business aspects of their field. Another professional track that draws many Pisces is that of medicine, while others will find themselves pulled toward theology and ecclesiastical studies. I encourage parents and caregivers of these magical Fish to watch out for a propensity to wander without direction. Wandering is part of the Pisces experience and should not be curtailed, but these children do best when wandering is accompanied by a specific aim.

Physical Activity

Parcival's quest for the Grail is a true quest with all of the action that such an endeavor demands. Piscean children are often not the first ones to sign up for physical activities, especially of the sports variety, but if coaches, parents, and caregivers can make physical activities feel like a quest, they have a much better chance of convincing the Pisces child to get up and get moving. Because of their Parcival-like drive, these children tend to be more cooperative and less competitive, and they do not always see the logic or need for a team at all. However, Pisces children benefit the most from sports and other physical endeavors. This is in part because physical exertion supports the Pisces child in gaining some distance and perspective on their feelings and placing their attention on their physical bodies. Sports and physical activities are also good for these little Fish, who sometimes are too reliant on their comfort zones and might worry that doing something hard will be their undoing. Physical challenges teach the Pisces child that they can be uncomfortable and perfectly fine at the same time. These children are often very coachable—that is, they listen to what is being asked for and then do their best to do it. Although developmentally there may be areas where they are not the best, these little Fish can demonstrate surprising abilities in the world of athletics. Moreover, playing on a team gives the Pisces child a lot of opportunities to interact with different people and to make some good friends. Sports that require a level of finesse, like soccer or swimming, are particularly good for the Pisces child.

Art and Creativity

The way that the Pisces child goes about healing is noteworthy. They quest, they serve, and they create. We see Parcival doing all of these things: questing in service to something greater (the Grail) and then getting creative in his answer to the Fisher King's question.

Healthy Pisceans often have a balanced spiritual path. Ritual observances may be part of their daily household routine, and these children are capable of great reverence and maturity when it comes to complicated theological questions. Many of the Piscean child's efforts—creative to spiritual—are made to heal something or someone. This is the case long before they are even aware of what they are doing or what healing means. They feel drawn to help, nourish, calm, and soothe, and they worry when one of their friends is unhappy or hurting. For this reason many Pisceans find themselves called to healing professions, and there is great healing potential in creative pursuits like art and music. These areas of interest are also of good benefit for the little Fish, who can easily suffer from a poor self-image, but can gain the admiration of others and experience a strong boost to their self-esteem when they share their artistic talents with the world.

Pisces children take to art and creative work the way a Fish takes to water! These children are incredibly gifted when it comes to art and creativity, and they are often good at more than one art form, such as learning an instrument and painting and drawing. The Pisces child may not seem too confident in social situations or academics, but when it comes to creative endeavors the Pisces child is at their most confident. They know they have abilities in this area, and most importantly they are ready and willing to help their less artistically gifted friends get the hang of things. Creativity is an arena in which the Pisces child can feel popular, sought out, and well liked, and Pisces children often make their first friends through mutual artistic endeavors.

Extracurricular Activities

Children influenced by Pisces are uniquely gifted, so naturally they have a good deal of extracurricular activities: music practice after school, followed by a drama club meeting, and then the next day a basketball game. The Pisces child who does not have a naturally busy extracurricular schedule is probably not enjoying themselves as much as they could be, especially when it comes to creative work.

As with all children, however, it is important for there to be breaks, treats, and moments of silence during which the Pisces child can recharge. If your child is a Pisces, watch out for a period, usually in late middle school or high school, when they want to quit everything. You can see this tendency in the story of Parcival. The things knights normally devote themselves to are not the things he thinks are worthwhile, and he is willing to give up all of that, even if it means he will be harmed. This is the Pisces anti-institutional tendency kicking in, and it is also a fulfillment of their particular purpose, like when the Fish swims one direction and then suddenly switches directions and does the polar opposite. The Pisces child at this point might need a break, but in many cases parents and caregivers do their children a service by encouraging them to follow their commitments through to the end. At the same time, one of the little Fish's gifts is their intuitive knowing of when something is not the right fit. In these cases their impulse to reverse course is exactly what is needed. So parents and caregivers will have to consider each situation on its own merits and listen to the reasons their Pisces child gives them for making those decisions.

Technology

In the tale of the Fisher King, the Grail is the technology—the magic—that brings healing to the realm. This story gives us powerful insight into the Pisces child's relationship to technology: in short, the technologies they are most interested in are those that have the ability to heal, repair, and restore. The Pisces child often shares the same preference for analog approaches that we find among Virgos and Capricorns. There is always something alluring about the classics and history for the Pisces kid, so they often prefer old-fashioned modes of communication and connection. However, it is possible for the Pisces child to get interested in technology, especially in how it works from the inside out and how it might be put to good use to save the world. (Pisceans are always interested in what is potentially salvific.) Cutting-edge technologies in medicine and environmental efforts will be of special interest to these little Fish. Pisces children are also drawn to new inroads in water purification and conservation as well.

There is a shadow side to the Pisces child's relationship to technology: the potential for her to fall into the trap of technology addiction, especially when it comes to overconsumption. These children are not the most likely to seek out video games, but they will absolutely lose themselves playing them, and hours can go by without them realizing what has happened. For this reason, it is especially important for parents and caregivers to monitor their Piscean child's screen time.

Sleeping and Waking

Related to a Pisces child's intuition is their liminal quality. "Liminal" is a Latin word that refers to the threshold of a building. To be liminal is to be in a state where you are in the waking world but simultaneously in another realm altogether: one of magic and mystery like the realm of "The Fisher King." Piscean children often convey the feeling that they are in both worlds at the same time because in a very real way they are. This comes through in their dream lives, which are often quite vivid and powerful. These little Fish tend to be night owls, as they are listening (and talking) to dreams and dream figures while the rest of us are dozing off.

Piscean children tend to be very sensitive to noise and "busy energy." They need to be able to turn off and tune out the busy world, and the middle of the night is a great time to do that. As a result, getting up in the morning can be hard for Pisceans. They need to wake up gradually, with plenty of time and space to get themselves sorted out before walking out the door. One of the best ways to wake up a Pisces child is with music. While their child is younger, parents or caregivers can put on their favorite music to lure them out of bed. As the child gets older, however, try suggesting that they practice music in the mornings before school. Practicing often has the effect of immediately waking them up and improving their mood. Making sure they eat a solid breakfast, have their school supplies ready, and their clothes for the day within easy reach all really help the process.

The Pisces child easily loses himself in wandering thoughts and feeling. He may start playing the piano or working on a drawing and forget that he actually needs to be getting ready for school. Or he might pose an interesting question or want to engage in a conversation while standing half-naked in the hallway. Parents and caregivers can move things along by allowing Pisces children to divert themselves in whatever ways seem most appealing *after* they are completely ready for school.

Discipline

Parcival is a good knight, but he is not a perfect knight. We know from our tale that he has made mistakes and grave errors. Years before the final part of "The Fisher King" story takes place, Parcival had the opportunity to win the Grail but failed to do so. This is reflective of the relationship between the Pisces child and discipline.

In early childhood Pisceans appear to be mild mannered, kind, compassionate, and easy to work with—and they truly are all of those things! However, as they get older they may reveal another aspect to themselves: the rebellious, antiauthoritarian, and antiestablishment bias that all Pisces carry. These compassionate souls love humanity as a whole, but they are often weary of individual people and the institutions that people create.

Pisces children have the same difficulties with rules that many Aquarian kids have—it just shows up later and in a slightly more elegant and less overt form. The Pisces child might coast through elementary school, but once they hit middle and high school they might find themselves on the wrong side of the administration more than once. A Pisces man that I know and love wore a jacket to his high school that was embroidered with flowers on the back and the succinct phrase "F**k War." He didn't say anything, but then again, he didn't have to.

This is a prime example of what acting out looks like from a Pisces. How to deal with this? Despite their good nature, Pisces do *not* like to be told what to do, so if they feel forced to do or be a certain way, they will absolutely do the opposite. However, if parents, teachers, and caregivers can make a concerted argument for *why* it is better for the Pisces child to do X, Y, or Z, then they can be persuaded to consider it. An awesome quality of Pisces is their willingness to admit when they are wrong. In fact, sometimes Pisces children find themselves too willing to say that they are wrong or made a mistake; as a result it is not uncommon for these children to get bullied. In those cases, the Pisces child needs to be encouraged to speak up and stand up for themselves, and adults need to intervene swiftly and decisively so that these children feel safe and supported.

How Best to Connect

There is a spiritual truth that's part of Grail lore and "The Fisher King" tale. It is resonant with the Pisces child, who is deeply spiritual and is often called to serve in that capacity as they get older.

Although Pisces children sometimes have the reputation of being cold fish, they are deeply loving, thoughtful, and feeling souls who like nothing so much as to curl up with their beloveds at the end of the day. Pisces children often feel insecurity more keenly than many of the other signs, so it is especially important for parents and caregivers to take time out of their busy schedules and spend it with their little Fish! Pisces enjoy snuggling up and listening to stories or watching a good movie or show, and they love doing anything creative with their parents or caregivers, including making music and art. Because of their spiritual feelings, Pisces children often feel very connected to their families when they are attending church, temple, mosque, or other spiritual services.

Polarity: Virgo

Virgo looks at Pisces's disorganized space and brings her own magic to bear in creating the right structures and containers that make it possible to take an idea or vision and turn it into something real. Virgo reminds Pisces to take care of their physical health and to mind the practical details that can make a big difference in one's ability to enjoy life.

Pisces Ascendant

Children with Pisces at the Ascendant usually have gorgeous eyes, beautiful skin, and a kind and gentle approach to others. They come off as magical, romantic, artistic, and a little bit vacant, ditzy, or even aloof. They flow. There is an innocence and sweetness about them even as they mature into adulthood. These children find the most satisfaction when their gifts are channeled into creating art or music, or when they are engaged in spiritual pursuits with an eye toward healing the soul.

Pisces Moon

The child with Pisces Moon is highly sensitive and often psychic. They are dreamers and need to talk about their dreams. They often give their dreams physical shape in some way. They are calmed by beautiful art and music. These children are easily overwhelmed by their surroundings and by books they read, shows they watch, and what they eat. That's why it's important for parents and caregivers to monitor what they consume. When the child with Pisces Moon is healthy, they are deeply empathic and able to connect with anyone. When they are overwhelmed, they will seek out ways to self-medicate.

Activity
Musical Mornings

Starting the day can be tough for Pisces children. Help them out by working with one of their favorite mediums, music! Every time they wake up have a ritual greeting for them, then ask what song they would like to hear and sing or play it for them. This will get them ready to greet the day and will give you great information about how they are feeling emotionally.

Ritual
Sacred Bathing

Sacred bathing is basically taking a bath with intention and a few magical ingredients thrown in for good measure. Every Pisces of any age will love this luxurious ritual. Just run a bath as you normally would, but ask your Pisces child before they get into the tub what they want to wash away today. They will feel into it for a while, think about it, and then come up with something. (They may or may not share what it is with you.)

Allow your child to pick out what they would like to add to the bath (oils, bath bombs, shower gel, etc.) and then let them take a bath. Pisces children like to linger in the tub, so allow that to happen. When they get out and dry off—or are helped to dry off—you can ask what they want to call into the evening now that they have washed away the gunk. Again, your child may or may not share that with you. Give them a little lotion or oil to massage into their palms and heart center before putting on their pajamas, and they will be able to go to sleep in a sweet emotional state.

Ritual for the Inner Pisces Child
Divine Divination

Grown-ups who are healing their inner Pisces child really hate being told how *sensitive* they are. Chances are, they have heard it throughout their whole lives—and they are over it! But the thing is, it's true. So, when addressing your inner Pisces child, put this tendency to good use by creating a simple divination practice. Sensitivity, after all, is just another way of saying "psychic, liminal, and magical." Pick your favorite divination tool—tarot, pendulum, the *I Ching* or the like—and work with it every morning for a month. Note how it changes your relationship to yourself and your day.

Epilogue

Let Them, Above All, Be Good

"To go in the dark with a light is to know the light.
To know the dark, go dark. Go without sight."

**from "To Know the Dark" by Wendell Berry, *The
Selected Poems of Wendell Berry***

*You are standing in a field of waist-high native grassland
under a star-pierced sky. Before you, rising up out of the tall
grasses, is a blasted-out Live Oak tree, struck by lightning at
some point in its past and yet growing around those scorch
marks and providing both shade and shelter. The tree
stretches its lowest branches generously across the ground
so that a toddler in your care can grasp and clamber his
way up into a natural saddle on the lowest branch. He
climbs his first tree not long after he takes his first steps.*

*The field before you opens up into hills and woodland
edge. If you were to walk a few yards, you would come
across armadillos to your left, patiently nosing through the
tall grasses, prickly-pear cactus patches, and clumps of
barrel cactus looking for a juicy snack of grubs. Were the
armadillos to sense your presence, they would retreat to
one of their dugouts, sometimes only going halfway in so
that their scaled, rounded bottoms reflect the starlight.*

From that same field might emerge the deer that has lived here as long as you can remember. A seasoned doe, she has always had a wounded foreleg—a compound-complex fracture that mended in its own way and on its own. She has outlived most of the other deer on this land and has a new fawn every Spring. Now, tonight, you do not seek out either creature. You are here on this night to listen. Take a deep breath and catch the scent of horsemint, mesquite, oak, bitterweed, and so many species of grass that you cannot name. This is the scent of the lands where you grew up, the scent of home.

The scent of home is still full in our noses when we hear traces of a voice. The voice is not deep or sonorous or even female, as you might have expected. It is the voice of, say, your oldest son, or a child in your care, the voice he uses when he is patiently explaining something that we should probably already know, something that we should have remembered like the speed of light or the difference between obsidian and granite.

"You know . . ." A pause. Owl call. "I am not only a mother. Not just. Not most of all." Coyote yip, bat flutter, moth kiss.

"I am also a child."

Silence.

"Your child."

Thunder greets you over the hills and valleys as a Spring storm moves across the land. "I am everyone's child." Lightning flash.

"How are you raising me?"

The sweet scent of the land gives way to the sharper one of ozone. It is the voice of the Earth, asking a question, expecting a response.

I'm sitting with a group of mom friends, munching on homemade pizza and sipping a nice rosé. It is the weekend before school is about to start. Our kids are having a pool playdate while we catch up after a busy summer. We are talking about the fall activities we are signing our children up for, the teachers and classmates they will have, and what their schedules will be like. But underneath that happy chatter we are also finding moments to bring up our fears and worries. There has just been a shooting in El Paso not so very far away. Would our children be safe? Was there anything we could do, any prayer we could make to ensure our children's well-being? We do not yet know words like "coronavirus" or "COVID-19." The idea of a pandemic is theoretical for all of us. But we find plenty of reasons to worry. I'm reminded of the question asked by the Earth itself: how are we raising them? It seems that one way to make an answer to that question is in the language of prayer.

I know these prayers. I, like every other parent in my generation, say them every day, in one form or another. I know too that every parent and teacher and caregiver has blessed their children throughout time. But my elders tell me that our time of parenting is especially fraught, for our prayers mark the line of defense not just against disease or community drama or accidents on the playground, but also school shootings, cyberbullying, and predators who hide their identities behind a flat screen and a picture of a cute kitten.

We want our children to be protected, but let us also ask that they be protectors of those not as strong or well favored. We want them to be safe, but let us also pray that they have the smarts and wit to see, identify, and steer clear of predators seen and unseen, macro- and microscopic. We ask that our children never experience a school shooting and that if they do—all angels forbid—that they survive it. Let us also petition that our children not be the ones to pick up the gun; to hide their pain, anger, and fear until it is too late; to hurt themselves or someone else. These are the soul-songs I would have us sing over the innocents and younglings.

The question confronting parents, families, caregivers, teachers, and all who care for children is not "How do we raise our children to become successful adults?" It is, rather, "How do we raise our children to live a flourishing life—to be good?" *Good* kids. *Good* adults. "Good" can sound staid and boring. It sounds "Goody Two-shoes," as many a Virgo will attest. It sounds like never coloring outside the lines, like making other people happy by jettisoning your own dreams and desires. But this is a shallow and relatively recent way of holding the word. In ancient Greek texts, the word "good" is often paired with the words "noble" and "beautiful," and all three are understood to refer to inner character, to what our Ancestors called "virtue."

"Good" is always rooted in what is wild but not feral. It does not exclude hell-raising or wandering, but it gives direction and purpose to each. Good children will inevitably find themselves in the time-out zone or penalty box. They will blurt out answers, talk over their peers, trip over themselves in enthusiasm. They will come home with torn jeans, messy hair, and rocks in their pockets that might knock the washing machine balance out of whack. There will be fibs from the lips of these "good" kids, stammering and delightful tall tales. All of this is part of the innate goodness of our children. We find in them care, empathy, and maturing development that does not ever seek to excise the child within but rather relies on it as a source of enthusiasm, deep wisdom, and boundless joy.

Children raised in recognition of their goodness grow into good adults. I have been blessed to meet them from every conceivable walk of life, of every skin color and culture. I stand strong in the knowledge that we who recognize and foster the good in ourselves and others far outnumber the unkind, the cruel, and the heartless. What can we do to nurture and call out that goodness in our children? There are so many ways, but among them I see a theme, a red lifeline leading out of the labyrinth: to see our children, to really see them, not as we would have them be nor expect nor desire them to be, but as they, in and of themselves, are. To see their natures, likes, dislikes, passions, and preferences and to know that between the hair-pulling and tattle-telling and driving us to drop into bed dead with exhaustion at the end of the day, they will grow and change and reveal marvel after marvel. This is why

I love looking to the birth chart, that one-of-a-kind heavenly star map, when I seek to understand and better relate to a child. The stars and Planets and the stories they tell are each unique. They are decidedly not my story, but the story line of the child, their path, a celebration of their particular gifts and knowings. Stars, Moon, Sun, Planets: they are all luminous bodies, all shining light that reveals what needs to be seen, revealing a whole child with many stories and many adventures awaiting. When we see that child clearly, then possibility opens and we have done something truly good.

Ordinarily we think of ourselves as free agents, individual actors—and this thought of ours applies to our children as well. But allow your perspective to slightly shift, and what do you see? Our links to each other, especially our lineages extending from the past to the future. No person is an island. If we remember who we really are, a whole community of people including other living beings, past and future, emerges. We are a community of souls that supports one another, that inspires each other, and that makes life possible for one another. Our community need not be restricted to biological inheritance; it can also be one of spirit, which can include adoptive parents, friends, living creatures, teachers, artists, or important historical figures.

From this wider and richer perspective, you are a Descendant of the Ancestors who came before you and whose names you likely do not even know. But you are also an Ancestor in the making, here and now. Someday we will be Ancestors, in the full meaning of the word, to our Descendants. The children in your life one day will also be Ancestors. To be an Ancestor is a thing to celebrate and honor, not to fear. It is a thing to aspire to and be worthy of.

As you have learned how to work with the stars for the children in your life, I encourage you to activate this wider sense of things; of Earth, of Home, and of the lineage and community of which we all are a part.

When we embrace this vaster way of seeing, we become aware of a need to take care of those who come after us: the Descendants. This is important for the work of seeing our children in themselves, and for seeing our own selves objectively. We look longer and further out onto the horizon, into the future, so that decisions made today are weighed by their effects not only tomorrow but for five, seven, twenty, and one hundred years later. Awareness of our Descendants—the children we have and the children who are to come—requires us to root our young ones into the rich knowing of the Earth and its people while raising them up to a bird's-eye vision of the whole that not one of us can afford to ignore or forfeit at this time. We must raise them all the way to the stars.

This is audacious work and not for the faint of heart. Every single Zodiac Sign can bring its unique medicine and giftedness to this endeavor, and that is a good thing. It will take every single Star Child to answer Earth's question, which is the question of our children too: *How will you raise me?* Our answer and our prayer? We will do it as best we can, and we will do it together.

Acknowledgments

Star Child was not a book I was intending to write, but it appeared—to a large degree fully formed—and demanded that I write it. As I have said from the very beginning of this endeavor, this book is one that I wrote for myself and for all of my beloved friends and family members who have Star Children in their lives. And as always, the writing of the book was not a singular endeavor but one made possible by a wide village of beloveds.

Thanks first of all to Mom and Dad, an intrepid Aries and Virgo combination who raised two daughters with so much love, generosity, grace, and wisdom. The best qualities in my own parenting come directly from the two of you.

Thanks to my Nana who has not only been an amazing Grandmother throughout my life but also a truly incredible Great-Grandmother to my two little boys.

My sister (and Aries polar opposite) Brittany gets thanks for always cheering me on with boundless enthusiasm, and for showing me the pieces I was missing.

Thanks to my extended family: you are home base and tribe, and I feel each of you with me on this journey.

One of the biggest influences in *Star Child* are the many, many conversations I have had with parent friends about our children and this whole parenting thing. These include Roxana, Colleen, Myra, Jordan, Carla, Paul, Jimmy, Cristina, Sarah, Darcy, Holly, Kara, Leslie, and Kylie. There are so many more, and you all are the brightest and best of lights.

Big thanks also to my nonparent friends who nevertheless love my children and are the best aunties and uncles that a mom could ask for, including Marion, Heather, Valori, Leslie, Arlene, and Fairy Godmother Felicia. You are the ones who inspired me to write this book—not just for parents but for all of those who care for our little ones.

Thanks to my colleagues in magic-making and stargazing: Theresa Reed, Heidi Rose Robbins, Jason Miller, Aidan Wachter, Fabeku Fatunmise, and Elizabeth Barrial. A tip of the hat to the wonderful storytellers I have been blessed to know and learn from, including Terri Windling, Dr. Martin Shaw, Esmé Wang, Dr. Clarissa Pinkola Estés, and so many elders within my own family.

Love and many blessings upon Jennifer Yvette Brown, editor par excellence and dear friend, who polished this manuscript until it shone, well, like a star!

Deep thanks to my Ancestors for reminding me daily that everything I do should point toward becoming a good Ancestor myself.

Thanks to Jasper and Heath—my very own Star Children—who keep me on my toes with questions, rituals, activities, celebrations, and suggestions and have taught me so very much about everything. Sweet boys, you both are my world.

And last but certainly not least, thank you to my husband, David. Without you there would be no Star Children in my life. You are beyond a blessing as both a husband and a father, and my love for you grows deeper with each day.

Additional Resources

BOOKS

Casey, Caroline W. *Making the Gods Work for You: The Astrological Language of the Psyche*. New York: Three Rivers Press, 1998.

Comstock-Gay, Claire. *Madame Clairevoyant's Guide to the Stars: Astrology, Our Icons, and Our Selves*. New York: HarperCollins, 2020.

Coppock, Austin. *36 Faces*. Rancho Boca de la Cañada del Pinole, CA: Three Hands Press, 2014.

Goodman, Linda. *Linda Goodman's Love Signs: A New Approach to the Human Heart*. New York: HarperCollins, 2011.

Goodman, Linda. *Linda Goodman's Sun Signs*. United Kingdom: Pan Books, 1972.

Greene, Liz. *Saturn: A New Look at an Old Devil*. Newburyport, MA: Red Wheel/Weiser, 2011.

Hand, Robert. *Planets in Transit: Life Cycles for Living, Second Revised Edition*. Atglen, PA: Schiffer, 2002.

Hand, Robert. *Planets in Youth: Patterns of Early Development*. Atglen, PA: Schiffer, 1997.

Nicholas, Chani. *You Were Born for This: Astrology for Radical Self-Acceptance*. San Francisco: HarperOne, 2020.

Reed, Theresa. *Astrology for Real Life: A Workbook for Beginners (A No B.S. Guide for the Astro-Curious)*. Newburyport, MA: Weiser Books, 2019.

Shesso, Renna. *Planets for Pagans: Sacred Sites, Ancient Lore, and Magical Stargazing*. Newburyport, MA: Redwheel/Weiser, 2011.

Woods, Mecca. *Astrology for Happiness and Success: From Aries to Pisces, Create the Life You Want—Based on Your Astrological Sign!* Avon, MA: Adams Media, 2018.

MAGAZINES

The Mountain Astrologer magazine: mountainastrologer.com/tma

FREE NATAL CHARTS

Astro.com, free daily horoscopes and free birth charts: astro.com

Astrolabe, free birth chart and astrology report: alabe.com/freechart

ASTROLOGERS

Below you will find a list of practicing astrologers. I only recommend astrologers whom I have worked with personally or whose work I am adequately familiar with to know that they provide accurate information paired with kindness and discernment. I can safely say that each of these individuals has a unique and excellent approach to Astrology, and you can learn a lot from any of them.

Chris Brennan, Hellenistic Astrology: hellenisticastrology.com

Austin Coppock: austincoppock.com

Kaitlin Coppock, Sphere and Sundry astrological-based
ritual and ceremonial supplies: sphereandsundry.com

Robert Hand, Arhat Media: arhatmedia.com

Jessica Lanyadoo: lovelanyadoo.com

Mystic Medusa: mysticmedusa.com

Chani Nicholas: chaninicholas.com

Dayna Lynn Nuckolls (The People's Oracle):
thepeoplesoracle.com

Anne Ortelee: anneortelee.com

Amelia Quint: ameliaquint.com

Theresa Reed: thetarotlady.com

Sam Reynolds: unlockastrology.com

Heidi Rose Robbins: heidirose.com

Mecca Woods: mylifecreated.com

Jenn Zhart: jennzahrt.com

Chris Zydel: creativejuicesarts.com

About the Author

Briana Saussy is a storyteller, writer, teacher, spiritual counselor, and ritualist dedicated to the restoration and the remembering of the Sacred Arts. Her first book, *Making Magic*, captures her approach to spirituality, which integrates the riches of the perennial world religions, contributions of modern psychology, and the wisdom contained in divination, folk magic, and storytelling practices. She holds a BA and MA in Eastern and Western classics, philosophy, mathematics, and science from St. John's College (Annapolis and Santa Fe), and she is a student of Ancient Greek and Sanskrit. Briana lives in her hometown of San Antonio, Texas, with her husband and two sons. You can learn more about her work at brianasaussy.com

About Sounds True

Sounds True is a multimedia publisher whose mission is to inspire and support personal transformation and spiritual awakening. Founded in 1985 and located in Boulder, Colorado, we work with many of the leading spiritual teachers, thinkers, healers, and visionary artists of our time. We strive with every title to preserve the essential "living wisdom" of the author or artist. It is our goal to create products that not only provide information to a reader or listener but also embody the quality of a wisdom transmission.

For those seeking genuine transformation, Sounds True is your trusted partner. At SoundsTrue.com you will find a wealth of free resources to support your journey, including exclusive weekly audio interviews, free downloads, interactive learning tools, and other special savings on all our titles.

To learn more, please visit SoundsTrue.com/freegifts or call us toll free at 800.333.9185.